The Democratic Foundations
of Policy Diffusion

The Democratic Foundations of Policy Diffusion

How Health, Family and Employment Laws Spread Across Countries

KATERINA LINOS

OXFORD

UNIVERSITY PRESS

OXFORD
UNIVERSITY PRESS

Oxford University Press is a department of the University of Oxford.
It furthers the University's objective of excellence in research, scholarship,
and education by publishing worldwide.

Oxford   New York

Auckland   Cape Town   Dar es Salaam   Hong Kong   Karachi
Kuala Lumpur   Madrid   Melbourne   Mexico City   Nairobi
New Delhi   Shanghai   Taipei   Toronto

With offices in

Argentina   Austria   Brazil   Chile   Czech Republic   France   Greece
Guatemala   Hungary   Italy   Japan   Poland   Portugal   Singapore
South Korea   Switzerland   Thailand   Turkey   Ukraine   Vietnam

Oxford is a registered trade mark of Oxford University Press
in the UK and certain other countries.

Published in the United States of America by
Oxford University Press
198 Madison Avenue, New York, NY 10016

© Oxford University Press 2013

Library of Congress Cataloging-in-Publication Data
Linos, Katerina.
The democratic foundations of policy diffusion: how health, family
and employment laws spread across countries / Katerina Linos.
pages cm
Includes bibliographical references and index.
ISBN 978-0-19-996786-5 (hardback : alk. paper)—ISBN 978-0-19-996787-2 (pbk. : alk. paper)
1. Law—International.   2. International Law.   3. Health care reform.   4. Family policy.
5. Comparative law.   6. Democracy.   7. Public opinion.   I. Title.
K590.5.L56 2013
344.03′21—dc23
2012046808

3 5 7 9 8 6 4 2
Printed in the United States of America
on acid-free paper

To my parents,
Dimitrios Linos and Athina Linou,
for their endless support

CONTENTS

LIST OF FIGURES AND TABLES

Figures

Tables

ACKNOWLEDGMENTS

In the course of this project, I have benefited from the wisdom and kindness of many wonderful people. Peter Hall's research on the influence of ideas inspired me to start this project, and his generosity in advising and commenting on many versions of the project kept me going. Torben Iversen's undergraduate seminars showed me that great research could be done in the field of social policy; I have profited from his insights and his support for more than a decade. Beth Simmons' work on compliance and diffusion critically shaped my thinking. This project draws heavily from her work, and her detailed comments on many drafts have pushed it much further than it would have otherwise gone. Ryan Goodman's research on socializing states inspired me to think carefully about how to connect diffusion research to debates about the design of international institutions. He has combed through multiple drafts over many years, with very helpful suggestions each time. Jack Goldsmith has been an amazing mentor, and helped me to develop provocative ideas, even when he disagreed with them. Martha Minow and Amartya Sen cheered me on in my three years at the Society of Fellows, and provided much guidance over delicious meals.

Since coming to Berkeley, many generous colleagues have offered their time and advice. KT Albiston, David Caron, Pradeep Chhibber, Andrew Guzman, Gillian Lester, Jonah Levy, Saira Mohamed, Paul Pierson, and Alison Post each spent a full day to help me redraft an early version of the manuscript. Harlan Cohen, Tom Ginsburg and Larry Helfer flew across the country to join in this book manuscript workshop and offer me their counsel. Anne O' Connell and Andrew Guzman have each spent countless hours discussing my research. Alison Post, my writing partner, read every chapter multiple times. Dean Christopher Edley and Associate Dean Gillian Lester not only gave me substantive advice, but also helped me find funds and mental space to complete this project. Many, many, thanks to Michelle Anderson, Bobby Bartlett, Eric Biber, Dick Buxbaum, Lauren Edelman, Dan Farber, Prasad Krishnamurthy,

Taeku Lee, Cal Morrill, Melissa Murray, Bertrall Ross, Andrea Roth, Eric Schickler, Jason Schultz, David Sklansky, Talha Syed, Eric Talley, Karen Tani, Victoria Plaut, and Jen Urban, for their very helpful advice.

I have also benefited from extensive comments from colleagues and friends in law and and political science in different parts of the world: Daniel Abebe, Chris Adolph, Bill Alford, Jim Alt, Ben Ansell, Fiona Barker, Elizabeth Bartholet, Erik Bleich, Gabby Blum, Tanja Börzel, Anu Bradford, Rachel Brewster, Daniela Caruso, Daniel Li Chen, Gráinne de Búrca, Anna di Robilant, David Dolowitz, Zach Elkins, Margarita Estévez-Abe, Gerda Falkner, Robert Fannion, Cary Franklin, Robert Franzese, Fabrizio Gilardi, Jane Gingrich, Jacob Hacker, Oona Hathaway, Mark Hallerberg, Dan Ho, Jennifer Hochschild, Bert Huang, Christopher Jencks, Derek Jinks, Christine Jolls, Andreas Kakridis, Andrew Karch, David Kennedy, Odette Lienau, Andrew Martin, Tim Meyer, Jonathan Miller, Kimberly Morgan, Aziz Rana, Brian Ray, Ivan Reidel, Jim Salzman, Kyoko Sato, Jasmin Sethi, Steve Shavell, David Sloss, Randall Smith, Paul Starr, Matthew Stephenson, John Stevens, Holger Spamann, Duane Swank, Mike Tomz, Joel Trachtman, Elina Treyger, Carolyn Tuohy, Carlos Vazquez, Pierre-Hugues Verdier, Kent Weaver, Jim Whitman, Jason Yackee, David Zaring, Nick Ziegler, and Kathrin Zippel. I am particularly grateful to Chris Adolph, who was always ready to help me through methodological quandaries, and to Andreas Kakridis, who helped me through multiple theoretical stumbling blocks. Finally, I wanted to thank the anonymous Oxford referees for their very helpful guidance.

The qualitative portion of the research was only possible due to the help of many librarians and interviewees. While I cannot publically acknowledge them, I am extremely grateful for all the time and information they offered me. The Juan March Institute in Madrid, the LSE Health and Social Care Program in London, and the European Commission Social Policy Cabinet in Brussels hosted me for extended and very enjoyable research stays. Marci Hoffman and Leslie Stone helped me track down obscure materials. Grants from the National Science Foundation, the Multidisciplinary Program in Inequality, the Justice, Welfare and Inequality Program, the Harvard Center for European Studies, the Harvard Weatherhead Center for International Affairs, the Olin Foundation and the Harvard Society of Fellows supported my research and travels. In addition, grants from the Berkeley Committee on Research, the Berkeley Institute for International Studies, the Berkeley Center on European Union Studies, the Hodgen Fund, and the Hellman Family Fellowship gave me significant support to complete this research, and prepare the manuscript.

I gratefully acknowledge research assistance from Eda Pepi, Michael Jordan, Susana Kim, Sergio Montero, Won Hee Park, Ruchira Saha, Henry Hauser and Katie Yablonka. Kim Twist, Annie Hilby and May Whitaker each edited earlier versions of the entire manuscript, and greatly improved its organization and flow. At Oxford, David McBride, Alexandra Dauler, and Pete Mavrikis supported and edited this project enthusiastically.

Over the years, my family has provided large amounts of emotional and practical support. My sisters Elizabeth Linos and Natalie Linos each reviewed multiple chapters. The love and unwavering support of my husband, Stavros Gadinis, made it all worthwhile.

The Democratic Foundations of Policy Diffusion

1

Introduction

Theoretical Claims

From environmental regulations to fundamental human rights, from market liberalization efforts to pension and health reforms, states imitate laws developed by other states or championed by international organizations. Diverse laws spread quickly within regions and around the globe, reaching the most remote corners of the world. This much is known and is well documented in large literatures in law, sociology, political science, and beyond.[1]

But why do international models wield so much influence? And who decides whether to borrow laws from abroad? Much prior work is silent on these questions and pays no attention to the actors involved in spreading laws across countries. Scholars who do offer an answer focus on networks of policy elites—international organizations and informal networks of sophisticated experts who formulate policy proposals that incorporate orthodox solutions to shared problems. Their narrative goes as follows: central bankers, police chiefs, environmental regulators, and judges meet regularly with their foreign colleagues. They devise common policy recommendations and build long-term relationships with their foreign counterparts. Socialized into international networks, key decision-makers become accountable largely to each other. They develop reputations for carrying out the promised reforms in the face of domestic opposition and draw strength from their foreign colleagues to resist pressures from domestic constituencies.[2] Globetrotting economists and other experts are sent by the World Bank and the International Monetary Fund (IMF) to the world's parochial backwaters to spread these orthodox ideas.[3] In short, the dominant account is a story of diffusion through technocracy.

In this dominant account, ordinary citizens provide no real input; their interests, concerns, and objections get scant attention. Policy diffusion "unfolds largely inside the bureaucratic agencies of the state and is not driven in any direct way by electoral incentives and calculations."[4] Poor, small, developing countries face the greatest pressures to conform. But even superpowers

1

like the United States are not immune, as "globalized elite bourgeois values" are imposed on ordinary Americans.[5] According to these traditional accounts, international norms and domestic democracy are in tension.

This conventional story is not only normatively troubling, it is also inconsistent with large literatures that explain how domestic policies are formulated. Under these domestic policy accounts, elected leaders pay great attention to what ordinary citizens and domestic interest groups want in order to maintain their popularity and win reelection.[6] From the domestic perspective, it seems unlikely that elected leaders would follow their foreign colleagues or international organizations on a broad range of issues if this hurt them at the ballot box.

This book asserts that, contrary to the conventional wisdom, international norms and democracy are mutually reinforcing. I argue that policies spread across countries not only because of the backing of technocrats, but also because of the support of ordinary voters. Technocrats still play a critical role in canvassing diverse ideas, bringing proposals to leaders' attention, and developing policy details. But elections and other democratic processes are an engine, not an obstacle, for the spread of policies across countries and can provide critical domestic legitimacy for these policies.

My theory is built on the intuition that foreign governments' policies and international organization proposals can serve as benchmarks against which voters can judge their government and its laws. Voters often worry that politicians are not competent and propose poorly thought-out laws that are unlikely to succeed. Voters also worry that politicians design laws in ways that enrich special interest groups and cater to fringe ideologues. Information that foreign governments have adopted similar laws can help politicians signal that their decisions are competent and mainstream. Foreign models have two distinct advantages as compared with endorsements from domestic groups, such as industry associations, unions, think tanks, and academics. First, because it is costly to adopt a law, foreign governments can send especially strong signals that they expect a proposal to succeed.[7] Second, foreign governments are outsiders; they don't stand to benefit directly from election results or policy choices in a neighboring state. When many foreign countries make the same policy choice, and when an international organization articulates this consensus and promotes it as the dominant international model, the influence of foreign models is at its peak.

There exist additional mechanisms through which voters could influence the diffusion of laws. For example, voters could collect information about policy models in neighboring countries and build bottom-up coalitions to pressure politicians for similar reforms. This is not the mechanism I propose, because voters are typically less invested in the policymaking process than are politicians. In my theory, politicians are the active (but constrained) agents. Politicians decide whether or not to introduce a law, and how to frame it in ways that will appeal to voters. Politicians end up imitating laws from countries familiar to voters disproportionately, because this allows politicians to present their proposals as competently designed and mainstream. My theory does not require voters to know much about other countries' policy choices— it only requires voters to have some general impressions about a few proximate countries heavily covered in the media. Chapter 2 spells out exactly how this theory works.

Diffusion through democracy produces different results from diffusion through technocracy; different international models are likely to resonate with these two groups. For theoretical clarity, I contrast these two mechanisms sharply in the paragraphs that follow. As I outline below, in some circumstances, we might also observe hybrid types, and see diffusion through democracy and diffusion through technocracy operate side-by-side.

Technocrats can collect detailed information from many sources, including diverse countries and international organizations. They can investigate not only whether a foreign country adopted a policy, but also whether this policy succeeded or failed abroad. If the policy succeeded abroad, technocrats can study whether it will transplant smoothly into their home country, or whether the two contexts are too different for successful transplantation. In short, technocrats can accumulate information and design a policy that closely fits their goals. What is not clear, however, is whether technocrats will use this information to serve the goals of the public at large, or whether they will select a policy that serves their professional interests narrowly defined, a policy that suits their future employers, or one that pleases their international peers.

Voters are very different from technocrats; they seek policies consistent with their interests and values, but do so with little information, and limited patience for further research. Voters rely heavily on the media for information. Large, rich and culturally proximate foreign countries receive extensive and favorable media coverage; the rest of the world remains invisible to voters. It is these countries that resonate positively with voters, and it is these countries that politicians reference to secure voter support.

Many studies of policy diffusion emphasize learning from policy success or failure; they argue that a foreign country's experience with a policy after this policy's adoption determines whether the policy spreads. For example, some argue that hospital financing reforms associated with reduced health expenditures are particularly likely to diffuse widely.[8] Experts can in fact review policies from very diverse sources and select the most successful ones, even if they come from distant and unfamiliar countries. I argue instead that, from the voters' perspective, discussions about a policy's success or failure abroad may be as confusing and partisan as debates about its likely domestic effects. As politicians from opposite camps fight over the policy's benefits, costs, and overall effectiveness in a foreign country, they muddy the waters for voters.

Instead, I argue that, even though voters remain unclear about a policy's success or failure abroad, they can place confidence in the fact that this policy was adopted by rich, proximate, and familiar countries. Many sociologists and constructivists call this diffusion pathway emulation, and document that it occurs often.[9] This book develops micro-level foundations for these patterns of policy emulation, and explains why the policy choices of large, rich, and proximate countries receive great weight in national policymaking, even when the success of these policies is in doubt. This is because politicians can signal the policy's desirability to voters by highlighting earlier adoptions by high-status actors. Conversely, it is hard to get voters to pay attention to the choices of distant or unfamiliar countries, and to find these convincing, even when technocrats believe that models from these countries are most successful.

The electoral power of simple, verifiable information that is easy to convey and hard to contest makes models that have already been widely adopted particularly influential. If many familiar countries have made the same policy choice, and better yet, an international organization has promoted this policy as the international standard, an incumbent who borrows this policy will send a strong signal of competence and mainstream values. If, instead, familiar countries are evenly divided, with some adopting one model and others a competing model, politicians should expect their choice to be contested, and should enjoy smaller electoral advantages from imitation. Note that under diffusion through technocracy, the opposite pattern should hold: technocrats cannot draw useful inferences about what works and what doesn't if all foreign countries have made the same choice; diversity is useful for social scientific inquiry.

The appeal of clear information that is easy to transmit also gives great power to international organizations. International lawyers have long wondered why nonbinding recommendations, declarations, and other international organization proposals are influential.[10] I argue that politicians are inclined to adopt these recommendations domestically to gain electoral advantages by clearly signaling their competence and mainstream values. Table 1.1 summarizes some of the key distinctions between technocracy and democracy as channels of policy diffusion.

As Table 1.1 outlines, diffusion through technocratic elites differs in key ways from diffusion through democratic channels. First, the two accounts differ on who responds to information from abroad. In diffusion through technocracy, voters are, at best, indifferent to international models; only elites are receptive. In diffusion through democracy, voters welcome foreign models,

Table 1.1 **Channels of Policy Diffusion**

	Diffusion through technocracy	*Diffusion through democracy*
Voter and elite response	Voters are indifferent or hostile to foreign models; only elites respond positively	Voters are receptive to foreign models and use them to benchmark elites
Countries considered	Diverse countries canvassed	Large, rich, and culturally proximate countries resonate
Influential features	Results matter	Adoption matters
Dominant arguments	Learning from policy success	Emulation
Ideal setting	Diverse models allow experimentation	Single global model sends a clear signal

and use these models to benchmark government performance. Second, the two accounts differ on which foreign models matter. While technocrats are free to consider reforms from around the world, elected politicians focus on a few large, rich, and culturally proximate countries that they can use to appeal to voters. Third, the features of foreign models that are most influential differ. Whereas technocrats can examine policy details, and study policy success and failure abroad, politicians focus on simple facts that are easy to convey and hard to contest, such as the widespread adoption of a particular policy. Fourth, the arguments about foreign models differ. For appeals to experts, arguments about policy consequences work best. For appeals to voters, simpler emulation arguments work better, arguments of the type "everyone else does X and so should we." As a result of these features, the ideal setting for diffusion through technocracy is a policy area where significant cross-national variation exists, as this allows for experimentation and hypothesis testing. In contrast, diffusion through democracy is most powerful when there exists a dominant international model. Chapter 2 develops these theoretical claims further, and explains the conditions under which we would expect to observe diffusion through democracy, diffusion through technocracy, and combinations of these two mechanisms.

Empirical Analysis

This book's empirical analysis turns to cases that are unlikely to confirm the proposed theoretical claims. "Least-likely" cases provide strong "support for the inference that the theory is even more likely to be valid in most other cases, where contrary winds do not blow as strongly."[11] The empirical setting for this book is the development of social policies across rich industrialized countries. Citizens' experiences of major life events, including illness, unemployment, disability, childrearing, and retirement, depend critically on public social policies. Across rich countries, governments devote almost half their budget, on average, to pensions, health care, unemployment, and family benefits.[12] By studying these fields, the book illustrates that international law, international norms, and other countries' policies are influential even when the stakes are very high, and when well-organized interest groups fight over very large sums of money. In addition, rich data on government spending on social policies allow me to investigate whether governments follow international models in practice, or whether governments only claim to follow international standards, but never actually implement these promises.

Rich democracies provide a hard test for my theory for another reason: they possess strong domestic policy-building capacities that reduce the need to draw inspiration from foreign developments. In developing countries, citizens have more worries that their governments are incompetent and corrupt, and more to learn from international comparisons. Yet, this book shows that rich democracies are also open to international benchmarking.

Scholars in international law and international relations have paid little attention to social policy questions, focusing instead on questions of war and trade. Conversely, a large literature in domestic and comparative social policy has largely ignored international forces, such as cross-national policy diffusion. Instead, this literature emphasizes domestic factors, such as conflicts between employers and employees, and right-wing and left-wing parties.[13] This inattention is surprising given the anchoring finding of social policy research in the past two decades—Gøsta Esping-Andersen's conclusion that geographically proximate countries have adopted very similar social policies, and cluster into three "worlds of welfare capitalism."[14] Policy clusters extend beyond rich countries: Figure 1.1 illustrates when countries around the world adopted their earliest social insurance program.[15] Light shades mark early adopters and dark shades mark late adopters. The map shows that European countries first developed social insurance programs in the late nineteenth century. North and South American countries followed the Europeans' lead in the 1900s and 1910s, while many Asian and African countries adopted social insurance programs in later decades.

Policy clusters could result from independent developments in proximate countries: neighboring countries might have similar domestic actors and institutions, and might respond similarly to common economic shocks. Such clusters could also reflect policy diffusion, defined here as a process in which

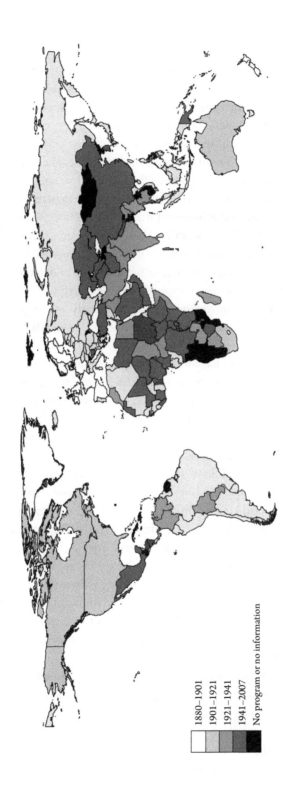

Figure 1.1 Adoption of Earliest Social Insurance Programs

1880–1901
1901–1921
1921–1941
1941–2007
No program or no information

one country's adoption of a policy, or an international organization's proposal, changes the probability that another country will adopt the same policy. This book uses cross-country regression models and qualitative techniques to estimate the impact of domestic factors and the effect of international influences. It finds that, even as domestic considerations remain important, countries are more likely to adopt a policy that their neighbors have previously adopted or that international organizations recommend.

This book concentrates on two areas of social policy: health policy and family policy. Health policy exemplifies a field where domestic interest groups—medical and pharmaceutical associations—are particularly powerful, while international organizations have only made limited efforts to define and spread international models. Yet, I show that foreign countries' experience with health policy models resonates with voters. The book begins with the U.S. health reforms of 2010. It uses original public opinion data to demonstrate that even American voters change their support for these reforms as they receive information about other countries' policies. It then analyzes campaign statements and the congressional record to show how both Democrats and Republicans used foreign models to promote their ideas.

The book then moves back in time to study an even more radical transformation: the diffusion of the National Health Service (NHS) model. The NHS model involves not only universal coverage, but also public provision of health care funded centrally through general taxation. The book documents how the British adoption of an NHS reverberated throughout Europe. International organizations have so far avoided recommending a specific model of health system organization and financing. The most important international instrument in this area is not a binding convention, but a nonbinding recommendation, the 1978 World Health Organization's (WHO's) Alma-Ata Declaration. This declaration did not call for the adoption of an NHS, but made some steps in this direction, by recommending universal coverage and a move away from specialized care and toward primary care. Nevertheless, I show that this instrument, though limited in scope and nonbinding in nature, was very influential in shaping national health systems. A combination of cross-national statistical evidence with case studies of reforms in southern Europe illustrates how foreign countries' choices and international organizations influenced national health reforms.

After examining major health policy reforms, the book turns to family policy, a field that underwent an even larger transformation in the last few decades. Across developed countries, governments that once encouraged women to stay at home and rear many children now promote women's workforce participation.[16] Maternity leaves, once unpaid and mandatory, are now compensated and flexible. Moreover, in many cases maternity leaves have been transformed into parental leaves, to encourage men's involvement in child care. Family allowances, once designed to promote fertility and encourage women's home-making roles, have also been restructured. Universal family allowances that depend on children's birth order, consistent with the older model of promoting large families, are among the few social benefits that left-leaning governments have cut back explicitly. Where they persist, family allowances are now pro-moted as gender-neutral poverty reduction tools, offered only to families that meet stringent means tests.

The book traces the influence of international organization proposals and other countries' experiences in these transformations. Family policy was an area of early and extensive international activity, in contrast with the limited input of international organizations in designing health systems. Starting in 1919, the International Labour Organization (ILO) has advocated for the adoption of maternity leave laws. Unlike the WHO, which included only broad guidelines in its declarations, the ILO developed very specific policy templates through its maternity leave conventions. Moreover, the ILO focused its efforts not only on pressing states to ratify these conventions, but also on lobbying nonratifying states to conform.[17] In parallel with the ILO advocacy, many rich countries introduced maternity leaves in their domestic legislation. As a result, maternity leave became the established international norm in reconciling work and family conflict. Subsequently countries around the world adopted mater-nity leaves quickly and with far less domestic contestation than we would oth-erwise expect. I contrast the ILO strategy with that of the European Union (EU), which reached agreement on a binding directive on maternity leave only in the mid-1990s. I show that, while the EU had much stronger tools at its disposal, including extensive financial and legal resources, the ILO was much more effective at shaping national laws in Europe because it started promot-ing a norm decades earlier, long before Europeans could agree on a binding EU directive. This outcome demonstrates that international organizations can greatly influence national policies by defining and promoting certain policies as international standards.

To examine the proposed theory, the book combines three types of empiri-cal evidence. First, experimental public opinion data show that even American voters respond favorably to international models. Second, cross-national regressions analyze policy reforms across eighteen rich democracies over sev-eral decades. These models allow me to predict the policies a country is likely to adopt based on its domestic socioeconomic conditions, the ideology of its government, the strength of key interest groups, and other domestic factors, and to carefully estimate whether and how much foreign models shape this choice. Third, qualitative case studies comparing early and late policy adopt-ers allow us to see how voters, politicians, and interest groups change positions when international models become available. These case studies show that international models do not only influence expected supporters, but also presumptive opponents of particular reforms. Combining three methods allows us to put the theory to many rigorous tests.

Chapter Outlines

Following this introduction, chapter 2 develops the book's theoretical argument: I explain the mechanisms through which international law and international norms can influence policy areas involving significant sums of money and well-organized domestic constituencies.

Chapter 3 examines two key assumptions of the theory: that ordinary voters respond strongly to information from abroad, and that politicians anticipate and mold this response. Americans are considered particularly unresponsive to international norms, and thus constitute a difficult case for the theory. The chapter presents original experimental public opinion data about Americans' views on health and family reforms. Surveying representative samples of US respondents shows that even American voters respond substantially to information from abroad, and that United Nations (UN) recommendations trigger stronger responses than information about the practices of foreign governments. Consistent with the proposed theory, voters predisposed to be skeptical of redistributive social policy initiatives—self-identified Independents and Republicans—and voters with limited information about social policy programs, respond especially strongly to information from abroad. This chapter also examines whether politicians anticipate and work to elicit this positive response. It presents policy debates surrounding the two most recent major reforms in these areas: the adoption of the 2010 Patient Protection and Affordable Care Act, and the adoption of the 1994 Family and Medical Leave Act. Qualitative data on the U.S. adoption of universal health care and family leave show that members of Congress and the president often refer to foreign models, but not necessarily to the most successful or relevant foreign models. Instead, U.S. politicians systematically refer to countries that are prominent in the U.S. media.

Chapter 4 reviews health systems across rich democracies, traces the rise and fall of the NHS as an international model, and uses cross-national regression evidence to show how international models contribute to the development of national health care policies. The great majority of countries around the world, and all rich democracies, have adopted some form of public health insurance. However, health systems differ on important dimensions, notably the breadth of health insurance coverage, the source of health financing, and the method of health care provision. This chapter explains how, starting in the 1950s and ending in the early 1980s, an international health model developed, focused on universal access, primary care, centralized financing, and public provision. The introduction of the British NHS and the WHO's Alma-Ata Declaration were key steps in the development of this model. Regression models show that governments were substantially more likely to adopt an NHS when the international environment was favorable. More specifically, these reforms are particularly likely to happen when foreign countries disproportionately covered in the press had already adopted an NHS, when evidence of an NHS success abroad was stronger, and when trade competitors had already adopted an NHS.

Chapter 5 continues the analysis of health reforms and uses case studies to clarify how international models shape domestic actors' positions. A comparison of NHS adoption in Britain, a pioneer, to NHS adoption in two late adopters, Greece and Spain, illustrates that the availability of foreign models permitted these late adopters to introduce radical reform under less favorable circumstances. In the two late adopters, politicians of all stripes repeatedly referenced Britain, France, and Germany, as well as the WHO, in election campaigns and parliamentary debates; this shows politicians' expectation that voters respond positively to the choices of familiar and respected bodies covered in the news media. Politicians focused in part on the success or failure of health policies abroad, but also argued that particular choices were modern and legitimate because they were endorsed by international organizations and rich and familiar European democracies. Notably scarce were references to other south European countries with similar economies and societies: fit and competitiveness considerations appeared less relevant in the quest to modernize. Foreign models also divided medical associations, an interest group that would have otherwise strongly opposed the reforms.

Chapter 6 begins the analysis of international influences on family policy reforms by presenting cross-national statistical evidence drawn from 18 countries over 25 years. Governments have been trying to shape women's employment and fertility patterns for decades by regulating leaves for parents and subsidizing families with children. What explains which laws they adopt, and how much they invest in implementing these laws? This chapter explains why international organization and country-to-country influences prove surprisingly powerful in explaining domestic regulatory and spending patterns. It compares two areas of family policy where there is significant variation in international organization activity. Maternity leaves have been the subject of substantial international efforts; both the ILO and, much more recently, the EU have promoted international and regional instruments in this field. In contrast, there has been little international activity in the field of family benefits; the ILO and EU have been constrained by their mandates to handle only aspects of family policy related to employment. I find that even though the EU has significantly more tools at its disposal, it ended up being much less influential than the ILO, because member states could not agree on a binding directive for many decades.

Chapter 7 presents qualitative evidence, and, in particular, case studies of various family reforms in Greece and Spain, to show how international models shaped family policy. Greece and Spain both developed similar policies on leaves, where international models were strong, long before relevant domestic pressure groups developed, using the rhetoric of joining and international community. Greece and Spain developed different policies on family benefits, where the international community offered diverse models, with Spanish Socialists explicitly cutting back a redistributive but highly stigmatized policy. Analysis of the timing and content of reforms, and of the rhetoric that accompanied policy change, highlights the centrality of foreign ideas to the development of family policy.

Chapter 8 concludes and spells out policy implications of the proposed theory. Two main types of policy implications follow from the findings that domestic constituencies substantially influence how international models spread. First, international organizations, nongovernmental organizations (NGOs), and others interested in spreading messages across countries could follow particular strategies to increase their influence. For example, an important choice that states, international organizations, and NGOs face is whether to design international instruments that involve binding obligations, or focus instead on creating nonbinding norms.[18] This study departs from prior work by suggesting that soft law may be substantially more effective in changing state behavior than previously believed, and that even the strongest form of binding international law we know, EU law, has important limitations. Second, citizens, scholars, and leaders concerned about the democratic deficits of international organizations could use this research to design international institutions that are both effective and legitimate.

2

A Theory of Diffusion Through Democratic Mechanisms

Extensive evidence in law, sociology, political science, and other disciplines documents that similar laws often spread within countries, within regions, and across the globe.[1] Foreign states' laws and international organizations' templates shape national constitutions,[2] corporate codes,[3] criminal prohibitions,[4] environmental regulations,[5] employment laws,[6] and administrative[7] and court structures,[8] among many other areas. These studies have identified three general objectives that states pursue when adopting laws from abroad. Some argue that states competing with each other for capital, trade, or labor also imitate each other's policies. Others propose that states learn from the success or failure of other states' policy experiments. Finally, some scholars claim that states emulate the policies of states considered "modern," "advanced," or "developed."[9]

But who, exactly, within the state makes the decision to pursue one objective or another, and for what reason? Much of this literature is silent on the question of agency. Scholars who offer an answer focus on technocratic networks of policy elites. Bureaucrats, policy experts, and politicians mingle in international circles, absorb orthodox policy ideas, and bring these lessons home. Yet, theories of elite networks cannot explain how the preferences of an enlightened minority win the day in modern democracies if these are distasteful to the majority of ordinary voters.

This is the starting point for this book's theory. International models, I argue, can help politicians rally voter support behind proposed reforms. International models are defined as policies already adopted by foreign governments or endorsed by international organizations. To win elections and garner support for legislation, politicians convince voters that their proposals are well-designed and mainstream. One way in which politicians can convey this information credibly is by referencing international models. Such references can help politicians signal to voters that a proposal has been carefully vetted by disinterested outsiders and is not an ill-thought-out experiment or a giveaway to fringe ideologues or special interest groups. Voters can use international models as benchmarks against which to judge their own government's proposals. However, voters are only familiar with a few foreign countries: these tend to be the large, rich, and culturally proximate countries disproportionately covered in national media. Politicians are more likely to reference these countries to appeal to voters. Thus these countries' policies are most likely to spread widely, even if more successful policies have been pioneered in small, poor, and remote states.

This chapter lays out in greater detail the theoretical claims of the book. I first summarize the insights of the existing literature on diffusion and show how they clash with our understanding of policy reform in democratic regimes. I then propose a theory of policy diffusion that explains how international models shift voter preferences. I explain, step by step, the key propositions of this theory, highlighting the role of the main participants in democratic contests: voters, politicians, domestic interest groups, and media outlets. Finally, I formulate empirical predictions for a democracy-based diffusion theory, setting the scene for the chapters that follow.

Insights from the Diffusion Literature

Theorists have suggested three broad pathways through which foreign models influence domestic laws: competition, learning, and emulation. Competition between two states for capital, markets, or other resources may lead countries to imitate their competitors' policies.[10] In the area of social policy, some have argued that governments competing with one another to attract mobile firms will lower labor regulations and will reduce social benefits funded through taxes on labor.[11] I test for this theory in the empirical chapters that follow, but find that the theoretically prominent pathway of competition played a moderate role in the diffusion of social policies across rich countries. Learning and emulation theories claim that information from abroad is critical to social policy diffusion. Foreign models can convey different types of information, including information about the content and consequences of particular policies, as well as information about the fact that a policy was promoted by a particular government or international organization. The type of information transmitted through foreign models distinguishes theories emphasizing learning from theories focusing on emulation. In learning theories, governments examine the effects of other governments' policy choices and imitate their policies when they correlate with positive outcomes. For example, downsizing policies correlated with gross domestic product (GDP) growth[12] or hospital financing reforms associated with reduced health expenditures[13] are particularly likely to diffuse.

While learning theories emphasize a policy's on-the-ground success as the main determinant of diffusion, emulation theories focus instead on the identity of prior adopters. The policy choices of high-status countries are emulated regardless of their policy consequences. Claims about emulation come in diverse forms. In sociological institutionalist diffusion models, actors enact a global script. They pursue choices that appear legitimate, appropriate, and modern, rather than pursuing goals instrumentally;[14] several constructivist scholars make related claims.[15] In informational herding models, agents have some private information and can also observe other agents' choices. Herding results when the amount of public information, gleaned from the choices of prior decision-makers, overwhelms any private information and actors all make the same choice, following the public information and disregarding private cues.[16] According to herding models, the fact that a particular government has adopted a policy will lead other governments to imitate this policy. In models based on cognitive biases, known as cognitive shortcut models, individuals make systematically biased choices: they place excessive weight on available information, draw overconfident predictions from limited observations, and attach disproportionate importance to initial anchoring values.[17]

A fourth mechanism, conditionality, posits that when the adoption of a practice is a condition for the receipt of some material benefit, such as aid, loans, or membership in an international organization, governments are more likely to adopt the practice.[18] Conditionality is discussed only occasionally in this book, because before 2010, international organizations had rarely tried to shape social policies in advanced industrialized countries through conditionality. Since 2010, the European Union (EU) and the International Monetary Fund (IMF) have required European states, including Greece, Portugal, and Ireland, to reform public spending and cut back social policies in order to receive bailout funds. Post-2010 reforms are still being negotiated, and are not the main subject of this book. However, there are important similarities in the political rhetoric accompanying very different reforms. In the 1970s and 1980s, politicians in Europe's periphery justified the expansion of social programs as a way for their countries to become modern and European, as chapters 5 and 7 explain. Today, politicians in these same countries are making deep cutbacks to social programs. Voters shudder at these bitter austerity measures, but still desperately want their countries to remain modern and European. Thus politicians frequently reference Europe, and highlight that balanced budgets constitute the new European model, in their efforts to make unpopular cutbacks more palatable.

The three mechanisms described above—competition, learning, and emulation—share a key limitation: they say little about the domestic actors who eventually determine policy adoption. Several scholars have criticized different strands of the diffusion literature for this reason. For example, a large literature on legal transplants documents similarities and differences between host and home country legislation but does not discuss in great detail what drives such transplants.[19] As a recent review of this literature concluded, progress in the field of legal transplants requires adding "to the 'macro' explanations of legal change currently available an analysis of the 'micro' level of individual action which is implicated in the transplant."[20] A different large literature in sociology—the sociological institutionalism literature—argues for the existence of a global script and shows strong correlations between diverse countries policies.[21] Again, however, this literature tells us little about individual agency; this theoretical tradition understands actors as "enactors of multiple dramas whose texts are written elsewhere."[22] The same criticism raised in the legal transplants is the main criticism facing the sociological institutionalism literature, namely that "the mechanics of social influence have so far been grossly underspecified."[23] Similarly, a large and growing literature on diffusion in political science employs correlations between countries to infer causal pathways on competition, learning, and emulation. The political science literature is criticized for identifying structural relationships while saying less about process and agency; it shares the same blind spot as the literature in law.[24]

A few groundbreaking studies delve into the process of policy diffusion and highlight the role of individual actors in spreading norms. Anne Marie Slaughter identified networks of judges, central bankers, and policemen as central to spreading laws across countries.[25] Michael Mintrom surveyed policy entrepreneurs and highlighted their role in spreading policies across U.S. states.[26] Kurt Weyland highlighted the role of domestic and international experts in the diffusion of pension and health reforms across Latin American countries.[27] Weyland's informational herding and cognitive shortcut models argue that individual policymakers suffer from severe cognitive, psychological, or informational limitations: they face uncertainty, learn, make cognitive mistakes, mimic others, and seek peer approval. The international political process aggregates these individual decisions in a way that preserves, rather than correcting, these biases.

These new works bring a much-needed focus on agency to the study of policy diffusion. In so doing, they build on important older traditions on how communities of lawyers, accountants, economists, and other professionals develop unified approaches to new problems and spread these ideas across countries.[28] However, these studies present policy diffusion as "a process that unfolds largely inside the bureaucratic agencies of the state and is not driven in any direct way by electoral incentives and calculations."[29] The focus is on government leaders and on national bureaucracies rather than the broad array of domestic constituents. Undoubtedly, leaders' informational shortages and psychological biases shape political decision-making to some extent. However, two additional assumptions are necessary for technocrats' biases to drive policy diffusion across diverse policy areas, including contexts where huge monetary sums are at stake. First, these biases must be very widely shared among technocrats, politicians, and other elites—otherwise enterprising bureaucrats, investigative journalists, or opposition politicians could decide to challenge and correct these biased views. More importantly, this unified elite must be able to impose their preferred views on unsuspecting citizens.

However, in democracies, government leaders are not free agents, able to translate their preferences into policy choices without constraints. Government leaders are also politicians who must win and maintain the support of ordinary voters. Voters' views constrain democratic governments' choices across a broad range of issue areas, as empirical studies in both the United States and the comparative literature confirm.[30] The salience of particular issues to voters, the structure of interest group preferences, and the nature of partisan competition all influence how constrained politicians feel.[31] This book provides a theory that explains how diffusion processes work in settings where decisions are made by elected politicians responsive to voters and interest groups. The following section examines what we can learn about these actors from the literature on the domestic politics of social policy.

Domestic Politics of Social Policy

A vast literature explores why some countries adopt social policies that redistribute income and risks while others do not: we have more than 400 quantitative estimates of the influence of left-wing parties on the development of redistributive policies.[32] A clear narrative focused heavily on domestic conflicts emerges from this literature. To explain why governments adopt social policies, political scientists first ask what voters want. Much of this work begins with voters' material interests, and argues that governments pursue economic policies in accordance with the interests of their "class-defined core political constituents."[33] Next, political scientists examine how unions, employer organizations, and other powerful interest groups position themselves. Strong labor unions encourage governments to develop policies that insure citizens against many risks and redistribute income.[34] More recent work emphasizes that employer groups do not always fight such initiatives, but sometimes form coalitions with labor unions to increase the provision of insurance[35] and facilitate investments in skills.[36]

Having explained how material conditions shape actors' preferences and bargaining power, the literature on the welfare state also explains how actors' preferences are channeled into policy outputs.[37] Policies of any kind, including social policies, are hard to introduce in countries where many politicians can block change. Arguments about veto players specify these conditions, by exploring the number and structural position of decision-makers required for change to happen.[38] But once introduced, social programs tend to stick. Path dependence arguments explore why early choices have determinative impacts on later outcomes.[39] And arguments in the varieties of capitalism tradition explain how particular social policies fit with other national institutions.[40]

This model of social policy development is very neat. But as with many neat models, it doesn't always match the data. Voters, in particular, tend to disappoint: they often vote in ways that deviate substantially from their material interests. Big predictions of comparative political economy are thus turned upside down. To take one prominent example, Allan Meltzer and Scott Richard argue that unequal societies should be most willing to enact redistributive social policies, because in unequal societies the decisive median voter has an income below the mean income and would benefit from redistribution.[41] But contrary to these predictions, many empirical studies find that the most unequal societies are often the least likely to adopt redistributive social policies.[42] Organized interest groups behave in more predictable ways. But even organized interest groups do not often identify the policy that would best serve their interests; they face cognitive and informational limitations and might choose a policy that is good enough rather than optimal.[43]

The more we believe that material incentives lead politicians to adopt natural, functional, and unique solutions to satisfy the preferences of their constituents, the less space exists for ideas of any kind, foreign or domestic, to influence policy. In contrast, the broader the range of alternatives consistent with voters', unions', employers', politicians', and other actors' material incentives, the more relevant arguments about ideas, and thus about foreign models, become. In contexts where such flexibility exists, foreign countries' choices can matter by making particular alternatives plausible options, and by changing actors' evaluations of these alternatives.

Proposed Electoral Theory

The electoral framework I propose explains how politicians who are severely constrained by voters and interest groups can benefit from introducing foreign models into their domestic politics. Politicians often have a set of preferred reforms that track their personal and partisan beliefs. However, democracy constrains them: politicians must balance their desire to enact their preferred reforms with their fear of losing the next election; this drives politicians away from their preferred policies and toward policies attractive to voters.[44] A key insight of the proposed theory is that foreign models do not necessarily conflict with prior policy positions voters have developed. Indeed, voters may have only vague ideas about the policies they want to see enacted, and strong worries that politicians may design policies that benefit special interests alone, and not the public at large. When voters are uncertain about whether a policy proposal will benefit them or not, politicians can reduce voter uncertainty by referring to the example of other countries or by pointing to an international organization proposal. Thus borrowing foreign models helps politicians improve their reelection probabilities.

The theoretical schema below also abstracts away another critical dimension of the diffusion process, that is, variation in the competitive environments politicians face, and thus in the degree to which politicians feel constrained to implement popular policies. Some politicians feel less constrained than others, because, for example, electoral rules lead them to expect to win with a large margin. Other politicians are at the end of their careers and are not seeking another term. Politicians in such situations have much greater leeway to deviate from what voters want and can behave more like technocrats. Conversely, while technocrats in general have substantial freedom to select their preferred policies, some may also seek to have popularity with mass audiences, and may behave more like politicians as a result. Interest groups are in the background for now. While interest groups play a critical role in the development of social policy, their positions often derive from material interests, and tend to be more stable and less amenable to the influence of foreign models, as compared to voter beliefs. I return to these and other variations after outlining how foreign models enter the electoral cycle, and identify how well this theory fits different policy areas, countries, international models, and other conditions. The proposed model involves four stages, outlined in Figure 2.1, and is presented in more detail below.

Media Cover Large, Rich, and Proximate Foreign Countries Disproportionately

Across countries, both print and broadcast media devote substantial space to foreign developments. Smaller countries devote even more attention to developments abroad than larger ones. The most comprehensive available study, commissioned by the United Nations Education, Scientific, and Cultural

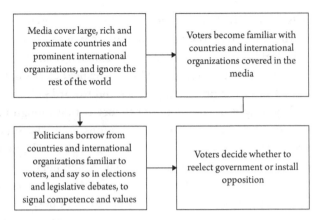

Figure 2.1 Proposed Electoral Theory

Organization (UNESCO), involving 13 national teams and presenting data for 29 countries, reveals the following patterns. Large industrialized countries, such as the United States, Germany, and Australia, devote about 20% of the evening television news to developments abroad.[45] Smaller industrialized countries, such as Finland and The Netherlands, devote approximately 40% of their TV news to foreign developments. Radio stations show similar patterns to TV stations, while print media typically devote even more space to foreign news.[46]

In turn, coverage of foreign developments is very uneven geographically. Diverse studies indicate that news coverage in television, radio, and print media tends to focus on proximate countries, where proximity is understood in geographic, linguistic, and cultural terms. Not all proximate countries benefit from equal coverage; large economies receive disproportionate coverage.[47] In contrast, small, distant, culturally dissimilar, and poor countries get very little news coverage; much of the world is invisible. This emphasis on large, rich, and proximate countries occurs not only in news coverage, but also in the domestic coverage of foreign political and economic conditions,[48] deaths abroad,[49] and even foreign arts and culture.[50] Similarly the media only cover prominent international organizations.

Voters Become Familiar with Countries and International Organizations Covered in the Media

Most voters do not actively collect information about domestic and foreign developments most of the time. They get information passively: voters spend many hours watching television, listening to the radio, reading newspapers, and browsing the Internet.[51] Moreover, family, friends, and others often echo what is covered in the media.

As a result of this media coverage, voters have a general, vague sense about the world. Voters are likely to become aware of countries covered in the media, and remain unaware of other countries. Voters get their impressions not only from news coverage, but from all kinds of media portrayals. For example, many people around the world watch Hollywood movies, and get a general sense that America is a rich, capitalist society. Similarly people around the world may hear that European societies are wealthy, while African countries are war-torn. Citizens of small, open countries are especially likely to hear about large and wealthy neighbors that share a language and culture. For example, Austrian voters hear a great deal about Germany; Irish voters hear a great deal about Britain. Note that at this stage, voters get a general sense about the few foreign countries covered prominently in the media—not necessarily about the policy choices these countries have made.

One way prior public opinion studies have captured this general sense is by asking citizens how warmly or coolly they feel toward particular countries on a feelings thermometer. For example, Americans' views of foreign countries range from warm feelings toward Britain, followed by moderately warm feelings toward other rich industrialized countries, followed by cooler feelings toward many developing countries, and ending with very cold feelings toward North Korea.[52] Similarly, the World Health Organization (WHO) and the United Nations (UN) receive moderately warm thermometer readings, while the World Bank and the IMF receive more tepid readings.[53]

Politicians Borrow from Countries and Organizations Familiar to Voters, and Say So in Elections and Legislative Debates, to Signal Competence and Mainstream Values

Politicians have much greater incentives and capabilities than voters to collect information about policy options. Interest groups and advocacy organizations will often present politicians with information about policy alternatives they prefer, including information about what foreign countries are doing. The easier it is to obtain information about foreign models, the more likely politicians are to consider foreign models.

Politicians will base their policies in part on what serves their personal and partisan goals, and on what best serves the interest groups on whose support they count. Concerns about winning elections, however, will constrain them. Politicians must ultimately explain their policy choices to voters; politicians thus design policies they can sell.

Politicians continuously seek to present their work in the best light possible, and media coverage of politics is ongoing. But there are two moments when we might be especially likely to see references to foreign models: during election campaigns and during debates on major legislative proposals. At these moments, media coverage of politics reaches a particular fervor, and voters pay greater attention to what politicians are saying. However, voters receive a barrage of competing information. Voters do not know exactly what to believe, as they can see that much of this information comes from partisan sources and serves partisan ends. As I explain below, references to foreign models can help politicians send credible signals to voters that their proposals are well-thought out and mainstream.

First, I present a few examples from election campaigns to give a flavor of the arguments politicians use. In their first electoral manifesto following Spain's transition to democracy, the Spanish Socialists pledged "to turn our country into a society similar to that of our neighbors in Europe, raising the standard of living of our fellow citizens, surpassing the limits of underdevelopment, to enter into a type of life proper for an industrial society of the European type."[54] Chapters 5 and 7 outline how such references were repeated and made more specific in subsequent elections and legislative debates, both in Spain and in other countries in the European periphery. While such pledges resonate strongly among citizens who are aware that culturally proximate neighbors enjoy a higher standard of living, they are sometimes heard even in rich superpowers like the United States. For example, when candidate Bill Clinton first campaigned for office, he challenged President George H. W. Bush in a televised debate by arguing that "[working families] deserve a strong economy, and I think they deserve a family and medical leave act. *Seventy-two other nations have been able to do it. Mr. Bush vetoed it twice because he says we can't do something 72 other countries do.*"[55] Candidate Clinton continued to defend his health care proposal in similar terms: "*I say if Germany can cover everybody and keep costs under inflation, if Hawaii can cover 98 percent of their people at lower health care costs than the rest of us, America can do it, too.*"[56] Chapter 3 outlines how Presidents Bill Clinton and Barack Obama used international models in their efforts to introduce family leave and health policy reforms, and how ordinary Americans responded to these references.

Politicians seek to persuade voters that they are governing competently, and that they are enacting proposals consistent with voters' values.[57] Borrowing foreign models can help with both of these tasks. First, politicians can borrow foreign models *to signal that they are governing competently.* Voters who receive information that a particular proposal has been adopted by foreign decision-makers may gravitate toward that proposal in the expectation that it will bring about better outcomes, domestically, than a new, untested proposal. A politician might identify prior adopters and highlight that "unlike other proposals, this plan is not an experiment."[58] Note that voters do not necessarily demand from politicians detailed evidence of the proposal's on-the-ground success or failure. If such evidence of clear success is widely available, it is likely to resonate strongly with voters and be invoked frequently by politicians. However, in many policy areas evidence of success is unclear or unavailable: the innovation may be too recent for its effects to have unfolded, there may be sharp disagreement on how to define and measure success, the innovation may have both advantages and disadvantages relative to alternatives, and any information about policy success that exists may not be widely available.[59] Where evidence of success is not clear and uncontroverted, voters rely on the fact that another—familiar—country has adopted the proposal as a signal of that proposal's qualities. Information that a foreign country adopted a legal reform is not cheap talk. It is a costly, and thus strong, signal that foreign leaders have vetted a particular proposal. This signal indicates that a foreign government evaluated the proposal and found it to be a good enough reform to adopt in their country.[60] Unlike most domestic endorsements, it is a signal unlikely to be issued for the purpose of influencing the domestic election; in most fields, foreign governments care too little to invest in domestic reforms in order to create policy incentives for their neighbors.

Second, politicians can borrow foreign models *to clarify that a proposal coheres with voters' values.* Governing parties want to signal that their policies are not radical proposals designed to please partisan extremists, but are instead mainstream policies, consistent with the values of the swing voters they want to attract. When a dominant international model exists, references to this model can help persuade voters that a policy proposal is mainstream. For example, in introducing the Spanish National Health System, Socialist members of parliament (MPs) emphasized that their proposal reflected not personal and partisan values, but values shared by hundreds of countries and endorsed by the WHO.[61] Similarly, in introducing family leave in the United States, Democrats, and even some Republicans, emphasized that hundreds of countries had already adopted the policy.[62]

A different pathway, not emphasized in this book, posits that international models can be influential in cases where some voters are concerned not only about the domestic consequences of a proposal, but are also directly concerned with how foreign countries are acting and with what international organizations are proposing. These voters may prefer that their country conform with international norms because this is intrinsically desirable or because it confers benefits abroad. The mechanisms emphasized above assume that voters care primarily about the domestic consequences of policy proposals. This assumption is based on a large literature suggesting that voters are far more concerned with the domestic consequences of policies than with their effects abroad.[63] However, this last pathway could become relevant in some policy fields, for example, for policies that have minor domestic consequences and major consequences abroad.

In the subsequent paragraphs I develop the proposed theory further, to explain which foreign models are most likely to be referenced and how they are likely to be featured in election campaigns and legislative debates. The next section spells out additional scope conditions and testable implications of the proposed argument.

Some foreign models will confer greater electoral advantages than others. At one extreme, a model adopted by a small, distant, and poor country, a country not prominent in the media and thus unfamiliar to voters, is unlikely to be useful to politicians. Constituents may worry that the politician is cherry-picking—that she designed a proposal to suit partisan preferences and then looked far and wide to find a country that had adopted it. At the other extreme, a dominant international model adopted by many prominent countries and endorsed by an international organization can help a politician signal both that she is governing competently and that she is not pursuing an agenda reflecting partisan values alone.

In busy, contentious reelection campaigns, simple and verifiable claims are likely to get communicated; nuanced statements can get lost. For example, a politician may want to offer a nuanced report of a foreign model to indicate not only that a foreign government adopted a policy, but also to highlight that it experienced great success with this policy. This additional information could be valuable to voters. However, voters' short attention span, and voters' worry that politicians are biased, may make it very hard to credibly communicate information that a policy was successful abroad. In contrast, the media can easily verify whether a policy has been widely adopted by foreign countries and endorsed by international organizations. For this reason, information about the fact that foreign governments adopted a policy becomes especially significant.

Foreign models are important both when a politician first seeks office and when she seeks reelection. When challenged on a particular policy area, incumbents who borrowed foreign models will make this clear to voters, to signal as best they can that they are governing competently and pursuing mainstream values. Imagine that a major environmental disaster brings environmental regulation to the forefront during an election. A government may defend its record by highlighting that it followed dominant international regulatory standards. It can portray the environmental crisis as an exogenous and entirely unforeseeable event, as evidenced by the fact that foreign regulators did not foresee it. A government may also assert that it was not unduly deferential to the industry that caused the environmental disaster, as evidenced by the fact that regulators in familiar foreign countries balanced safety concerns with concerns about industry profitability in the same way.

Opposition politicians will challenge incumbents' assertions in any way they think effective. If they anticipate that references to foreign models will resonate among voters, they will try to contest these references. Opposition politicians may argue that governing parties are misinterpreting international organization advice, that multiple foreign models exist, and that the incumbents are selectively referencing the wrong countries. Where there exists a coherent foreign model, adopted by many countries and forcefully promulgated by international organizations, these challenges will not work well. In contrast, where a diversity of foreign models exists, and international organizations have not settled on a clear template, opposition politicians will have ample space to contest the government's choices.

Here are some examples of contestation from the social policy cases discussed in this book. In Spain, politicians from the center-right contested the assertion that the WHO recommended a National Health Service (NHS), and instead argued that the WHO endorsed multiple models.[64] Similarly, in American health care debates, Republicans emphasized that multiple health models existed, and that Democrats were incorrectly borrowing ideas from Socialist countries.[65] In contrast, in debates about family leave, where clear consensus on an international model existed, and this model had been adopted by almost every country in the world and promoted by international organizations for decades, many Republicans chose to be silent on the question of international norms, and a few ended up supporting the policy and referencing international norms favorably.[66]

Voters Decide Whether to Reelect Government or Install Opposition

After the campaigning ends, voters decide whether to reelect incumbent politicians or not. Could efforts to borrow foreign models influence electoral results? Some voters have very stable views: committed conservatives and committed progressives will likely vote predictably, whatever the incumbent's record and campaign strategy. For this reason, both election campaigns and policymaking efforts focus greatly on swing voters.[67]

The theory developed in this book predicts that foreign models should have a large impact among voters who have doubts about the government's competence and about the government's values. Many swing voters fall in this category. This increases the electoral incentives for politicians to borrow foreign models.

The prediction that voters who face a lot of uncertainty will be most responsive to foreign models is a particularly distinctive one; prior diffusion studies suggest that foreign models only resonate among persons predisposed to support the foreign model on ideological grounds. In addition, and more predictably, foreign models should have large effects among voters who are internationally oriented, and who see the foreign countries referenced as reflective of their values. The discussion below explores in more detail the types of voters and politicians most likely to respond to foreign models, the countries most receptive to ideas from abroad, the international models most likely to resonate, and the ways in which foreign models and domestic politics intersect.

Before explaining in more detail the conditions under which foreign models are more or less influential, I summarize the key features of the theory. Voters and other constituents who face uncertainty about whether a proposal serves them well might be reassured if told that credible outsiders, with skin in the game, have vetted the idea. In addition, voters who believe that certain countries' choices are consistent (or inconsistent) with their values are likely to find information about foreign models useful in situating particular domestic proposals. Not every foreign model is likely to resonate with voters. To gain electoral advantages, politicians will have incentives to borrow the policies of countries and international organizations familiar to voters, and ignore useful information from other sources not visible to voters. Relatedly, politicians who have personal doubts about dominant international models will nonetheless have incentives to publicly embrace these models to win reelection.

This proposed principal-agent dynamic, in which politicians reference foreign models to assure key constituencies that they are pursuing policies that serve their interests, also applies to constituencies other than voters. Ultimately, even the best-financed interest group with the best available research faces some uncertainty about the consequences of policy proposals. However, organized interest groups, unlike voters, tend to have far less uncertainty about whether a proposal is likely to suit their interests. Organized interest groups might shift their views given new evidence from abroad, but because they already often have significant information at their disposal, and well worked-out positions, these shifts should be smaller than for voters. As a corollary, we should see foreign models matter the most to interest groups whose views are in flux, perhaps because they formed recently or are experiencing a generational shift.

When Do Foreign Models Resonate? Scope Conditions and Testable Implications

The proposed theory has implications for many aspects of the diffusion process: the *actors* likely to respond to information from abroad, the *policy areas* where diffusion should be strongest, the *countries* most receptive to foreign models, the *international models* most likely to spread, and the ways in which *international models and domestic politics* intersect. The claims that follow help develop the theory. They can be understood as scope conditions; that is, the proposed model will work better under some circumstances than others. In addition, these claims also function as testable implications of the theory, and start off a discussion about empirical facts that confirm and facts that challenge the proposed theoretical model. In the discussion below I contrast the predictions of my theory with the predictions of other theoretical perspectives. Figure 2.2, at the end of this section, summarizes these predictions and notes the chapters that explore particular implications.

Actors Involved in the Diffusion Process

As described above, many diffusion studies do not specify which actors are involved in the diffusion process. Studies that speak to this question of agency tend to focus on networks of policy elites. In contrast, this book's central claim is that electoral incentives reinforce and change the diffusion processes. In my account, bureaucracies and expert networks are critical to bringing foreign models to politicians' attention. However, politicians ultimately decide whether or not to introduce foreign models based on whether this will help them win domestic elections—not based on whether this will please their foreign counterparts. The proposed theory has several testable implications regarding the agents of policy diffusion. Three are particularly distinctive because they run counter to much of the diffusion literature. First, we should see inexpert voters, who know and care very little about politics, respond strongly to international models. Second, foreign models should resonate not only among persons predisposed to favor a particular idea, but among diverse groups. Third, we should see politicians—who are very constrained by domestic elections—respond to foreign models more strongly compared to decision-makers who operate outside the electoral process, such as judges, central bankers, or leaders of autocratic regimes.

Many academics, judges, and commentators emphasize how references to foreign law reflect elite predilections antithetical to the views of ordinary voters, especially ordinary Americans. Justice Antonin Scalia tells us that borrowing from foreign law involves imposing the views of a "small cream at the top," "not the views of America at large."[68] Kenneth Anderson describes the process as "the promotion of a shared set of globalized elite bourgeois values."[69] Steven Calabresi contrasts the culture of the "elite," who eagerly borrow from abroad, with "another culture among ordinary Americans that holds that Americans are a special people, in a special land, on a special mission."[70] The list of writers who echo this theme is long; in addition, many other countries have streaks of exceptionalist rhetoric.[71] And, as discussed above, many scholars who are not explicitly interested in the divide between ordinary voters and elite decision-makers deflect our attention from ordinary voters by emphasizing that networks of policy elites drive policy diffusion.[72]

In contrast, this theory predicts that ordinary voters will respond significantly to information from abroad precisely because, unlike sophisticated elites, voters know little about many policy issues. According to the proposed theory, the fact that a foreign government has adopted a policy conveys information that someone with skin in the game has vetted the policy, and that it is likely to bring about better results than a new, untested policy. In addition, when a proposal follows a dominant international model, this can suggest that the proposal reflects mainstream values. These informational signals can be very valuable to someone who knows little about a topic. They are much less valuable to an expert who already knows an issue area very well. Just as an additional piece of information should shift ordinary voters' views more than experts' views, so we should see variation among voters, depending on their prior information levels. That is, we should see voters who know less about an issue area respond more strongly to foreign models than voters who are better informed.

Additionally, the proposed theory implies that voters who face significant uncertainty about their government should respond more than voters who are confident in their government's policies. Independents and moderate conservatives face significant uncertainty about left-leaning governments; independents and moderate progressives face significant uncertainty about right-leaning governments. Committed conservatives and committed progressives know which way to vote; their views on policies and politicians should not respond strongly to information about international developments, or to information about domestic developments for that matter. The prediction that left-wing governments can borrow foreign models to signal to independents and moderate conservatives that they are competent and mainstream is counterintuitive, as is the corresponding prediction about right-wing governments. Many writers believe that foreign models resonate only among committed progressives.[73]

Finally, the proposed theory implies that voters who hold positive views of foreign governments and international organizations should respond more strongly to foreign models. This expectation is consistent with a large literature in communications, which indicates that endorsements are more persuasive when audiences perceive these to come from credible, high-status actors.[74]

In addition to implications about voters, the proposed theory also implies that we should see certain patterns among decision-makers. If the proposed theory is correct, we should observe elected decision-makers making many references to foreign models, and we should expect these references to concentrate on a handful of countries familiar to voters. In addition, as outlined above, we should see these references both during elections and during debates on major legislation. We see these patterns in the chapters that follow—politicians in the United States, Greece, and Spain concentrate their references to countries familiar to voters, even when other references would better suit partisan ideology or identify more suitable foreign models.

This theory should apply best to decision-makers operating in very competitive electoral environments, in which every vote counts. It should apply to some extent to decision-makers in moderately competitive environments, and should not apply to decision-makers who do not have any domestic audiences to please. Few decision-makers are entirely unconstrained by domestic audiences; dictators in personalistic regimes perhaps approach this point.[75] However, some democracies have party systems that are not very competitive and see the same party consistently gaining the support of a majority of voters.[76] And across many democracies, some decision-makers are deliberately shielded, to some extent, from public opinion—judges, central bankers, and other important appointees might fall in this category.[77] Additionally, some elected officials have long terms, or have no plans for reelection. The more decision-makers are shielded from public scrutiny, the more freely they can enact their preferred policies. Unconstrained decision-makers have many more choices than elected officials facing tough competition as regards foreign models: they can borrow foreign models only to the extent they think this is best for their country, or for their personal interests.

In addition, some decision-makers face audiences that are different from the general public. For example, judges face a second key audience: the legal community. Because this community is more educated than the electorate at large, judges are less constrained to reference the very few countries familiar to the public at large. Indeed, lawyers' education might prevent judges from referencing obviously unsuccessful and irrelevant foreign models. As a result, we should see more diverse, and more pertinent, references to foreign models.

Diffusion Across Policy Areas

According to the proposed theory, we should expect to see strong diffusion patterns, especially in areas where decision-makers are severely constrained by electorates. More specifically, if politicians anticipate that an issue will capture voters' attention with high probability, the effect of foreign models should be large. If voters might one day care, but only if a crisis focuses their attention on the issue, there should be some effect of foreign models on policy design. Imitating foreign models is a type of insurance; if the risk is unlikely to materialize, and if insurance is costly, politicians may not purchase it. That is, if voters are unlikely to scrutinize a particular policy decision, and if borrowing a foreign model would require deviating significantly from what the politician would otherwise choose, politicians may not purchase the insurance. In addition, this mechanism should not be relevant if a policy effort is likely to produce immediate and uncontroverted success domestically. That is, if a policy is likely to yield clear positive results before the next election, it will be easy for a politician to claim credit on the basis of these domestic results. In contrast, references to foreign models are more useful signals if, domestically, policy results are likely to be incomplete or ambiguous come election time. The full costs and benefits of many important policies, including the social policies examined in this book, unfold over many years, if not decades.[78]

In fields where unaccountable decision-makers can make decisions with independence from voters' wishes, the proposed electoral mechanism should not be relevant. While there are few such fields, across many policy areas, decision-makers are more accountable to voters for the overall policy outlines and major goals, but have substantially more leeway in determining exactly how these policies will be implemented. Because of this, we should expect diffusion through democracy to be more important in determining broad policy goals, and diffusion through technocratic networks to be more pronounced in policy details, rather than in broad policy goals. Many prior diffusion studies document decoupling; that is, public adherence to international norms combined with only partial implementation of the international model. Decoupling is consistent with the proposed electoral theory; politicians may adopt the broad outlines of international models to reassure the general public, but allow powerful interest groups to have more say in less visible aspects of policy implementation.[79]

Countries Receptive to Foreign Models

Countries vary in how receptive their citizens are to foreign models and to international organization proposals. If the proposed theory is correct, and foreign models serve to reassure voters who face uncertainty about their government's policy proposals, we should see strong diffusion effects in countries lacking domestic sources of credible information. Countries with histories of incompetent, partisan, and corrupt government, countries that lack independent domestic information producers, and countries that are unitary, and thus lack experiments from subnational governments, should rely especially heavily on foreign models. Small and poor countries might be especially likely to lack good domestic sources of information. In contrast, in countries with credible domestic sources of information, such as countries with well-established independent bureaucracies or federal states with strong local experimentation, foreign models provide one additional piece of information among many others, and should thus be less influential. Relatedly, countries experiencing transitions should respond more strongly to foreign models than countries experiencing periods of stability. This is because in transition periods citizens are likely to experience more doubts about their government and its policies, and politicians may make greater efforts to borrow foreign models to reassure their constituents.

Additionally, countries vary in how much exposure their citizens have to foreign developments. As outlined above, citizens of small countries receive more coverage of developments in neighboring countries than citizens of large countries. This phenomenon is likely to be especially pronounced if their neighbors are perceived as richer and more modern. Moreover, different countries' national media focus on different countries: as described above, national media tends to focus on large, rich, and culturally proximate countries. As a result, countries should be especially likely to borrow from their large, rich, and culturally proximate neighbors. Countries that lack such neighbors, perhaps because they are culturally or geographically isolated, or because they are very rich, should be less responsive to foreign models.

Three countries studied in depth in subsequent chapters—the United States, Spain, and Greece—differ along the dimensions outlined above. The United States is a particularly hard test case for the proposed theory, both because it is a large federal state with excellent domestic sources of information, and because the United States is very rich, and few Americans see other countries as significantly more modern on policy dimensions they care about. In contrast, we should see stronger diffusion effects in Spain and Greece, both because these are smaller countries with fewer credible sources of domestic information and because Greeks and Spaniards perceive many European countries as more modern than their own societies. In addition, in the course of the twentieth century, both Greece and Spain have experienced regime change many times; in periods of transition to democracy, these countries should be especially receptive to foreign models.

International Models that Resonate

The influence of foreign models should be especially strong if voters believe the foreign decision-maker to be competent. However, foreign models should resonate in a wider range of circumstances, even when voters have no particular reason to believe that a foreign decision-maker is particularly competent. When a single international model exists, adopted by many foreign governments and promulgated by an international organization, the influence of this model should be extremely strong. The paragraphs below develop each of these three claims.

When voters believe that international models reveal high-quality information, they should be strongly influenced by them. This situation might arise, for example, in areas where international organizations are considered to have particular technical expertise. Recent game theoretic models illustrate how, in such circumstances, international organizations can provide valuable information to voters and create electoral incentives for leaders to conclude trade treaties,[80] comply with environmental agreements,[81] and seek UN Security Council approval on military questions.[82] Analogously, the yardstick competition literature suggests that within federations, voters compare tax policies in neighboring states in deciding whether to reelect incumbents.[83] Similarly, if voters believe a foreign country to be well governed, as evidenced, for example, by its high-growth rates, the influence of this country's policies should be great.

However, foreign models should also be influential in a broader set of circumstances, including in circumstances where voters have no particular reason to think that foreign leaders are wiser or better informed than domestic politicians. To clarify this point, I draw an analogy to models from financial economics. The key assumption that drives a large set of these models is the assumption that when competent decision-makers are independently vetting similar proposals, they are likely to come to similar conclusions. It gradually becomes known that more decision-makers align behind one particular proposal. Once this happens, subsequent decision-makers must think twice before supporting a proposal that deviates from the choice prior decision-makers have made, as they risk being perceived as incompetent.[84] Substituting elected politicians for financial analysts allows me to apply this model to policy diffusion. Two clarifications are necessary to make the transition from finance to politics. First, voters must believe that the countries are similar in some respects. If voters believe that the countries are entirely different, such that a policy expected to succeed abroad is no more likely to succeed or fail domestically, they again should ignore the choices of the foreign government. Second, the voters must believe that the foreign government uses any private information it has in a non-evil fashion: it is likely to enact policies when it has information that the policy will lead to positive outcomes, and it is likely to avoid policies when its information indicates that the policy will lead to negative outcomes. When these conditions hold, even minimally, borrowing should follow.[85] To summarize, game theoretic models predict that references to foreign models should allow politicians to improve their reelection chances under a wide range of circumstances.

When a policy area is dominated by a single international model, adopted by many foreign governments and promulgated by an international organization, the influence of this model should be especially strong. When multiple foreign governments make the same policy choice, voters gain more information that the policy has been vetted than when a single foreign government has adopted the policy, or than when different foreign governments have made different policy choices. Similarly, when an international organization collects and articulates law reforms in multiple countries in the form of a policy recommendation, voters receive a particularly strong signal that the policy has been vetted. And when a policy has been widely adopted, it becomes harder and harder for opponents of a policy to portray it as an effort to curry favor with party extremists, and as inconsistent with mainstream values.

The health and family policy reforms studied in this book differ in the extent to which a single, unified international model existed at the time, and there is also some variation within the field of family policy. In family policy, a single, unified international model dominated the field of maternity leave. This model was first promoted by the International Labour Organization (ILO) in 1919, and by the time Greek, Spanish, and American decision-makers considered the policy, most of the world had already introduced it. As a result, even ideologically conservative politicians supported a policy that pushed women away from the home and into the workforce, and called for additional regulation and redistribution. In contrast, in areas of family policy where the international model was weaker, as, for example, on the question of cash benefits for families with children, we see much more diversity in policy positions within and across countries. Contrast maternity leave with health policy. While a norm that rich countries should offer some type of health care to all their citizens may be emerging, there is no consensus on the type of health organization and health financing that should allow for this. Rich countries have diverse structures, ranging from NHSs, to social insurance systems, to systems that allow for significant private insurance and provision. In health policy, opponents of NHSs point to this diversity of national practices and accurately describe the WHO recommendations as allowing for multiple models. This multiplicity of models substantially weakened the influence of international models.

How International and Domestic Forces Interact

Theories of diffusion have implications about the politics of late and early developers. Standard domestic models of social policy assume that the same domestic input will yield the same output across countries. Estimating a single coefficient for all countries for the effect of unionization on social spending, for example, represents exactly this assumption. The theory of cross-national influences proposed here, however, implies that domestic politics differ in late and early developers. Specifically, domestic forces should be especially important for early developers, while late developers should rely less on domestic forces and more on foreign models. Late developers should be able to adopt policies under less favorable conditions than pioneers.[86]

Let me explain why this is so. The standard domestic policy model should apply best to early developers. For example, for an early developer, perhaps a strong left-wing government coupled with a highly unionized workforce is necessary to bring the issue of social insurance to the domestic agenda, to bargain with employers and right-wing parties, and to enact a social insurance law. By definition, a pioneer has no or few international models available, and will not adopt a social insurance law until these favorable conditions are met. According to the information-based theories of diffusion proposed above, once social insurance laws are adopted by large, rich, and proximate countries, are promulgated by international organizations as global models, or are shown to correlate with good outcomes, they become useful templates. These diffusion theories predict that the existence of a foreign model puts this policy solution on the domestic agenda more quickly than it would otherwise enter, and may also provide positive information about this solution. Given this boost, late developers may be able to adopt social insurance laws with a weaker left-wing government or a less unionized workforce than pioneers.

The theoretical prediction that foreign models allow late developers to introduce policies under less favorable conditions than pioneers is not a distinctive prediction of the proposed electoral mechanism—other diffusion mechanisms could also result in this pattern. I highlight this implication, however, because it is of great practical importance and allows us to better reconcile two literatures that developed at some distance—the literature on domestic policy development and the literature on policy diffusion. To preview the empirical findings, I find that late developers adopt both health and family policy under less favorable circumstances than pioneers. Figure 2.2 presents a summary of the empirical implications of my theory and points the reader to the chapters that explore each implication.

Actors Involved in the Diffusion Process

Voters who know little about an issue, voters who have doubts about their government and its policies, and voters who are favorably disposed to international bodies should respond particularly strongly to foreign models. (Chapter 3)

Elected politicians are constrained to borrow from and reference the few foreign countries familiar to voters. We should expect such references both during election campaigns and during debates on important legislation. The more competitive the political environment politicians face, the stronger the effects of the proposed diffusion mechanism should be. In contrast, decision-makers who are less constrained by elections, including experts, technocrats, and leaders of authoritarian regimes, need not be especially receptive to foreign models familiar to voters. (Chapters 3, 5 and 7)

Diffusion Across Policy Areas

Electoral incentives should influence policy diffusion both for reforms that are very salient politically and also for reforms whose political salience is more moderate. (Chapters 6 and 7)

Electoral incentives should influence the diffusion of broad policy goals more than the diffusion of policy details. (Chapters 5 and 7)

Countries Receptive to Foreign Models

Countries lacking good domestic sources of credible information and countries experiencing transitions should be especially receptive to foreign models. Many small and poor countries are likely to lack good domestic sources of information. (Chapters 3, 4, 5, 6, and 7.)

Countries should be especially receptive to the policy reforms of rich and culturally proximate foreign countries covered prominently in the news. (Chapters 3, 4, 5, 6, and 7)

International Models Likely to Spread

Policy proposals already adopted by many countries, and promoted by international organizations, should spread especially quickly. Health and family policy differ on this dimension. (Chapters 3, 4, 5, 6, and 7)

Interactions Between Domestic and International Models

Foreign models should allow late adopters to introduce policy reforms under less favorable policy conditions than pioneers. (Chapters 5, 6, and 7)

Figure 2.2 Key Empirical Implications

How Americans View Foreign Models

The previous chapter spelled out the main theoretical claims of this book: that policy diffusion is often not driven primarily by elites' internationalist preferences, as many other writers suggest; instead, ordinary voters' uncertainties, and politicians' reelection concerns are critical to policy diffusion. Voters use international models as benchmarks to figure out whether domestic proposals are competently designed and reflect mainstream values.

Voters base their decisions on very limited information, and politicians can communicate only a few key facts clearly and credibly. As a result, diffusion through democracy leads to the emulation of the policies of large, rich, and culturally proximate countries, not to unbiased learning from policy successes and failures from around the world. Moreover, diffusion through democracy places a premium on the existence of a single and coherent international model; in fields where such unified models exist, ideas from abroad become hard to resist.

This chapter begins the empirical investigation of the proposed informational theory of policy diffusion, an investigation that unfolds over many chapters and across many countries, time periods, and types of evidence. This chapter examines some key steps in the proposed theory. Do voters in fact tend to respond positively to information from abroad? What types of voters respond more positively, and what types of voters respond more negatively? Do politicians reference foreign countries frequently? And do they concentrate on countries prominently featured in the media? Table 3.1 outlines the theoretical predictions I begin to investigate in this chapter. Subsequent chapters continue to test these and additional implications outlined in chapter 2 and summarized in Table 2.2.

The empirical analysis begins in the United States, which is a particularly hard test case for my theory. The proposed informational theory suggests that foreign models should be most relevant in countries where domestic sources of information are of low quality and in which the media cover foreign models prominently. In contrast, American voters benefit from diverse, high-quality

Table 3.1 **Empirical Implications Examined in Chapter 3**

	Diffusion through technocracy	*Diffusion through democracy*	
		Consensus international model (e.g., family policy reforms)	*Diverse international models (e.g., health care reforms)*
Public opinion	Ordinary voters are indifferent and even hostile to foreign models.	Ordinary voters receive foreign models positively; public opinion effects are largest because there is a single international model. Foreign models have the greatest influence on persons who doubt their government.	Ordinary voters receive foreign models positively; public opinion effects are moderate because diverse models exist. Foreign models have the greatest influence on persons who doubt their government.
Legislative record	Countries with greatest success in each area are referenced. Learning arguments predominate. Learning is objective; priors and partisanship play limited role.	Countries familiar to voters are referenced across issue areas. Emulation arguments predominate. Partisanship is muted by dominant foreign model. Advocates reference dominant model frequently; some opponents accept model, but many stay silent.	Countries familiar to voters are referenced across issue areas. Both emulation and learning arguments are heard. Partisanship shapes foreign references. Advocates and opponents both reference foreign models, and disagree on what lessons to draw.
Ideal setting	Diverse models permit learning.	Single global model sends clearest signal.	Diverse models send noisy signals.

domestic sources of information: nonpartisan governmental agencies evaluate many policy proposals, leading universities produce research on U.S. policies, and 50 state governments offer up their experiences. Moreover, the United States is significantly wealthier than most countries in the world and is geographically and culturally distant from potential rivals such as Germany and Japan. In addition, American citizens are more conflicted about international institutions than are citizens of other countries. In a recent Pew Survey, only 55% of Americans expressed support for the United Nations (UN), as compared with 84% of Swedes and 70% of Canadians.[1] However, surveys of elites' opinions show that U.S. politicians do not always accurately predict how supportive Americans are of international institutions and international cooperation efforts—if anything, politicians systematically underestimate voter support for these efforts.[2]

Contrary to the perception of Americans as hostile to international models, the empirical evidence in this chapter highlights that even Americans respond very positively to information from abroad. To examine whether foreign models resonate with ordinary Americans, I conducted public opinion experiments on representative samples of the U.S. public. Experimental methods allow us to identify causal pathways clearly and to separate out citizens' baseline views on a particular policy from citizens' views on the same policy once information from abroad is presented. These experiments show that foreign models resonate with a wide range of Americans. Indeed, an endorsement from the UN elicits stronger positive responses than a range of other endorsements, including endorsements from domestic experts. Moreover, these effects are not concentrated among liberal elites. Diverse groups of Americans respond strongly to a UN endorsement, including a particularly strong response among self-identified Republicans. These distinctive findings are consistent with the proposed theory in which foreign models serve to reassure voters who doubt their government and its policies. The next section presents these experiments and outlines their advantages and limitations.

To study how politicians use foreign models to advance their projects, I compare debates on the Obama administration's major legislative proposal, the Patient Protection and Affordable Care Act of 2010, with debates on the Family and Medical Leave Act of 1993 (FMLA). These two social policy proposals raise similar concerns about risk, redistribution, and labor market regulation, but differ on a key dimension: by the time of their respective U.S. debates, a single international model existed for family policy but not for health policy. In both fields, politicians made many references to foreign models—far more than to U.S. states. The *Congressional Record* reveals more than 290 references to foreign models in the FMLA debates and more than

140 such references in the health care debates. In both fields, politicians focused on countries prominent in the media and familiar to voters, not on countries with the most successful or appropriate reforms for the U.S. to emulate. For example, in the family policy debates, politicians focused on Germany and Japan. Neither country had particularly successful family policies, but in the late 1980s and early 1990s, both were very prominent in the national media and relevant to voters. In the health care debates, politicians focused on Canada and Britain, even though experts highlighted reforms in the Netherlands and Switzerland.

In both areas, reform advocates sought to frame their policy proposals as basic rights offered by all rich-country governments. Advocates' efforts to cast the FMLA as an issue of minimum rights succeeded because they could point to a consensus international model adopted by almost all countries and forcefully promoted by international organizations. Opponents' efforts to raise questions about whether family leave worked well in other countries fell on deaf ears. A common emulation argument was repeated by Democrats, and even by some Republicans, and ultimately carried the day: everyone offers leave, therefore we should too. Democrats also tried to frame health care reform as an effort to grant Americans a fundamental benefit afforded by all other rich countries. However, Republicans successfully used the diversity of foreign models to contest the Democrats' framing. Democrats could not simply point to an international consensus but had to engage with Republicans in debates about policy success and failure abroad, debates that diluted the signaling power of the international model.

That being said, and consistent with my theory, the United States remains the hardest case for the diffusion of foreign models. In both health care and family policy, the United States adopted reforms long after other rich Western countries had done so. And the precise form of these reforms differed from other countries' policies in significant ways. Nevertheless, the adoption of family leave and universal health care in any form in the United States is striking. A decade ago, Charles Blake and Jessica Adolino highlighted how unlikely the United States was to adopt universal health insurance. The United States, uniquely among industrialized countries, had a strikingly negative context for all of the cultural, economic, institutional, and political variables they studied.[3] Absent international models, universal health care and family leave may never have been placed on the U.S. policy agenda. To see how diverse international and domestic forces contributed to the adoption of health care and family leave laws, I analyze data on health care and family leave reforms across advanced rich democracies over several decades in chapters 4 and 6.

Public Opinion Experiments—Methodological Advantages and Caveats

This chapter combines two types of evidence: I start with public opinion experiments of representative samples of U.S. citizens and continue with studies of politicians' statements from the *Congressional Record* and beyond. Public opinion polls are an important tool social scientists have used for decades to answer questions about voters' views. More importantly, politicians commission similar polls frequently to determine which legal reforms to propose to their constituents and, once they select those reforms, which arguments to use to effectively persuade voters to support those reforms.[4]

This chapter applies experimental techniques used in other fields to the study of the cross-national diffusion of legal reforms. Experimental designs have been introduced recently in social science and legal scholarship to identify causal pathways clearly.[5] Nonexperimental, observational studies might show that politicians reference certain foreign models frequently and might even show a correlation between frequent references to foreign models and reelection probabilities. Such data would suggest that a politician believes that certain foreign models are likely to resonate among voters. But it is hard to use these data to pinpoint causal patterns exactly. For example, a politician might get reelected despite, rather than because of, his frequent references to certain foreign models. Experimental studies allow us to manipulate one variable at a time and keep everything else constant in order to more clearly identify how references to foreign models shape voters' views. There are important limitations to such public opinion experiments, which I discuss immediately after presenting the results.

Results from two original public opinion experiments follow: I examine how Americans respond to information from abroad in evaluating health policy and family policy. Both policies fit well in the proposed informational theory, as it is plausible that information about foreign countries' experiences might shift at least some voters' minds. However, it is important to note that health policy was a headline issue in 2008, when the questions were fielded, whereas family policy was not. Because Americans received a barrage of information on health policy prior to the survey, one can use health policy as a difficult test case to examine the limits of the proposed theory.

I first describe the experiments and present aggregate results. I then explore how different groups respond to information about foreign models.

Experiment 1—Questions on Health Policy

In the first experiment I commissioned, respondents were asked their views about health policy reform. A representative sample of 2030 U.S. adults was used, and the questions were fielded in 2008.[6] Respondents were randomly assigned to one of four groups. Respondents in the first group were asked the "baseline" question: "To what extent do you agree or disagree with the following statement: 'The United States government should increase taxes in order to provide health insurance to all Americans.'" Response options were "strongly agree," "somewhat agree," "somewhat disagree," and "strongly disagree."

Respondents in groups 2 through 4 received the same baseline question, prefaced by different introductions. For group 2 the preface was: "Most developed countries provide health insurance to all their citizens." For group 3 the preface was: "The United Nations recommends that all countries should provide health insurance to all their citizens." For group 4 the preface was: "Many American health policy experts believe that the United States government should provide health insurance to all its citizens."

Figure 3.1 presents the basic results of this experiment. For the baseline, where no introduction was given, support for a tax increase to introduce universal health insurance was moderate; about one-third of Americans agreed with this proposal. However, aggregate support for a tax increase to introduce universal health insurance increased by 16 to 18 percentage points when it was presented as the policy choice of most Western countries or as the recommendation of U.S. experts. Aggregate support increased even more—by 24 percentage points—when the policy was introduced as a UN recommendation. As the regressions below document, the differences between each of the introductions and the baseline are highly statistically significant and persist when a variety of control variables are included in the models.

By showing that even Americans respond positively to endorsements from abroad, these aggregate results support my theory. What is most striking is how strongly the UN recommendation resonated. The large effect of the UN recommendations supports the claim that foreign models presented as universal solutions resonate especially strongly with voters.

Experiment 2—Questions on Maternity Leave

The second experiment was very similar to the first one and focused on Americans' views on maternity leave. This second experiment involved a sample of 1291 U.S. adults, selected as representative of U.S. citizens. From this

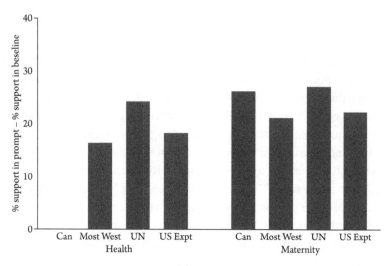

Figure 3.1 Responsiveness to Prompts by Issue

sample, respondents were randomly assigned to one of five groups. Respondents in group 1, the baseline group, were asked: "To what extent do you agree or disagree with the following statement: 'The United States should increase taxes in order to provide mothers of newborn children with paid leave from work.'" Response options were "strongly agree," "somewhat agree," "somewhat disagree," and "strongly disagree."

Respondents in groups 2 through 5 received the same baseline question, prefaced by different introductions. For group 2 the preface was: "Canada provides mothers of newborn children with paid leave from work." For group 3 the preface was: "Most Western countries provide mothers of newborn children with paid leave from work." For group 4 the preface was: "The United Nations recommends that all countries should provide mothers of newborn children with paid leave from work." For group 5 the preface was: "American family policy experts recommend that the United States should provide mothers of newborn children with paid leave from work." Figure 3.1 also presents the basic results of this experiment.

For the baseline, no-introduction condition, support for a tax increase to introduce paid maternity leave was limited; only about one-fifth of Americans agreed with this proposal. However, aggregate support increased by 21 to 22 percentage points when this proposal was presented as the policy choice of most Western countries or as the recommendation of U.S. experts. Aggregate support increased even more—by 27 percentage points—when the policy was introduced as a UN recommendation. Similarly, the Canada prompt resonated strongly with Americans as a whole, increasing support by 26 percentage points. The differences between each of the introductions and the baseline are highly statistically significant and robust to the introduction of diverse control variables, as the regressions illustrate.

The aggregate effects in the maternity leave survey are larger than the effects of the health policy survey; this is consistent with the expectation that Americans who had received a great deal of information about health policy at the time of the survey from the media would respond less to information from abroad. Nevertheless, the effects in both surveys are large in absolute terms and entirely consistent. In both cases, what is most striking is how responsive Americans are to the UN recommendation prompt.

The very strong endorsement effects of the UN recommendation is particularly notable given that Americans are somewhat ambivalent about this institution. In this and in other studies of public opinion, a majority of Americans expressed favorable views of the UN, but a large minority expressed unfavorable ones. Prior studies of attitudes toward the UN help us put the surprising UN endorsement effect I report in context. While experimental polls are novel, the Chicago Council on Global Affairs, among other bodies, has been conducting detailed polls of Americans' views toward international institutions since 1974. They conclude that Americans are strongly supportive of the goals international organizations are pursuing, but are ambivalent about how well international organizations are performing in their efforts to reach those goals.[7]

Moreover, while some international organization efforts are controversial, the development and promotion of human rights and of basic health care and labor standards are overwhelmingly popular among Americans (as well as among citizens of other countries). For example, in recent polls, 70% of Americans supported UN involvement in the promotion of human rights, even when concerns about national autonomy were raised.[8] Similarly, 93% of Americans supported the inclusion of minimum labor standards in trade agreements.[9] One way to interpret these findings is that the UN endorsement transforms health care and family benefits, which might otherwise be seen as controversial and partisan social welfare proposals, into basic labor standards and universal human rights.

An important extension of these experiments would be to examine how Americans respond when the UN is replaced by other international bodies, such as the World Health Organization (WHO) or the International Monetary Fund (IMF) and when Canada is replaced by diverse other country names. Nonexperimental public opinion work tells us that Americans feel very warmly toward the WHO, are lukewarm toward the UN, and are cold toward many international financial institutions.[10] Similarly, Americans feel quite warmly toward proximate, rich, and industrialized countries like Germany and Japan, but less warmly toward countries like China.[11] We might expect the size of the endorsement effect to vary depending on how warmly or coolly Americans feel toward the endorser. Indeed, a new study by Zachary Elkins reports that U.S. undergraduates significantly increased their support for a policy proposal when they were told that England had adopted it, and they significantly decreased their support for a policy when they were told that Nigeria and Brazil had adopted it.[12] These findings are consistent with the theory I propose here and support the claim that only a handful of rich and culturally proximate countries resonate with American voters. However, we should keep an important caveat in mind and be cautious in moving from undergraduates to the population at large. As the next section explores, messages from abroad resonate differently with different demographic groups.

Different Groups' Responses to Foreign Models

How do different types of Americans respond to information from abroad? Some writers emphasize the expectation that only liberal elites respond to foreign models, and ordinary Americans are quite hostile to them.[13] However, my experimental data suggest that foreign models resonate among diverse groups of ordinary Americans: well-educated and poorly educated people, rich and poor, men and women, whites and minorities.[14]

The analysis that follows helps further clarify the theoretical mechanisms that explain policy diffusion. The proposed theory posits that foreign models can reassure skeptical voters that particular policy proposals are not radical, ill-thought-out experiments, but mainstream, tried-and-true solutions. This theory gains further empirical support if the data show that the effects of foreign models are particularly large among people who lack information about an issue area and among people who are concerned that a proposal is radical.

Respondents in both experiments were asked how familiar they were with social policy issues, to separate out people who believed they had high and low levels of prior information. Specifically, respondents were asked: "Employers and employees pay taxes and fees for benefit programs such as health insurance, pensions, and child care. In general, how well informed are you about the costs and benefits of such programs? Would you say you are very well informed, somewhat well informed, not too well informed, or not at all informed?" About half of the respondents answered that they were either not too well informed or not at all informed. This suggests that voters face important informational limitations in evaluating social policy proposals, as my theory assumes.

To identify voters likely to be especially skeptical of the policy proposals examined here, questions about voters' ideological leanings are useful. We would expect voters who identify with the Republican Party to be particularly skeptical of these redistributive policy proposals. This is because both paren-tal leave and (especially) universal health care have been promoted heavily by Democratic politicians. Moreover, the question wording highlighted this left–right cleavage by presenting a trade-off between a tax increase and the introduction of a redistributive social program. The data confirm this expec-tation; as described above, Republicans are much more skeptical about both policies on average. However, the analysis that follows also suggests that low-information voters and Republicans respond at least as strongly—and often more strongly—than other voters to foreign endorsements. These pat-terns are consistent with the proposed theory.

To examine how information levels and party affiliation condition shifts in attitudes, logit models predicting support for an increase in taxes for the purpose of introducing universal health care are presented in Table 3.2. Similar logit models predicting support for an increase in taxes to introduce paid maternity leave are presented in Table 3.3. In both tables, model I pre-dicts baseline support based only on the experimental treatments; model II predicts baseline support based on the experimental treatments and a set of demographic controls; model III examines how information about social pol-icy conditions the impact of the experimental stimuli; model IV examines how party affiliation conditions the impact of these stimuli; and model V, the final specification, includes both types of interactions.

To interpret these effects, predicted values and first differences were cal-culated using simulations.[15] Model V in Table 3.2 indicates that when other values are held at their mean, support for a tax increase to introduce uni-versal health insurance is 25 points lower among Republicans than among Democrats,[16] 9 points lower among people in the top 20% of the household income distribution as compared with less wealthy people, and 4 points lower among 50-year-olds as compared with 30-year-olds. Model V in Table 3.3 indi-cates that when other values are held at their mean, support for a tax increase to introduce paid maternity leave is 8 points lower among men as compared with women, 13 points lower among 50-year-olds as compared with 30-year-olds, 10 points lower among whites as compared with nonwhites, and 20 points lower among Republicans as compared with Democrats. All these differences are in the expected direction and statistically significant.

Figure 3.2 shows how prior information about social policies influences responses to each of the prompts on health policy. This figure and Figures 3.3 through 3.5 are again based on model V, holding demographic variables at their means. Figure 3.2 suggests that people with high levels of information and people with low levels of information respond in similar ways to each of the prompts; the differences between these groups are not statistically signifi-cant. Figure 3.3 shows how partisanship influences responses to each of the

Table 3.2 **Models Predicting Support for Universal Health Insurance**

	I	II	III	IV	V
Group 2	.72***	.76***	.69***	.69***	.63**
(most countries)	(.17)	(.17)	(.24)	(.22)	(.27)
Group 3	1.00***	1.06***	.92***	.76***	.65**
(UN recommendation)	(.16)	(.17)	(.25)	(.23)	(.29)
Group 4	.78***	.75***	.71***	.64***	.61**
(U.S. experts)	(.17)	(.17)	(.24)	(.22)	(.27)
Women		−.01	−.01	−.01	−.01
		(.12)	(.12)	(.12)	(.12)
Children		−.13	−.12	−.14	−.13
		(.17)	(.16)	(.17)	(.17)
Age		−.01**	−.01**	−.01**	−.01**
		(.00)	(.00)	(.00)	(.00)
Education		.05	.04	.05	.05
(high school)		(.23)	(.23)	(.23)	(.23)
Education		.18	.18	.18	.18
(some college)		(.23)	(.23)	(.23)	(.23)
Education		.22	.22	.23	.23
(bachelors +)		(.24)	(.24)	(.24)	(.24)
White		−.02	−.02	−.01	−.01
		(.15)	(.15)	(.15)	(.15)
High income		−.34**	−.34**	−.34**	−.34**
		(.15)	(.15)	(.15)	(.15)
Republican		−1.00***	−1.00***	−1.39***	−1.38***
		(.12)	(.12)	(.27)	(.27)
Well informed		.04	−.10	.04	−.08
		(.12)	(.24)	(.12)	(.25)
Group 2 * well informed			.16		.15
			(.33)		(.34)
Group 3 * well informed			.29		.23
			(.34)		(.34)
Group 4 * well informed			.10		.08
			(.34)		(.34)
Group 2 * Republican				.28	.27
				(.36)	(.36)

(Continued)

Table 3.2 (**Continued**)

	I	II	III	IV	V
Group 3 * Republican				.82**	.80**
				(.35)	(.35)
Group 4 * Republican				.36	.35
				(.35)	(.35)
Constant	−.78***	−.05	.00	.08	.12
	(.12)	(.35)	(.37)	(.36)	(.38)
N	2,030	2,024	2,024	2,024	2,024

Standard errors in parentheses.
***$p < .01$, **$p < .05$, *$p < .1$.

Table 3.3 **Models Predicting Support for Paid Maternity Leave**

	I	II	III	IV	V
Group 2	1.22***	1.32***	1.75***	1.40***	1.82***
(Canada)	(.24)	(.25)	(.38)	(.31)	(.41)
Group 3	1.01***	1.15***	1.54***	.83***	1.25***
(most countries)	(.24)	(.24)	(.36)	(.30)	(.38)
Group 4 (UN	1.23***	1.30***	1.56***	1.11***	1.39***
recommendation)	(.24)	(.25)	(.37)	(.31)	(.39)
Group 5	1.05***	1.11***	1.19***	.97***	1.08***
(U.S. experts)	(.25)	(.26)	(.40)	(.31)	(.41)
Women		.33**	.34**	.33**	.34**
		(.15)	(.15)	(.15)	(.15)
Children		.03	.03	.01	.01
		(.18)	(.18)	(.18)	(.18)
Age		−.03***	−.03***	−.03***	−.03***
		(.01)	(.01)	(.01)	(.01)
Education		−.22	−.21	−.21	−.21
(high school)		(.28)	(.28)	(.27)	(.27)
Education		−.42	−.42	−.41	−.40
(some college)		(.28)	(.28)	(.28)	(.28)
Education		−.14	−.15	−.12	−.13
(bachelors +)		(.28)	(.29)	(.28)	(.28)
White		−.43**	−.42**	−.44**	−.43**
		(.18)	(.18)	(.18)	(.18)

(Continued)

Table 3.3 (**Continued**)

	I	II	III	IV	V
High income		.03	.03	.03	.02
		(.19)	(.19)	(.19)	(.19)
Republican		−.83***	−.84***	−1.29***	−1.41***
		(.16)	(.16)	(.42)	(.46)
Well informed		.26*	.77**	.27*	.86**
		(.16)	(.38)	(.16)	(.42)
Group 2 * well informed			−.87*		−.93*
			(.50)		(.54)
Group 3 * well informed			−.80		−.91*
			(.50)		(.52)
Group 4 * well informed			−.50		−.62
			(.51)		(.53)
Group 5 * well informed			−.14		−.24
			(.52)		(.54)
Group 2 * Republican				−.17	−.02
				(.55)	(.58)
Group 3 * Republican				.95*	1.08*
				(.52)	(.55)
Group 4 * Republican				.71	.83
				(.52)	(.56)
Group 5 * Republican				.52	.62
				(.56)	(.60)
Constant	−1.31***	.39	.14	.49	.23
	(.19)	(.42)	(.48)	(.43)	(.48)
N	1,291	1,284	1,284	1,284	1,284

Standard errors in parentheses.
***$p < .01$, **$p < .05$, *$p < .1$.

prompts. It suggests that both Republicans and Democrats responded in similar ways to each of the endorsements, with the exception of the UN recommendation, which resonated more strongly among Republicans. That is, when Democrats were told that the UN recommended that all countries should provide universal health insurance, they increased their support for this policy by 19 percentage points, whereas Republicans increased their support by 31 percentage points, a statistically significant difference.

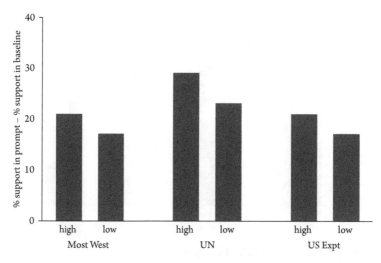

Figure 3.2 Health Policy Attitudes by Information Level

Figures 3.4 and 3.5 repeat the analyses for the maternity leave survey. Figure 3.4 suggests that people with low information responded more strongly to each of the endorsements from abroad, although the difference was not statistically significant in the case of the UN recommendation. For example, whereas people familiar with social policy issues increased their support for paid maternity leave by 16 points when they were told that most Western countries offered this benefit, people who were unfamiliar with these issues increased their support even more, by 30 percentage points, a statistically significant difference. Figure 3.5 suggests that Republicans responded more strongly than Democrats

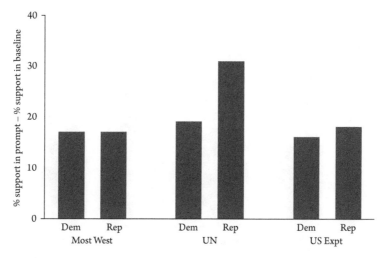

Figure 3.3 Health Policy Attitudes by Party

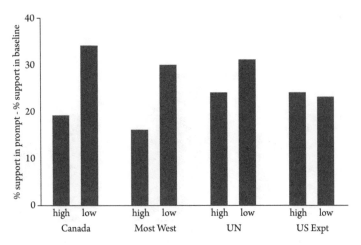

Figure 3.4 Family Policy Attitudes by Information Level

to information that most Western countries offer maternity leave; support for this policy increased by 19 percentage points among Democrats, and by 29 percentage points among Republicans, a statistically significant difference. Similarly, Republicans responded more strongly to information about the UN, whereas Democrats responded more strongly to information about Canada; however, these differences do not reach conventional significance levels.

The finding that people with low levels of information respond more to foreign endorsements than people with high levels of information, observed in each of the endorsements in the maternity leave experiment, is consistent with the proposed claim that information is a key pathway through which foreign models influence public opinion. However, I did not observe this differential

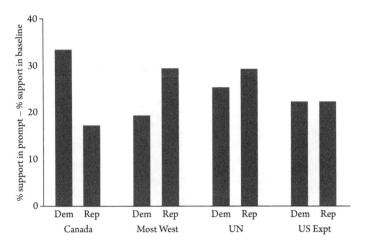

Figure 3.5 Family Policy Attitudes by Party

in the case of health care policy, possibly because health policy was a hotly con-tested issue during the 2008 presidential campaign, and thus all respondents had extensive information.

The finding that Republicans respond strongly to foreign models is coun-terintuitive—other theorists suggest that foreign models resonate only among liberals.[17] Yet this counterintuitive observation is consistent with my theory. My theory suggests that foreign models are particularly valuable to voters who worry that policy proposals are poorly designed or inconsistent with their values. Policies that raise taxes to introduce social programs tend to worry Republicans, not Democrats. Foreign governments and international organi-zations may not be Republicans' most trusted source of information, but they might be more credible than typical domestic advocates for social policy pro-grams—Democratic politicians, labor unions, and liberal think tanks. Foreign governments and international organizations enjoy an important advantage over other providers of information: they are outsiders with no stake in the next domestic election.

Importantly, while Republicans responded more strongly than Democrats to UN recommendations for all countries, and to information about the prac-tices of most Western countries, they did not respond more strongly than Democrats when given information about Canada's policies. These patterns are consistent with the idea that foreign models can have two, sometimes opposing, effects: they can signal that an idea has been vetted, and that an idea is consistent (or inconsistent) with voters' values. A reference to Canada indicates that a foreign government has vetted the proposal, evidence that should increase support for the policy across groups, for both Democrats and Republicans, a pattern we observe. On the other hand, Canada may also be shorthand for liberal values, values that increase support for the proposal among Democrats but decrease support among Republicans. References to most Western countries and to the UN may imply values that are broadly accepted, and thus mainstream, and thus trigger strongly positive responses, even among Republicans.

This logic suggests that endorsement effects should vary by policy areas. In fields in which Democrats worry that policies may be poorly designed or ideo-logically extreme, Democrats should respond more strongly to international endorsements. An experimental study on attitudes toward military interven-tion during the Bush years reveals exactly this pattern. Democrats, and more generally people who did not trust the U.S. president, shifted their views more in response to information that the UN and North Atlantic Treaty Organization (NATO) allies had endorsed a proposed military intervention.[18]

In summary, the tables show that foreign models do not resonate only among well-informed elites, or only among liberals, as was widely believed.

Americans in general respond strongly and positively to foreign models. If this is true, why did we get it so wrong? Why do we believe that Americans do not respond positively to foreign models or that only liberal elites do so? This could be because, in typical observational studies, we are not able to isolate the effects of foreign models from the effects of other variables. That is, in a typical observational study we might note that Republicans tend to disagree with proposals to increase taxes to introduce social programs, regardless of whether these proposals are presented with references to foreign models. Indeed, this conclusion is still what I find here: across all the scenarios studied, a majority of Republicans disagree with proposals to increase taxes to support universal health care or paid maternity leave. However, fewer disagree with these proposals once they are presented with a UN or other trusted foreign endorsement in support of the policy. In other words, in this experimental study I separate out the content of the policy proposal from the international endorsement and show that even (and perhaps especially) for a proposal that is otherwise unattractive to Republicans, a UN endorsement carries great weight.

Limitations of Public Opinion Experiments

How much are such effects likely to matter in practice, given that a large literature on political communication shows that voters respond differently to questions framed in different ways? A recent review of this literature concludes that there exists "a clear and systematic limit to framing," namely "perceived source credibility."[19] Indicatively, prior experiments show that an endorsement from the New York Times shifts voters' policy views, but one from the National Enquirer does not. Similarly, an endorsement from Colin Powell changes voters' policy views, but Jerry Springer's endorsement does not.[20] The evidence presented here adds to domestic research on endorsements by showing that the adoption of a practice by the Canadian government, or by many Western governments, is as credible an endorsement as the recommendation of U.S. experts, and that a recommendation from the UN that all countries adopt a practice can be even more credible.

While we can have some confidence in the direction of the reported effects (positive responses to foreign endorsements) and to the comparative magnitude of these effects, we cannot place great weight on the absolute magnitude of these effects. Prior research suggests that the magnitude of these effects will likely decrease when voters are presented with competing information, but that the endorsement effects will not disappear entirely.[21] In addition, the magnitude of these effects is likely to decrease because the method of information transmission differs in the real world and in the experimental world.[22]

In the survey experiment, respondents were directly presented with information about foreign models immediately prior to voicing an opinion. In the real world, voters get information from many sources, some clearer than others, and likely forget much that they hear before making key decisions.

Ultimately, public opinion data as such cannot show how much endorsements will influence voters outside a controlled setting. They cannot tell us how valuable politicians perceive these foreign endorsements to be or how willing politicians are to deviate from policies they would otherwise propose in order to gain these foreign endorsements. This chapter therefore continues by examining aggregate data on how health care and family policy develops by looking at politicians' rhetoric. Subsequent chapters examine how policy proposals change in light of foreign models.

Politicians' Use of Foreign Models—Theoretical Expectations

The prior section provided empirical support for a key step in my theory, the claim that diverse U.S. voters respond positively to foreign models. This part turns from voters to politicians. Do politicians also behave as the theory predicts, referencing foreign models to appeal to voters? To answer this question I examine how politicians advocate for their proposals in congressional debates and electoral campaigns.

I turn to the most important reforms in U.S. health care and family policy in recent years. I start with the major legislative proposal of the Obama administration, the Patient Protection and (Affordable Care Act) of 2010. To see whether the health debates were exceptional, I compare them with the debates on the FMLA and with the debates on President Clinton's unsuccessful health reform proposal, the Health Security Act of 1993. Both health care and family policy reform proposals were controversial and raised similar issues of social insurance, government regulation, and risk redistribution. Both proposals pitted liberals, eager to smooth out labor market risks equitably, against conservatives who were fearful of government regulation and interventionism.[23] However, as described earlier, health care and family policy differed on a key dimension of interest. A single international model existed for family policy, promoted by international organizations for decades and adopted worldwide, while rich countries had adopted a diversity of health care models.

Presidential campaign statements and the *Congressional Record* offer ample evidence that politicians referenced foreign models to gain voter support on both health care and family policy reforms. This evidence also confirms additional theoretical predictions developed in Chapters 1 and 2: politicians focused on foreign countries familiar to voters and often developed simple emulation arguments to send clear signals. As my theory predicts, in both health care and family policy debates, proponents of the legislation tried to depict their proposal as universally adopted abroad and thus consistent with mainstream values and likely to work well domestically. In the FMLA debates, this framing was not heavily contested, and it carried the day. In the health care debates, Republicans contested the framing with which Presidents Clinton and Obama started, that all rich countries offer universal health insurance in cost-effective way. Republicans highlighted the diversity of health financing and organization systems worldwide. Democrats and Republicans ended up discussing not only whether foreign governments had adopted particular models, but they also debated whether these policies had succeeded or failed. This helped dilute, but likely did not eliminate, the persuasive power of foreign models.[24]

While the following analysis focuses on politicians, advocates and opponents of reform also picked up on and popularized claims about foreign models. For example, Michael Moore's documentary *Sicko*, arguing that U.S. health care was inadequate relative to what foreign governments provided, reached millions of American viewers directly and grossed more than $24 million.[25] The media storm that followed ensured that even more Americans considered whether the U.S. health care was inferior or superior to that of foreign countries. A national poll by the Kaiser Family Foundation a month after the movie's release in August 2007 found that while only 4% of respondents had actually seen the movie, an additional 42% had heard or read about it. Of people familiar with the movie, "43 percent said the movie made them more likely to think that the U.S. healthcare system needs reform—liberals and conservatives both among them—and a little over a third said it swayed them to think that other countries do a better job."[26]

Foreign Models in the Clinton and Obama Campaigns

Both health care and family policy reforms failed many times before being finally adopted in the United States. American efforts to introduce universal health care and maternity leave began in the late nineteenth and early twentieth century. Historians have established how the Progressive movement, and Presidents Theodore Roosevelt, Woodrow Wilson, and Franklin Delano Roosevelt in particular, borrowed social reform ideas extensively from Europe.[27] Indeed, the popularity of social reform efforts in the United States waxed and waned with Germany's military choices. While in the pre–World War I years, "progressives had found it essential to turn to Europe for precedents," World War I changed this,[28] and "German ideas like Bismarck's

Social Insurance" became suspicious.[29] Both family policy and health care reform proposals were introduced repeatedly in the subsequent decades. Comprehensive health care reform appeared on the national agenda at least six times at various points in the twentieth century.[30] Family leave bills were repeatedly introduced in the 1980s.[31]

Many factors contributed to the ultimate adoption of the FMLA in 1993 and the Affordable Care Act in 2010, notably Democratic control of the White House and both houses of Congress and supportive positions by key interest groups, notably labor unions and the American Medical Association. This chapter does not aim to assert that foreign models were the driving force behind the adoption of these laws or even to assess the relative contribution of foreign and domestic influences on health care and family policy reform. Instead chapters 4 and 6 use cross-national regressions to show how both domestic and international factors contributed to health care and family policy reform across Organization for Economic Cooperation and Development (OECD) countries. The goal is to show how politicians advocating for controversial reforms used foreign models to appeal to voters in order to make reform proposals appear mainstream and well designed. I also highlight how reform opponents challenged these references in theoretically predictable ways.

This chapter concentrates on the most recent episodes of health care and family policy reform and begins with the 1992 election campaign, a watershed moment for both reforms. Candidate Bill Clinton drew attention to both health care and family policy reform proposals. In his first televised debate against President George H. W. Bush, Clinton called for family leave, emphasizing foreign countries' experiences: "[Working families] deserve a strong economy, and I think they deserve a family-and-medical-leave act. *Seventy-two other nations have been able to do it. Mr. Bush vetoed it twice because he says we can't do something 72 other countries do.*"[32] In that same debate, Clinton also campaigned for universal health care, again pointing to foreign countries' choices. Clinton argued:

> I've got a plan to control health-care costs. But you can't just do it by cutting Medicare. You have to take on the insurance companies, the bureaucracies and you have to have cost controls, yes. *But keep in mind we are spending 30 percent more on health care than any country in the world, any other county. And yet we have 35 million people uninsured.* We have no preventive and primary care. The Oregon plan is a good start, if the federal government's going to continue to abandon its responsibilities. *I say if Germany can cover everybody and keep costs under inflation, if Hawaii can cover 98 percent of their people at lower health care costs than the rest of us, America can do it, too.*[33]

Candidate Clinton repeated these themes throughout the campaign.[34] Once he won the presidency, he introduced health care and family policy reform proposals by inviting Americans to benchmark their governments against international standards,[35] and many congressmen echoed this rhetoric, as the discussion below illustrates. Family leave passed and was the first law President Clinton signed, doing so in a highly publicized Rose Garden ceremony.[36] In signing the FMLA, President Clinton concluded with the theme he started with, highlighting that "American workers in all 50 states will enjoy the same rights as workers in other nations."[37] Then, in campaigning for reelection in 1996, Democrats chose "Families First" as their slogan. Clinton repeatedly emphasized how he signed and sought to extend the FMLA, while his opponent, Senator Bob Dole, had voted against it twice and engineered filibusters to prevent its passage.[38]

While family leave was a crowning accomplishment for President Clinton, health reform was a stunning failure. Many factors likely contributed to this, including sustained attacks by the insurance industry and concerted Republican opposition.[39] Critically, however, Democrats interpreted this failure to be the result of political missteps, not a result of the content of the proposal.[40] Thus subsequent Democratic candidates, including most importantly Barack Obama, heavily promoted universal health care in their bids for the White House.

Obama used foreign models to frame his health care proposal throughout his campaign, starting with his very first speech introducing his health care plan, "The time has come for universal health care," in January 2007.[41] He argued: "[It's] wrong when 46 million Americans have no health care at all. In a country that spends more on health care than any other nation on earth, it's just wrong." He continued: "Some of the biggest corporations in America, giants of industry like GM and Ford, are watching foreign competitors based in countries with universal health care run circles around them, with a GM car containing twice as much health care cost as a Japanese car."[42] About a month later, in a civil rights rally in Selma, Alabama, Obama repeated these claims. He said: "We've got 46 million people uninsured in this country despite spending more money on health care than any nation on earth. It makes no sense."[43] He continued: "Some of the biggest corporations in America, giants of industry like GM and Ford, are watching foreign competitors based in countries with universal health care run circles around them, with a GM car containing seven times as much health care cost as a Japanese car."[44] Obama kept reiterating these and related ideas, over and over, throughout the campaign.[45] And once elected president, in his speech introducing health care to Congress, Obama argued: "We are the only democracy—the only advanced democracy on earth—the only wealthy nation—that allows such hardship for millions of its people."[46] He continued: "We spend one and a half times more per person on health care than any other country, but we aren't any healthier for it."[47]

Foreign Models in Congress

Democrats in Congress picked up on and repeated the themes that Presidents Clinton and Obama had campaigned on, arguing in favor of both health care and family leave reform. How did the Republicans respond? Republicans were initially opposed to both health care and family policy reform. In the health care debates, Republicans successfully used the diversity of foreign models to weaken Democrats' framing of health care as a universal right, afforded by rich governments to all their citizens. In contrast, in the family policy debates, Republicans were faced with a coherent and widely adopted international model. In response, Republican politicians either remained silent on the question of foreign models or joined the Democrats in calling for the United States to adopt leave rights guaranteed the world over. In the tables below, I analyze the *Congressional Record* because, as the official record of debates in Congress, it offers a comprehensive compilation of the arguments Democratic and Republican politicians want their constituents to hear.

Frequency

In the development of health care and family policy, arguments about international models occupied center stage in congressional debates. There were 135 references to international models in the 2009–2010 health care debates, 224 in the 1993 health care debates, and 287 in the FMLA debates.[48] That references to foreign models were especially frequent when health care reform was first proposed by the Clinton administration is consistent with evidence from other diffusion studies suggesting that foreign models are most relevant in the early, agenda-setting stages of the policy process. References to foreign countries were even more frequent in the FMLA debates than in the health care debates.[49] In addition, in the FMLA debates there were repeated references to groups of countries ("all countries," "the industrialized world," "even the third world"). These likely reflect senators' and representatives' correct and shared understanding that only a single global model was available for family leave, whereas multiple foreign models were available for health care.

These references are particularly frequent in comparative perspective; I also examined how frequently U.S. states were referenced in these debates for comparison. The 50 U.S. states are often described as "laboratories for democracy," test grounds where policies can be introduced on a small scale before they are adopted nationwide. U.S. states had experimented with both family leave and universal health care prior to the introduction of these policies at the national level. By the time the FMLA was introduced, more than a dozen states had adopted some version of family leave.[50] And before the Affordable Care Act, Massachusetts had pioneered a very similar reform in 2006, while several other states had also experimented with expansive health care reforms.[51] Yet references to foreign countries were substantially more common than references to these state-level efforts, even though senators and representatives are generally eager to reference their home states.

Partisanship

Partisanship is a regular feature of debates on health, family, and related social policy issues, as redistributive issues often define and distinguish conservative and progressive politicians. My theoretical model helps explain when these partisan differences carry over to the use of foreign models. As Chapter 2 explains, in fields where a single foreign model exists, this often becomes the dominant solution and mutes partisan debates. In contrast, where diverse foreign models coexist, partisanship thrives, as reform opponents and proponents advocate for the model that best suits their partisan beliefs. In turn, these partisan debates complicate matters for voters, weakening the signal that foreign models send.

Partisanship was very strong during both in the 1993 and 2009–2010 health care debates. Republicans typically incorporated foreign references in comments hostile to the legislation, while Democrats incorporated them in comments friendly to the legislation. However, regardless of party affiliation, senators and representatives frequently engaged in, rather than refraining from, international comparisons. For example, Democrats argued that the Canadian health care system was cost effective, while Republicans argued that the Canadian health care system involved long wait times. Many senators and representatives, as well as Presidents Clinton and Obama, highlighted that their preferred policy was consistent with American values. However, comments about the uniqueness of the US system and the irrelevance or illegitimacy of foreign comparisons were rare, even though conservative jurists have called for ignoring foreign models. The few positive comments Republicans made about foreign health care models emphasized limitations on litigation, an issue Democrats did not emphasize, and pharmaceutical pricing, an issue Democrats also raised.

In contrast, partisanship was far more muted in the discussions about foreign models and the FMLA. Democrats were overwhelmingly positive in their references to the FMLA. However, Republicans were in a bind because of the existence of a dominant international model. Many chose to remain silent—only 19 statements about foreign models came from Republicans during the FMLA debates, far fewer than in the health care debates.[52] More strikingly, half of these references were positive ones. And the types of arguments Republicans made in favor of the FMLA were very similar to the arguments Democrats made—namely that essentially every country but the United States had adopted family leave. This is not to imply that the FMLA was not controversial—after all, President George H. W. Bush had vetoed the Family Medical Leave Act of 1992. Instead, I suggest that the existence of a single prominent international model muted opposition, prompting conservative Republicans to stay silent and helping moderate Republicans explain to voters why they were joining the Democrats in support of the bill.

Most Referenced Countries

My theory suggests that, unlike technocrats, politicians will seek to persuade voters by referencing rich, proximate, and familiar countries rather than those countries that have been successful in particular issue areas. This is in fact what we see. While Democrats and Republicans made very different arguments in the health care and family policy debates, they referenced the very same countries to make these arguments. Many of these countries were only marginally relevant to the debate at hand, but they were familiar to ordinary Americans. In contrast, countries that experts consider most relevant to the U.S. debates were not mentioned frequently unless those countries were also prominent in the media. The data below support the proposition that legislators are constrained when referencing foreign models. Not only can they not select the countries that most help their argument, they cannot even focus on those countries that experts would consider most relevant to the U.S. debate at hand because of their success in particular policy areas, or because of their similarity to the United States in particular fields.

In the 1993 and 2009–2010 health care debates, both supporters and opponents of the legislation referenced Canada and the United Kingdom repeatedly while making very few references to the Netherlands and Switzerland, two countries on which health experts focused because of their success in managing health systems with significant private provision and insurance.[53] In the 1992–1993 FMLA debates, Germany and Japan figured prominently in statements by both opponents and proponents of the legislation. These countries were prominent in the news media in the 1980s and 1990s because of their rapid industrial development; however, their family policies never stood out as particularly successful. In contrast, references to Sweden, a country advocates of family leave have focused on, were far fewer.

Tables 3.4 through 3.6 present countries that were referenced five times or more in each debate. For these tables, the unit of analysis is the country, not the

Table 3.4 **2009–2010 Health Care Debate References by Country and Attitude**

Country/Region	Count	Positive	Negative
Canada	32	16	16
Europe	28	7	21
UK	24	12	12
France	10	9	1
Japan	9	8	1
Germany	8	6	2
Sweden	5	4	1
Spain	5	5	0
Italy	5	5	0

References to foreign countries made fewer than five times: Australia (3); Denmark, Switzerland (2); Belgium, the Netherlands, India, China, Ireland, Taiwan (1).

References to U.S. states: Texas (15); Massachusetts (13); California (10); Minnesota (8); Washington (4); Vermont, Arizona, Missouri (2); Oregon, Wisconsin, Alaska, Florida (1).

Table 3.5 **1993–1994 Health Care Debate References by Country and Attitude**

Country/Region	Count	Positive	Negative
Canada	105	42	63
(West) Germany	30	14	16
UK	25	11	14
Japan	16	9	7
France	10	8	2
Sweden	10	4	6
"Other countries"	7	6	1
Europe	6	1	5

References to foreign countries made fewer than five times: Italy, the Netherlands (4); Belgium (2); Israel, Mexico, Norway, South Africa, Switzerland (1).

References to U.S. states: Hawaii (11); Oregon (5); Washington (4); Tennessee (3); Florida (2); Arizona, California, Connecticut, Kentucky, Massachusetts, Minnesota, Missouri, Montana, New Hampshire, Pennsylvania, Utah, Vermont (1).

Table 3.6 **1992–1993 FMLA Debate References by Country and Attitude**

Country/Region	Count	Positive	Negative
Japan	46	42	4
(West) Germany	46	42	4
Canada	23	21	2
South Africa	20	18	2
Europe	19	13	6
Industrialized world	19	19	0
Sweden	13	9	4
France	11	8	3
UK	10	8	2
Italy	9	6	3
Third world	8	8	0
Austria	6	4	2

References to foreign countries made fewer than five times: "All countries," Asia, Chile, Finland, Iran (4); Australia, Cuba, Ireland, Korea, Libya, Switzerland, Middle East (2); Central America, Africa, Belgium, Burkina, Denmark, East Germany, Guinea-Bissau, Iceland, India, Indonesia, Iraq, Israel, Kuwait, Laos, the Netherlands, New Zealand, North America, Norway, Poland, South America, Spain, Sudan (1).

References to U.S. states: New Jersey, Oregon, Pennsylvania (1).

statement. For example, if a congressman stated that we should adopt health care reform because Germany and Japan offer it, this is counted as one reference to Germany and one reference to Japan.

Argumentation

The proposed theory also has implications for the types of arguments reform proponents and opponents are likely to employ. The diffusion literature distinguishes between emulation, learning, and competition. Emulation arguments, both positive and negative, focus only on the identity of the foreign country—that is, legislators merely highlight that Canada, or Socialist countries, or Western countries, adopted a law. Emulation arguments in the *Congressional Record* were very similar in structure to the prompts given in the public opinion experiments discussed earlier. Learning arguments offer some additional information about the success and failure of the policy abroad—they contain evidence that was not known at the time the policy was adopted abroad.

Competition arguments focus on what perceived competitors of the United States are doing.

When a single international model exists, advocates can rely on emulation alone and send a simple and coherent message. In emulation arguments, advocates can argue that everyone has this policy and so should we. However, when multiple foreign models coexist, conversations about which foreign models work better begin and discussions about what we can learn from abroad occur. While these learning arguments connect the adoption of a policy to a positive or negative consequence, they are often partisan, general, and unscientific—they are not the types of learning arguments that would persuade experts. That being said, learning arguments are more complex than emulation arguments; they can muddy the waters for voters and weaken the persuasive power of foreign models.

Tables 3.7 and 3.8 classify the types of arguments used in the health care and family policy debates. The unit of analysis in Tables 3.7 and 3.8 is the individual statement, and each statement might contain references to several foreign countries. The column "Only argument" includes statements that contained only one of the three types of arguments. The column "All arguments" includes statements that made more than one type of arguments. As described previously, emulation arguments were popular in both debates, but far outnumbered all other types of arguments in the FMLA debates. In contrast, learning arguments, that is, arguments that emphasized various dimensions of the policy supported by data (broadly defined), were very common in the health care debates.

Table 3.7 **FMLA Debate References by Nature of the Argument**

	Only argument	All arguments
Emulation	49	76
Learning	2	6
Competition	8	33

Table 3.8 **2009–2010 Health Care Debate References by Nature of the Argument**

	Only argument	All arguments
Emulation	22	30
Learning	27	35
Competition	2	2

Arguments in the Health Care Debates

In the 2009–2010 health care debates, arguments about learning and emulation were prevalent, but arguments about competition were surprisingly few.
Democrats supportive of the Obama reform echoed the emulation argument
that, since every industrialized country offers universal health insurance, so
should the United States. For example, Senator Kent Conrad (D-ND) argued:
"Every other industrialized country in the world has universal coverage. They
have figured out a way to provide health insurance to every family in their
countries. France, Germany, Great Britain, Japan, every other major industrialized country has figured out a way to provide health insurance for every one
of their citizens. It is time for America to do the same."[54] Relatedly, Democrats
used rankings developed by the UN and WHO to support an expansion in
health care access.[55] Interestingly, reform opponents felt the need to respond
to this argument by discussing the ranking methodology, while conceding that
the U.S. system did not provide the best possible health care for its poor.[56]

Additionally, several emulation arguments were negative. What distinguishes emulation from learning is the focus on identity of prior adopters
rather than the consequences of policy reform abroad. To take an example of a
negative emulation argument, opponents of health care reform criticized it as a
Socialist attempt to establish a European-style welfare state, with little further
elaboration on the drawbacks of such systems.[57]

In addition to the emulation arguments just discussed, lawmakers also
engaged in efforts to draw lessons from other countries' experiences. Learning
arguments were relatively simple and direct, designed to put forward a clear
message that ordinary Americans could easily understand. More specifically,
Democrats emphasized that foreign countries managed to spend significantly
less than the United States on health care and yet achieved comparable or better results.[58] They also identified various ways in which foreign health care systems are more successful in constraining costs. According to reform advocates,
foreign countries allow parallel imports of drugs,[59] spend more on prevention
and public health,[60] manage distinct stages of treatment in conjunction with
one another,[61] and discourage medical tort litigation.[62] Moreover, a key selling
point by reformers was that people with preexisting conditions easily get treatment in foreign countries but have difficulty in securing health insurance in the
United States.[63] For reform advocates, providing health care for everyone in
need was both a moral imperative and an institutional design achievement.[64]

Health reform critics referred to foreign countries' experiences in order to
highlight two main and related disadvantages of the proposed reforms: long
waiting lists and the rationing of health care. First, critics complained about
the long waiting lists by offering the slogan "care delayed is care denied."[65] To

back up this argument, critics provided information about how long it took to start certain treatments in various countries.[66] They emphasized that for illnesses such as cancer, where early treatment is key, the United States achieves better health outcomes.[67] The second key warning that health reform opponents raised was that foreign countries keep costs down by rationing, and ultimately denying, health care to some patients.[68] In addition, critics worried that government control would discourage private initiative in medical research and innovation.[69] While emulation and learning arguments were plentiful in the health care debates, competition arguments were scarce. This is striking given that health care expenditures constitute 17% of U.S. gross domestic product (GDP) and thus could clearly impact firm relocation choices. Neither proponents nor opponents of the reform highlighted this in Congress, even though competition had figured prominently in both the Clinton and Obama electoral campaigns.

Arguments in the FMLA Debates

In the FMLA debates, arguments about the emulation of foreign countries' policies dominated the discussion in Congress, from start to finish. "The U.S. is currently the only industrialized country in the world without laws mandating parental or maternity leave," said Senator Chris Dodd (D-CT) in introducing the legislation.[70] Dozens of senators and representatives echoed these themes. In signing the FMLA, President Clinton concluded with this theme, as described earlier. Emulation arguments were very prevalent in the FMLA debates—politicians offered very little information other than the fact that many foreign governments had adopted maternity leave policies. In the health care debates, many emulation arguments were positive and many were negative. In the family policy debates, almost all emulation arguments, even those made by Republicans, were positive. For example, Representative Olympia Snowe (R-ME) echoed a claim made by many Democrats and argued: "Until recently the United States was alone among industrialized nations, with that well-known center of enlightened government, South Africa, in lacking a family leave policy. Now even South Africa has adopted a more progressive policy than we have, leaving us in shameful isolation."[71] Proponents of the reform characterized maternity leave as a key feature of modern family policy that should be valued "in the 20th century."[72] They saw the lack of such a policy as "backwardness"[73] and as a "disgrace."[74] The few emulation arguments casting foreign countries in a negative light described these countries' laws as paternalistic regimes that do not respect freedom and individual choice.[75]

Competition between the United States and other industrialized countries was a second significant theme in the FMLA debates. Those worried about the

FMLA stressed the importance of flexible labor laws for job creation. In contrast, proponents of FMLA argued repeatedly that, since the two major competitors of the United States at the time, Germany and Japan, had both adopted generous maternity leave policies, maternity leave would not place the United States at a competitive disadvantage.[76] Others argued that maternity leave in fact confers a competitive advantage to Germany and Japan, because workers who enjoy a rich and stable family life will ultimately be more productive.[77] The presence of competition arguments in the context of the FMLA is surprising. Because the FMLA only provides for unpaid leave, it likely has a very small impact on firms' bottom line and relocation decisions. While sophisticated audiences would likely find competition arguments unpersuasive, voters concerned about the competitive position of the United States vis-à-vis Germany and Japan in the late 1980s and early 1990s might be reassured that their government is benchmarking its performance against key competitors, never considering that this policy area was unlikely to have a major impact on national competitiveness.

Learning arguments were also made, but infrequently. For example, Representative Curt Schroeder (R-PA) worried that "American families are breaking up at a 100-percent faster rate than any other country." In general, politicians seeking to draw lessons from other countries' experiences provided fact-based justifications for their positions. However, these justifications were expressed in simple and unscientific terms—they were arguments addressed to ordinary Americans, and would likely not persuade sophisticated audiences.

In summary, the patterns that emerge from the *Congressional Record* are consistent with the theoretical predictions outlined in Figure 3.1. First, references to foreign models were frequent. Second, they were colored by partisanship. Democrats used foreign models to support both health care and family policy reform. Republicans' responses differed in the two issue areas. In health care, where diverse foreign models were available, Republicans' references were primarily negative, while in family policy, where a single foreign model was dominant, Republicans' references were mixed. Third, both Republicans and Democrats focused on the same few countries familiar to voters rather than on countries that were most successful in particular issue areas. Fourth, emulation arguments were prevalent in both debates and dominant in debates on the FMLA. In this debate, Democrats and even some Republicans simply repeated the claim that since almost all other countries offer leave, the United States should as well. In the health care debates, both learning and emulation arguments were made, as Republicans highlighted the diversity of foreign models to weaken the rhetorical power of the Democrats' pitch.

Conclusions

This chapter has examined empirically two key theoretical propositions: the proposition that voters respond to information about foreign models and the proposition that politicians reference particular foreign models to show voters that they are pursuing desirable goals in a competent fashion. There is significant support for both claims. Original experimental data suggest that even Americans respond positively to information from abroad. This positive response is widespread, and not concentrated among liberal elites as previously believed. People with limited education and highly educated people, people with low and high incomes, men and women, whites and nonwhites all respond positively to foreign endorsements. Across these groups, recommendations from the UN resonate particularly strongly; indeed, UN endorsements are especially likely to shift Republican's views on contested issues of redistribution.

These experimental findings are novel to the academic literature, but they comport with politicians' intuitions. Politicians frequently reference foreign countries to increase support for proposals they support. Politicians who oppose policy proposals challenge these references, concerned about their persuasive power. In both the family policy and health care debates, references to foreign countries were made significantly more frequently than to U.S. states.

What these data do not tell us is how much influence foreign models ultimately have on policy adoption. What might have happened if many western European countries never adopted family leave or universal health care? Would these ideas have been adopted in the United States in 1993 and 2010?[78] Would they have been adopted much later with much greater tensions between their opponents and supporters? Or might they have never been on the table at all, rejected out of hand as Communist fantasies? The chapters that follow investigate these questions.

4

National Health Services Across OECD Countries

Health care markets changed dramatically in the decades following World War II. Many rich democracies introduced health insurance programs that covered their entire populations through centralized, government-run insurance funds. Some governments launched even more radical health reforms. They adopted the National Health Service (NHS) model, which also involved nationalizing many hospitals and turning many doctors and nurses into government employees. Existing explanations for major health care reforms emphasize health crises, strong left-wing parties, weak medical associations, and institutional structures with limited veto points as key determinants of reform.[1] However, while the following empirical analyses find some support for each of these factors, existing theories are incomplete. The diffusion of regional and global health policy templates provides the missing puzzle piece.

This chapter shows that a relatively weak international health care model had a major impact on national health policies across advanced industrialized countries, even though this model harmed powerful domestic interest groups. This chapter develops this argument in three steps: it first explains how international and regional models developed in the health policy field, then illustrates how these templates influenced the adoption of health policies across rich countries, and finally clarifies the mechanisms of country-to-country policy diffusion. The next chapter turns to southern Europe for more detailed case studies of the context and discourse used to introduce health reforms.

The chapter's first step is descriptive: it identifies the major actors involved in health care reforms, classifies the range of health policies advanced industrialized countries have adopted, and presents international health templates. International organizations' efforts to develop and promote specific templates were more limited in the area of health policy than in other fields, such as labor policy and family policy. Starting in the 1950s and ending in the early 1980s, a broad international health model developed, which focused on universal access, primary care, centralized financing, and public provision. The introduction of the British NHS and the World Health Organization's (WHO) Alma-Ata Declaration were key steps in the development of this international template. The WHO identified key goals for which all governments should strive in their health policies, just as the International Labour Organization (ILO) did for policies in the areas of employment, unemployment, pensions, and families. However, the ILO was much more specific in its policy advice: not only did it promote desirable policy tools, such as maternity leaves, but it also specified parameters for the implementation of policy, like desirable leave length and compensation rates.[2] In addition, while the WHO's efforts took the form of non-binding declarations, the ILO pushed for the ratification of specific conventions, creating legal obligations for ratifying states to introduce reforms. The ILO even asked countries that had not ratified these conventions to submit periodic reports. In contrast, the international health template was relatively weak because it was vague on key points and did not place any legal obligations on states.

In addition, the international health template also challenged the interests of medical associations, a key interest group. Medical associations are critical to the development of health policy, both because they function as powerful providers' unions and because doctors enjoy unique expertise and high social status. Medical associations often lobby against reforms that limit doctors' autonomy and compensation, such as the introduction of NHSs. Conversely, patients' interests in obtaining affordable care are typically not well represented in the political arena. This is because patients, like other consumers of goods and services, face severe collective action problems. This asymmetry between doctors' and patients' organizational capabilities distinguishes health policy from other social policy fields where either labor unions or employer associations (or both) benefit from proposed international models and thus have material incentives to be receptive to the spread of those policies. In contrast, the international health template could harm organized interest groups.

This chapter's second task is to document the impact of this international health template on policy development across rich countries. Event history models indicate that both domestic factors and international factors were critical to the adoption of NHSs across many countries. The analysis that follows highlights that countries with left-wing governments, countries with unified administrations, and countries facing a favorable international environment are particularly likely to introduce an NHS. This last finding—that international influences are critical to health policy development—challenges a large literature in comparative politics that explains social policy development on the basis of domestic actors' material preferences alone. It also responds to an international law literature that states that diffusion, international norms, and "soft" international law only result in symbolic and superficial changes, decoupled from actual domestic practices. If international models can precipitate policy change in a field such as health care, which involves large sums of money, advanced bureaucracies, and powerful interest groups, diffusion is likely critical to other diverse realms as well, as subsequent chapters comparing health policy to family policy illustrate.

The chapter's third task is to elucidate the mechanisms of policy diffusion. This book's key theoretical claim is that policy diffusion happens and takes particular forms because of, rather than despite, politicians' responsiveness to key constituencies. That is, politicians' reelection constraints and, in particular, their need to signal to uninformed voters that they are pursuing desirable goals competently, prompts politicians to borrow prominent foreign models and ignore other, less public information sources. Chapter 3 provided some support for the micro-foundations of this argument by showing that even American voters respond positively to information from abroad and that American politicians of all stripes reference a few prominent countries frequently. This chapter supports this claim through cross-national data on policy adoption: it illustrates that across rich industrialized countries, the probability that a country will adopt an NHS increases when countries covered prominently in the national media have already adopted this reform. This chapter also illustrates that two other diffusion mechanisms—learning from policy success and competition—shape national health care patterns. Governments are substantially more likely to adopt NHSs when countries whose news voters follow have already done so, when trade competitors have adopted these policies, and when evidence of NHS success is stronger. In addition, the key domestic factors influencing the adoption of an NHS are left-wing governments, unified administrations, federalism, and past policy choices. To preview subsequent chapters, similar, but not identical, diffusion mechanisms operate in the area of family policy. That is, imitation of countries covered in the news is a key diffusion mechanism in both fields, but learning from policy successes and competition are only relevant in the case of health care.

Health Reforms Across Advanced Industrialized Countries

The great majority of countries around the world, including all advanced industrialized countries, have adopted some form of public health insurance. However, health systems in Organization for Economic Cooperation and Development (OECD) countries differ on important dimensions, notably, the breadth of health insurance coverage, the source of health care financing, and the method of health care provision. Three main types of systems are presented here: predominantly private systems, social insurance systems, and universal systems. Most universal systems also take the form of NHSs.

In predominantly private systems, government involvement is limited to regulating and subsidizing market participants. Health financing and health provision are mainly private. Private spending is a substantially higher percentage of total health care spending in the two primarily private health systems—the United States and Switzerland—than in other OECD countries. Correspondingly, public spending is substantially lower than average in these two countries. However, while public spending is low in comparative terms in these two countries, it nonetheless constitutes more than 40% of total U.S. health spending and more than 50% of total Swiss health spending.[3] Historically, the fraction of the population benefiting from any type of health insurance varied substantially in predominantly private systems. However, recent reforms have lead to widespread health insurance coverage even in these systems.

Social insurance constitutes a second model, in which national legislation requires employers and employees to pay payroll taxes, and these contributions in turn determine benefits. Historically, social insurance programs offered no coverage to persons without a connection to the workforce and provided different benefits to different types of workers. More recently, however, many countries with social insurance programs have extended and standardized coverage. In social insurance systems, health care provision is regulated but is not predominantly public. Private and public hospitals coexist, and doctors are typically in contractual relationships with insurance funds rather than being government employees.

A third model is a universal, single-payer system. This system offers citizens uniform and universal coverage, regardless of contributions, and is heavily funded through general taxation. Most universal, single-payer systems rely extensively on the public provision of health services, and therefore constitute NHSs.[4]

The three health system models have different implications for equity, efficiency, and policymaking incentives. Primarily private systems and social insurance systems can leave substantial portions of the population uninsured, and did so historically. In recent years, however, the three health systems have converged on the question of health insurance coverage: coverage will soon be almost universal across the rich democracies studied here. Nevertheless, despite these recent reforms, both primarily private systems and social insurance systems allow for greater inequality in the quality of care provided than do universal single-fund systems. While heavy government involvement is considered inefficient in many policy sectors, in health care, single-payer systems are considered particularly cost effective as they consume substantially smaller fractions of gross domestic product (GDP) without substantial reductions in health care outputs and outcomes. This occurs because in single-payer systems, central governments are better able to control overall costs, using their power as sole purchasers to lower drug and technology prices and to collect revenue efficiently.[5] Yet, limitations on patient choice, queues for nonurgent procedures, and doctor dissatisfaction are frequent complaints about NHSs.[6] Finally, from a policymaking perspective, public sector monopolies generate very different policy dynamics than sectors organized according to corporatist or market principles.

Table 4.1 represents a broad categorization of advanced industrial countries on the basis of their health systems.[7] Figure 4.1 presents the same information on a map to highlight the geographic distribution of each type of system. While a clear social insurance cluster emerges at the center of western Europe, countries that have adopted NHSs seem dispersed across the European periphery. Table 4.1, however, which contains the dates of introduction of NHSs, shows that substantial regional clustering exists in the adoption of NHS policies as well.

Alternative classifications of health care systems exist. Although Switzerland is often classified as a private insurance system, on many dimensions it is more similar to the social insurance systems of continental Europe than to the United States. If Switzerland were reclassified in the social insurance column, the geographic clusters Figure 4.1 presents would be even more pronounced. A key debate also arises regarding which of the universal, single-fund health services are true NHSs. The theoretical distinction hinges on whether health care services are publicly provided or not. In practice, whether hospital beds are publicly owned turns out not to be a useful marker of NHSs; both countries with universal care and single-fund financing and countries with social health insurance systems have very high rates of publicly owned hospitals.[8] A more useful distinction concerns the payment method for general practitioners and hospital physicians. In some universal, single-fund health care systems, doctors are reimbursed on a fee-for-service basis similar to social insurance and private insurance systems. In others, they receive fixed salaries or salaries dependent only partially on the size of the populations they serve (capitation) or the services they provide (bonuses, combinations of salaries, and fees for services provided).

Table 4.2 includes all OECD countries with universal coverage through a single fund[9] and lists the year when they introduced a single-payer system, the predominant method of payment for general practitioners and hospital physicians, and the typical ownership structure of hospitals. OECD reports classify all these countries except for Canada and Australia as belonging to the "public

Table 4.1 **Health Systems in Advanced Industrialized Countries**

Mainly private insurance	Social insurance system	Universal, single-fund financing (including national health services)
Switzerland*	Austria	Australia
U.S.	Belgium	Canada
	France	Denmark
	Germany	Finland
	Japan	Greece
	Luxembourg	Iceland
	Netherlands	Ireland
		Italy
		New Zealand
		Norway
		Portugal
		Spain
		Sweden
		UK

*The Swiss health system shares many features with social insurance systems.

integrated model."[10] This term refers to government financing and provision of health care that is often financed through general taxation, and in theory corresponds to NHSs. A narrower definition of NHSs, in which only countries where physicians are in some way government employees are included, would result in largely similar classifications. Specifically, this classification would be the same as the OECD classification, except that New Zealand would not be classified as an NHS, and Ireland would only be considered an NHS since its 1989 reforms changed the form of physician payment from fee-for-service to capitation.

Table 4.2 lists countries by the year in which they adopted a single-payer system. We can divide them into three groups. In the first group, we find pioneering countries adopting policies in the 1930s, 1940s, and 1950s. These policies gave citizens free health care funded through general taxation. In this early era, both hospital and primary care services were limited. Moreover, the social insurance systems intended to help fund them were recently established and weakly institutionalized. The absence of entrenched medical interest groups and the relatively low cost of health care at the time facilitated the introduction of these reforms. Nonetheless, with the possible exception of Britain, the early adopters were timid and did not go as far as introducing NHSs. They permitted private medicine to flourish alongside public provision.

Table 4.2 **Provision of Health Care in Single-Fund Health Care Countries**

Country	Year of unified health fund/NHS adoption	Doctor payment method	Hospital bed ownership
New Zealand	1938	Fee-for-service	Majority of beds in public hospitals
UK	1948	Capitation and bonuses	95% of hospital beds in public hospitals
Ireland	1957	Capitation (since 1989)	Majority of beds in public hospitals
Canada	1966	Fee-for-service	Majority of hospital beds public
Norway	1969	Salary and fee-for-service	Vast majority of beds in public hospitals
Sweden	1969	Salary and fee-for-service	95% of hospital beds in public (county) hospitals
Finland	1972	Capitation and fee-for-service	Vast majority of beds in public (county) hospitals
Denmark	1973	Capitation and fee-for-service	Vast majority of beds in public (county) hospitals
Australia	1974	Fee-for-service	70%–80% of hospital beds public
Italy	1978	Capitation	80%–85% of beds are in public hospitals
Portugal	1979	Salary and fee-for-service	80%–85% of beds in public hospitals
Greece	1983	Salary	Majority of beds in public hospitals
Spain	1986	Capitation	Majority of beds in public hospitals

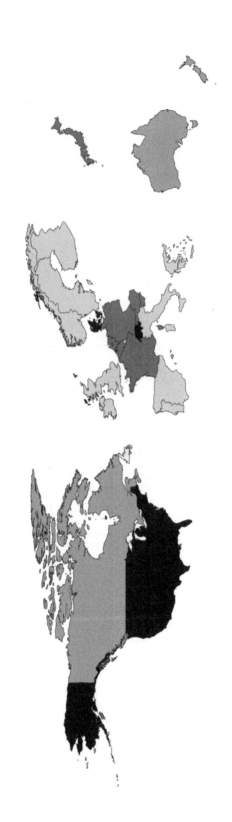

Legend:
- Mainly Private
- Social Insurance Program
- Universal Single-Fund Program
- National Health Services

Figure 4.1 Health Systems in OECD Countries

In the second group of countries, an even milder transition was necessary to establish NHSs. Here, the adoption of NHSs mainly involved a transition from a tax-funded system of hospital services with substantial regional variation in quality to a better-organized, tax-funded system providing more uniform and higher-quality public health services across the national territory. It is noteworthy that all Scandinavian countries introduced such laws shortly after Sweden made its Seven Crowns reform. This pattern is suggestive of policy diffusion.

In the final set of countries, introducing an NHS involved radical reform, as it meant switching from an established system of occupational health insurance to a tax-funded system. The sets of reforms adopted by this group greatly resembled the UK NHS and often called for substantial limitations on both private practice by NHS doctors and private hospital operation. Chapter 5 explores these surprising transitions in greater depth. The next sections examine what prompted countries across the OECD to adopt NHSs, beginning with a description of international models.

The Development of a Weak International Health Template

This section traces the rise and fall of the NHS model as an international template. In health care policy, international organization efforts to promote a single model were significantly more limited than in other social policy fields. Instead, international organization efforts focused on promoting universal coverage, equitable access, primary care, and prevention, goals that were consistent with NHSs, but also achievable through other health care systems. In the absence of a clear international template promoted forcefully by an international organization, country-to-country diffusion became a key mechanism of cross-national influence.

Prior to World War II, social insurance models of health financing were prominent. The idea of an NHS started to gain popularity as soon as Britain announced the Beveridge Plan in 1942. Indeed, Britain's reforms began to be publicized internationally even before they were adopted. As a prominent historian puts it:

> If the [Beveridge] report's impact at home was spectacular, it was also pushed heavily overseas by an initially enthusiastic Ministry of Information. Details of 'The Beveridge Plan' were broadcast by the BBC from dawn on December 1, [1942] in twenty-two languages. Copies were circulated to the troops, and sent to the United States where the Treasury made a $5000 profit on sales. More copies were

dropped into France and other parts of Nazi-occupied Europe where they caused concern at the highest level.[11]

Many features of the 1946 National Health Service Act, such as the one-step form of the reform, the format of the government publications surrounding it, and the (English) language in which they were written, likely facilitated the spread of UK policy ideas to international audiences.

By the mid-1970s, international experience with health care systems such as the British NHS had cumulated and been processed, and organizations such as the WHO took an important stance in promoting a health paradigm focused on prevention and equitable, universal primary care. This is in part because severe questions about the older, hospital-based model of care had been raised in the 1950s and 1960s. The provision of modern primary care required a substantial shift from the traditional model in which patients consulted with specialist physicians to cure particular problems. The new model called for physicians specializing in primary care, physicians working in teams with other health workers, the provision of continuous care, and prevention.[12] The WHO actively championed universal primary health care, as opposed to technical policies targeted to specific diseases, through a series of meetings and reports in the late 1970s that culminated in the 1978 Alma-Ata Declaration. The Declaration was the main result of the International Conference on Primary Health Care, organized by the WHO and attended by 3000 delegates, mostly health ministry officials from 134 countries and 67 international organizations.[13] The Declaration's far-reaching language enshrines primary health care as a human right and demands "an acceptable level of health for all the people of the world by the year 2000."[14] More practically, the Declaration urged national policymakers to ensure equal access to health services to people in rural and underprivileged areas. Governments were to create a "comprehensive national health system" that allocated resources evenly among the population and guaranteed that generally trained personnel were readily available to deal with immediate health concerns, while specialized personnel were proportionate to "the expressed needs of the community." Additionally, in the 1977–1980 period, former West German Chancellor Willy Brandt chaired a major international commission on development that echoed similar principles.[15] In summary, by the late 1970s the international health community had articulated certain parameters of health system success, conferred legitimacy on health policy features expected to lead to this success, and delegitimized the older model of specialized care.

The WHO's recommendations were consistent with NHSs. Indeed, the emphasis on equitable access and primary care resonated most with this system of health organization. However, these goals could also be achieved through other health systems, and the WHO did not forcefully advocate for the NHS as the only appropriate system of health organization. Moreover, WHO efforts took the form of a declaration; no formal legal obligations or monitoring systems were put in place. Indeed, throughout its history the WHO has shied away from the traditional tools of international cooperation through law; it developed its first international convention in 2009, 90 years after the ILO.[16]

As a result of this approach, the WHO's impact on the adoption of NHSs was muted. Case studies of Spain and Greece in chapter 5 illustrate that both proponents and opponents of NHSs referenced the WHO. However, proponents of NHSs interpreted WHO advice as an endorsement of the model, while opponents emphasized that the WHO believed that more than one health-financing model was appropriate. This suggests that the WHO had a smaller impact than its high status and legitimacy might have allowed for.

International organizations other than the WHO have also played a role in promoting health reforms, but have not prompted rich industrial countries to revisit core health finance and organization practices. For example, starting in the mid-1990s, the World Bank began extolling managed competition.[17] However, these World Bank efforts are both too recent and too heavily focused on developing countries to have shaped the introduction of NHSs in the OECD. The ILO has actively promoted labor law reform since 1919, including health and safety at work measures. The European Union (EU), which shapes the policies of its member states very directly in some fields, has had limited activity in the area of health. EU efforts have focused on cancer research, worker and consumer safety, and access to health benefits when workers migrate rather than on health finance or organizational design.

To summarize: in comparison to the family policy field described in subsequent chapters, the dominant international organization model in the field of health care was relatively vague, allowing for many variants. As a result, country-to-country diffusion became a key pathway through which ideas about health organization have spread.

Measuring the Influence of Foreign Countries Covered in the News

Policy diffusion research suggests that foreign models can shape domestic policy choices through three primary pathways: competition, learning, and emulation.[18] This book's key theoretical contribution is to clarify how emulation and learning work in practice and to suggest that politicians' electoral incentives and voters' informational limitations greatly shape patterns of policy diffusion. Chapter 3 examined micro-level implications of this theory for voter and politician behavior. The analysis that follows examines a macro-level implication: that policy adoption depends on the actions of countries covered in the news, which tend to be large, rich, and culturally proximate countries. More specifically, this chapter illustrates that, when countries covered in the news adopt an NHS, countries receiving this news are more likely to introduce such a service. Chapter 6 shows a very similar pattern in family policy. Because this theory is new, I spend several pages exploring the metrics used to test it and their validity. In health, but not in family policy, I also found support for other diffusion mechanisms, namely learning from policy success and competition, which I discuss below.

The regressions that follow use spatial lags to examine whether a country's policy choices depend on foreign countries' choices. A spatial lag has two components. The first component of a spatial lag is a spatial weight. A spatial weight specifies the relationship between particular country pairs. For example, to test the hypothesis that a country is influenced by the countries it borders, one could give a weight of one to country pairs where two countries share a border, and a weight of zero to all other country pairs. The second component of a spatial weight is a measure of the policy being examined. For example, this second component could reflect whether a particular foreign country has or lacks an NHS.

This section explains how I constructed spatial weights in the regressions that follow that reflect media connections between countries. Subsequent sections explain how I created spatial weights that capture trade relationships and policy success, and spell out in more detail how spatial weights are used to construct spatial lags. To examine whether countries whose news voters follow are imitated disproportionately, the regressions that follow use foreign newspaper and magazine sales as a measure of connectedness between two countries.[19] This measure of foreign newspaper sales is the best available measure for purposes of the regressions, because it is the only measure that has been consistently collected and compiled for all OECD countries over many decades. In the paragraphs that follow, I present this measure and validate it in two ways. First, I show that the measure used in the regressions is consistent with important regularities in the media studies literature on how domestic media cover foreign developments. Next, I show that the measure used in the regressions is highly correlated with other data I collected on national newspaper coverage of foreign countries and with public opinion measures of citizen familiarity with foreign countries.

The foreign newspaper spatial weight matrix reflects the same patterns as published media studies

Published media studies suggest that not all foreign countries receive the same coverage: in particular, rich, large, and proximate countries receive the most attention. All these patterns are present in the foreign newspaper sales spatial weight matrix used in the regressions that follow. Table 4.3 presents this matrix for the year 1975. Columns list exporting countries; rows list importing countries. Cells reflect the fraction of a country's newsprint import that comes from each exporting country each year. To construct these weights, the value of sales of newspapers, journals, and periodicals in U.S. dollars was used.[20] Amounts were row-standardized so that imports in each row total 100%.

Large and rich countries are especially prominent in Table 4.3. More specifically, the spatial weight matrix shows four countries to be the major exporters of newspapers: France, Germany, the United Kingdom, and the United States. In contrast, Japan, the second richest OECD country, exports very little newsprint. Each of the four major exporters is also the base of at least one major international newswire (Agence France Press, Deutsche Presse-Agentur, Reuters, and Associated Press and United Press International).[21] The role of these major newswires as dominant creators and gatekeepers of international news is well established.[22] In turn, wire services heavily overrepresent the countries from which they originate in the news they transmit.[23] In the media systems of western European countries, international wires have less agenda-setting power than in other regions because of the great availability of other information sources, notably foreign correspondents and foreign newspapers.[24] However, because these additional sources of information also overrepresent powerful countries, the net effect is asymmetric coverage.

The spatial weight matrix also reveals a second important regularity: that proximate countries exchange far more newspapers than distant ones. These two regularities—the prominence of rich and proximate countries—are similarly noted in all major studies of the domestic coverage of foreign events. The most comprehensive comparative study, commissioned by the United Nations Education, Scientific, and Cultural Organization (UNESCO), involving 13 national teams and presenting data for 29 countries, including 5 OECD countries, concluded that

> almost without exception, the data . . . from forty-two countries, derived from ten separate studies, are in perfect harmony with the

Table 4.3 **Weights Based on Newspaper Sales (1975)**

	Australia	Austria	Belgium	Canada	Denmark	Finland	France	Germany	Greece
Australia	0%	0%	0%	0%	0%	0%	0%	2%	0%
Austria	0%	0%	0%	0%	0%	0%	1%	97%	0%
Belgium	0%	0%	0%	0%	0%	0%	49%	21%	0%
Canada	0%	0%	0%	0%	0%	0%	8%	1%	0%
Denmark	0%	0%	0%	0%	0%	3%	2%	42%	0%
Finland	0%	0%	0%	0%	0%	0%	2%	15%	0%
France	0%	0%	40%	0%	0%	0%	0%	8%	0%
Germany	0%	3%	4%	0%	5%	1%	10%	0%	1%
Greece	0%	1%	0%	0%	0%	0%	28%	39%	0%
Ireland	0%	0%	0%	0%	0%	0%	0%	0%	0%
Italy	0%	3%	0%	0%	0%	0%	24%	56%	0%
Japan	0%	0%	0%	0%	0%	0%	6%	59%	0%
Netherlands	0%	0%	32%	0%	2%	0%	6%	38%	0%
Norway	0%	0%	0%	0%	19%	7%	2%	17%	0%
Portugal	0%	0%	0%	0%	0%	0%	47%	28%	0%
Spain	0%	0%	1%	0%	0%	0%	44%	38%	0%
Sweden	0%	0%	0%	0%	15%	28%	3%	26%	0%
Switzerland	0%	0%	1%	0%	0%	0%	27%	57%	0%
UK	0%	0%	0%	0%	1%	4%	13%	14%	0%
U.S.	0%	0%	0%	60%	0%	0%	7%	17%	0%

results of [this UNESCO study]. The pattern is so strong and so consistent in all of the studies that one wonders how impressions to the contrary could have gained acceptance. And the pattern is simple: regional news is emphasized in the media of countries in all parts of the world with all kinds of political and media systems; in second place, behind the dominance of 'own region', is news from Western Europe and North America.[25]

More recent studies of particular news genres also reflect these regularities.[26] We see similar clusters in the domestic coverage of foreign political and economic developments,[27] deaths abroad,[28] and even foreign arts and culture.[29]

Ireland	*Italy*	*Japan*	*Netherlands*	*Norway*	*Portugal*	*Spain*	*Sweden*	*Switzerland*	*UK*	*U.S.*
0%	1%	6%	0%	0%	0%	0%	0%	0%	57%	33%
0%	0%	0%	1%	0%	0%	0%	0%	1%	0%	0%
0%	3%	0%	25%	0%	0%	0%	0%	0%	0%	1%
0%	1%	0%	0%	0%	0%	0%	0%	0%	5%	86%
0%	3%	0%	4%	12%	0%	0%	21%	0%	7%	5%
0%	2%	0%	1%	0%	0%	0%	74%	0%	4%	3%
0%	33%	0%	8%	0%	0%	2%	0%	2%	5%	1%
0%	21%	0%	26%	0%	0%	2%	2%	13%	7%	5%
0%	9%	0%	4%	0%	0%	1%	5%	2%	7%	5%
0%	0%	0%	2%	0%	0%	0%	0%	0%	97%	1%
0%	0%	0%	3%	0%	0%	0%	0%	5%	3%	5%
0%	9%	0%	0%	0%	0%	0%	0%	1%	3%	21%
0%	5%	0%	0%	0%	0%	1%	1%	0%	5%	9%
0%	2%	0%	2%	0%	0%	0%	35%	0%	11%	5%
0%	6%	0%	1%	0%	0%	4%	0%	0%	9%	4%
0%	6%	0%	3%	0%	0%	0%	3%	1%	2%	1%
0%	3%	0%	2%	2%	0%	0%	0%	0%	9%	10%
0%	12%	0%	1%	0%	0%	1%	0%	0%	0%	1%
11%	28%	0%	5%	0%	0%	0%	0%	1%	0%	20%
0%	2%	2%	1%	0%	0%	1%	0%	0%	8%	0%

An important limitation of published media studies is that most report data by region and not by country—reporting, for example, U.S. coverage of western European news, not U.S. coverage of French or German news in particular. Because North America consists of two countries, Canada and the United States, it is possible to tease out country details. The UNESCO study reports that in 1979 in the United States, 62% of foreign news focused on other North American countries (i.e., Canada), while 38% focused on western Europe.[30] The spatial weight matrix shows very comparable weights. For the United States in 1979, 68% of foreign newspaper sales came from Canada, 30% from western Europe, and 2% from Japan.

Foreign newspaper sales correlate highly with domestic coverage of foreign countries and citizens' familiarity with foreign countries

The prior section showed that the foreign newspaper sales matrix reflected the same patterns as published studies of media coverage. I also collected original data to test in more depth the assumptions involved in using weights based on foreign newspaper sales in the regressions that follow. More specifically, use of this matrix reflects two assumptions: that countries from which many foreign newspapers come are also the countries covered heavily in the domestic press, and that this extensive coverage of particular countries leads citizens to become especially familiar with these same countries. To test these assumptions, I compiled news coverage data and public opinion data from the two case study countries examined in subsequent chapters, Greece and Spain.

Table 4.4 shows that the spatial weights measure based on foreign newspaper sales correlates highly with measures of domestic news coverage of foreign countries and with measures of Greeks' familiarity with foreign countries. In each case, I present data for the earliest year available. The first column presents the spatial weights I used in the regressions. These are based on foreign newspaper sales to Greece in 1975. The second column tracks references to foreign countries in *Οικονομικός Ταχυδρόμος* in 1975. *Οικονομικός Ταχυδρόμος* was a prominent Greek newspaper of the 1970s that was subsequently subsumed by *Το Βήμα*. The correlation between the measure of foreign newspaper sales and coverage in *Οικονομικός Ταχυδρόμος* is .84. Both measures show Germany and France to be the countries to which Greeks were most exposed. Italy, the United Kingdom, and the United States follow. Both measures show Greeks had very little exposure to a range of rich, developed countries, including Spain, Japan, Denmark, Belgium, Canada, Australia, Norway, Ireland, Portugal, Finland, and Luxembourg.

The third column reflects a measure of voter familiarity with foreign countries. In 1980 the Eurobarometer survey sought to capture ties between Europeans by asking about how much they trusted people from different countries. The question read: "Now, I would like to ask about how much you would trust people from different countries. For each country please say whether, in your opinion, they are in general very trustworthy, fairly trustworthy, not particularly trustworthy, or not at all trustworthy?" Eurobarometer researchers noted the number of "don't knows" in response to this question and commented: "The explanation is easy: Each individual has a sort of mental map of the world, distorted in varying degrees and containing some areas which are no more than a blur. If a particular individual has only an unclear picture of the country or people he is being asked about, he will probably not reply. There are

Table 4.4 **Greeks' Familiarity with Foreign Countries**

	Foreign newspaper sales	Οικονομικός Ταχυδρόμος references	Eurobarometer measure of unfamiliarity
Germany	.39	642	12
France	.28	618	17
Italy	.09	338	14
UK	.07	484	16
U.S.	.05	474	14
Sweden	.05	150	
Netherlands	.04	160	32
Switzerland	.02	217	30
Austria	.01	124	
Spain	.01	123	29
Japan	0	250	30
Denmark	0	183	36
Belgium	0	164	37
Canada	0	146	
Australia	0	125	
Norway	0	116	
Ireland	0	110	42
Portugal	0	90	36
Finland	0	57	
Luxembourg	0	27	42

therefore more 'don't knows' for people from a small country (Luxembourg) or an outlying country (Portugal or Greece) (positive or negative) than for the inhabitants of a large country (Germany, France, or the UK)."[31] So column 3 in Table 4.4 plots the number of Greeks who didn't know what to think of citizens of particular foreign countries. The correlation between this Eurobarometer measure and coverage in *Οικονομικός Ταχυδρόμος* is .90; the correlation between the Eurobarometer measure and the spatial weights matrix I use in the regression is .68.[32]

Table 4.5 repeats this analysis for Spain. As in Table 4.4, the first column in Table 4.5 lists the spatial weights used in the regression models that are based on foreign newspaper sales in 1975. The second column tracks references to particular countries in the newspaper *El País* in 1977, its first full year of circulation. The last column captures the fraction of Spaniards who answered

Table 4.5 **Spaniards' Familiarity with Foreign Countries**

	Foreign newspaper sales	El País references	Eurobarometer measure of unfamiliarity
France	.44	2518	28
Germany	.38	1848	35
Italy	.06	1489	36
Netherlands	.03	509	47
Sweden	.03	312	
Britain	.02	1121	37
U.S.	.01		38
Switzerland	.01	758	44
Belgium	.01	488	48
Portugal	0	944	36
Japan	0	355	45
Ireland	0	292	48
Canada	0	268	
Austria	0	262	
Greece	0	234	48
Denmark	0	219	51
Luxembourg	0	203	53
Norway	0	171	
Australia	0	143	
Finland	0	102	

I was not able to conduct the search for "Estados Unidos." *El País*'s search engine uses an approximate search and includes phrases such as "estamos unidos" (are together) "estaban unidos" (were together) in this search. The total for both the U.S. and the variants of "being together" for 1977 is 3881 references. The abbreviation for USA (EE UU) yields fewer than 100 references. It is possible that the *El País* references to Britain are inflated for similar reasons, but I did not see this problem in looking through the first few entries for "Reino Unido."

"don't know" to the Eurobarometer question about trust in citizens of particular countries outlined earlier.[33]

The correlation between the measure of foreign newspaper sales I use in the regression and coverage of foreign countries in *El País* is .87. Again, the Eurobarometer question is an imperfect measure of familiarity with foreign countries. That being said, the correlation between coverage in *El País* and familiarity according to Eurobarometer is .94. The correlation between familiarity and the measure of foreign newspaper sales is .72.

These correlations are very high. All three measures show that Spaniards had the most exposure to, and greatest familiarity with, France, Germany, and Italy, in that order. In addition, the measures show that Spaniards had little exposure to, and little familiarity with, a number of developed countries, such as Japan, Ireland, Canada, Austria, Greece, Denmark, Luxembourg, Norway, Australia, and Finland. The correlation is, of course, not perfect. To the extent my weight matrix has noise, which it does, we would expect that this would make the measure trend to zero, and that the true effect would be larger than the effect I report in the regressions. In sum, each of these measures helps validate the measure of foreign newspaper sales I use in the regressions that follow and in chapter 6.

Learning from Policy Success

Learning from policy success is the general hypothesis that policies that are implemented, evaluated, and shown to meet their goals are imitated disproportionately. Chang Lee and David Strang tested whether downsizing policies correlated with outcomes such as GDP growth, budget balancing, or positive trade balances were more likely to be copied.[34] Fabrizio Gilardi and coauthors report that one type of hospital financing reform—the shift from retrospective to prospective reimbursement based on diagnosis-related groups—is more likely to diffuse when correlated with cost savings.[35]

Policy success may also influence policy diffusion. Countries may look at which other countries succeed in reaching policy goals and imitate those countries' policies.[36] What does success mean in the context of health policy? Infant mortality and disability-adjusted life expectancy are the measures the WHO now promotes as ways to evaluate whether a population is receiving adequate health care.[37] Infant mortality depends critically on the health of the mother and thus reflects the health care available to a country's adult population, in addition to the health care available to infants. Infant mortality has a key additional advantage—it is a measure that has been widely used to compare health systems over several decades, and is visible to researchers and policy-makers alike. The success variable examines whether the policy choices of top performers in health care, defined as countries with the lowest (bottom 10%) infant mortality each year, were imitated disproportionately. Few researchers would accept aggregate correlations between particular policies and particular outcomes as evidence of policy success, but more nuanced evaluation data have not been widely available to policymakers. Therefore results should be interpreted as evidence of the influence of perceived policy success rather than actual success.

Competition

Competition between two states for capital, markets, or some other resource may lead countries to imitate their competitors' policies. For example, competition for foreign direct investment helps explain the proliferation of bilateral investment treaties,[38] the imitation of competitors' trade liberalization decisions,[39] and the introduction of market-oriented infrastructure reforms.[40] NHSs shift the payment of health care taxes from workers and employers to the general population (in countries that previously had social insurance programs) and also help control overall health spending. Countries whose competitors have already introduced NHSs might be disproportionately likely to introduce these same policies in order to attract firms interested in lower labor costs.

The Domestic Politics of Health Care Reform

In most accounts of welfare state development, actors' material positions determine their policy preferences, and actors' relative strengths along with national institutions determine the final form social policy compromises take.[41] The health policy literature emphasizes left-wing parties, medical associations, veto players, and demographic shifts as the key actors and institutions shaping these compromises in the health policy arena.

Specifically, left-wing governments are associated with redistributive policies and higher government spending on diverse social programs. NHSs are no exception, as they typically expand access to health care to the very poor and introduce substantial government control over the health care industry. They therefore fit more comfortably with left-wing ideology.[42] Indeed, many scholars note a strong positive correlation between left-wing administrations and the expansion of public health insurance policies.[43] Interestingly, John Huber finds no significant effects of left-wing governments on changes in health care spending.[44] This may result because programs such as NHSs contain both cost-increasing measures, such as broader coverage, and cost-control measures.

Medical associations are also critical to the development of health policy. Medical associations derive part of their power from their role as a providers' union that typically enjoys a monopoly over the provision of a vital service. In addition, doctors are substantially more professionalized than other providers of services: they expect and exercise more autonomy, enjoy high social status, and make decisions based not only (or even primarily) on profit maximization, but also on a code of ethics and best practice. Therefore, in addition to the bargaining force that medical associations have as a providers' union, they also have added clout in debates because other decision-makers are more likely to defer to physicians' status and expertise.[45]

Medical associations historically have lobbied for greater professional autonomy for doctors,[46] for fee-for-service rather than for salary methods of compensation,[47] and against the introduction of NHSs.[48] NHSs involve the nationalization of the health care industry: not only does hospital ownership revert to the state, but physicians once paid through fee-for-services arrangements often become salaried state employees. As Ellen Immergut puts it:

> Medical professions throughout Western Europe . . . fought each step toward greater government monopsony because they wished to avoid increasing government incentives and instruments for regulating the profession. They preferred programs subsidizing voluntary mutual aid societies to programs of national health insurance. In turn, they preferred programs of national health insurance to national health services.[49]

Different institutional arguments explain how the resources of key interest groups are channeled into policy outputs.[50] Having many veto players impedes governments from agreeing on and implementing radical changes.[51] Immergut applies this general argument to the field of health politics and identifies the independence of the executive from the legislature and a tradition of referenda as key impediments to national health insurance efforts.[52] Huber finds that cabinet reshuffling is associated with decreased success in efforts to contain health care costs.[53]

However, some authors argue that not all types of veto players have similar effects. Vicki Birchfield, Markus Crepaz, and Arend Lijphart argue that, although competitive veto points (such as regional players) impede the policy-making process, collective veto players (such as multiparty governments) facilitate cooperative policymaking and thus speed up the process.[54] In contrast, two qualitative studies of health care development in Canada and Spain argue that federalism facilitated, rather than blocked, health policy development in those countries because of regional governments' ability to innovate. Antonia Maioni argues that a federal structure in combination with a parliamentary system contributed both to health policy experiments in Canadian provinces and to the elevation of these proposals to the national level.[55] Similarly, Ana Rico claims that competition and imitation among Spanish federal regions, and between the regional and central governments, led to a rapid expansion of health policies.[56]

In general, much of social policy reform is incremental. Typically a country's position in one time period is heavily dependent on its position in the prior period.[57] While NHSs represent a break from the past, it seems likely that past policy choices would nonetheless matter, making the reform easier in some countries than in others. NHSs extend coverage to all citizens. How challenging this task is for a country depends in part on how extensive coverage was prior to the reform. Jacob Hacker, however, makes a somewhat contrary prediction. He compares the United States and United Kingdom and argues that the expansion of capacity prior to the expansion of coverage explains much of the difficulty that national health insurance proposals faced in the United States.[58]

Finally, demographic factors influence health spending directly and might also trigger health reforms. The elderly tend to experience more frequent and severe illnesses than younger people, and thus countries with older populations might have greater needs and desires for health care. As NHSs tend to reduce health care choices in order to control health care spending, it seems likely that these systems will be preferred by countries with younger populations. The intuition here is that the elderly will prefer a social insurance system to an NHS, as they are more likely to enjoy the benefits this offers and less sensitive to its costs. The health care literature provides mixed support for this argument.[59]

While several quantitative studies of health care reform examine health care spending, the dependent variable examined in the qualitative literature and in this chapter is the introduction of particular reforms. The theories examined here predict that domestic and international factors should directly influence policy adoption and indirectly influence spending. Spending on social policy depends heavily on demographic trends and is not immediately responsive to policy changes. Moreover, the domestic hypotheses typical in social policy do not apply well to the area of health spending and instead yield indeterminate results. For example, left-wing governments, strong unions, and centralized administrations should be associated both with reforms to extend coverage, which increases spending, and with reforms to increase government control over the health market, which reduces spending. For these reasons, studying policy adoption rather than spending patterns is an appropriate theoretical choice. An additional practical consideration is that missing data for certain countries prior to the 1970s makes analysis of spending changes in earlier periods challenging.

In sum, the strength of political parties, medical associations, and centralized institutions, as well as several other domestic factors, are very relevant in health policy reform. The following analysis includes them and describes how they are operationalized. Combining these factors, however, does not explain the original puzzle motivating this inquiry: why southern European countries switched from social insurance systems to NHSs. While left-wing governments introduced NHSs in Spain, Greece, and Portugal (but not Italy),[60] these left-wing parties had just come to power and were not strong.[61] More curious was the position of conservative and centrist parties, as well as medical associations, which were surprisingly divided, and even occasionally supportive, of radical reforms that were Socialist in content. And while governance is very centralized in some southern European states (Greece and Portugal), this is not the case for others (Spain and Italy). Similarly, the quantitative analysis exploring all OECD countries suggests that domestic factors are very significant, but cannot in themselves account for reform patterns.

Methods and Results

This section examines the health policy decisions of 20 OECD countries from 1960 to 1995. Countries included in the models are Australia, Austria, Belgium, Canada, Denmark, Finland, France, Germany, Greece, Italy, Japan, Netherlands, Norway, Portugal, Spain, Sweden, Switzerland, and the United States.[62] The models estimate how domestic and international actors and conditions influenced the probability that a country would adopt (1) or not adopt (0) an NHS in a particular year. Health spending, an alternative dependent variable used in other analyses, would not be appropriate here, as total spending aggregates diverse policy decisions that push spending in opposite directions, as well as demographic trends. For example, a left-wing party might expand health coverage, which increases health spending, while at the same time capping reimbursements for expensive procedures, which tends to reduce costs. Similarly, health care costs might rise merely because of an aging population or other demographic movements. Thus a change in this dependent variable may not indicate a policy shift. In family policy, these concerns are more muted, and thus the analyses in chapter 5 include levels of spending and the length of leaves as dependent variables.

Duration models are frequently used to estimate how much time passes until a particular event (such as the adoption of a policy) occurs. For analyzing processes measured in discrete time intervals, Nathanial Beck and coauthors propose using a grouped duration model.[63] This is essentially a logit or other binary dependent variable model that explicitly includes duration dependence through a hazard function.[64] This model is based on, and is very similar to, duration analysis of continuous variables. However, the grouped duration model has two advantages: it permits a flexible specification of the hazard function and it makes time-varying covariates easy to introduce.[65] Standard errors reflect clustering at the country level.

Diffusion variables are constructed by weighing countries' policies by measures of the relationship between countries.

The models estimated take the following form: $y = \rho Wy + X\beta + \varepsilon$.

y is an $NT \times 1$ vector (N units, T time periods per unit) of the dependent variable. ρ is the spatial autoregressive coefficient to be estimated. It captures the strength of the diffusion process. W is the spatial weight matrix. It can be time invariant ($N \times N$) or time varying ($N \times N \times T$). The elements of this matrix, $w_{i,j}$, reflect the degree of connectedness from unit j to unit i. This matrix need not be symmetric. For example, larger countries may have a greater influence on smaller countries than the reverse. The degree of connectedness between a country and itself is set to zero by convention, and the matrix is row-standardized.[66] Wy is the spatial lag. For each observation $y_{i,t}$, the corresponding element of Wy gives a sum of y_j (neighbors' policies), weighted by the degree of connectedness between the country and each neighbor. A spatial lag is similar to a temporal lag, except that it represents the weighted average of dependent variable values in a country's neighbors. To create this weighted average, the researcher must specify the structure of the weight matrix; estimating this from the data is generally not feasible.[67] X is an $NT \times K$ matrix of observations on K independent variables. β is a $K \times 1$ vector of coefficients. ε is the vector of error terms.

The following discussion explains how different theoretical approaches lead to different specifications of what constitutes a neighboring country. In the emulation theory described earlier, voters pay disproportionate attention to proximate and economically powerful countries. To examine whether countries whose news voters follow are imitated disproportionately, foreign newspaper and magazine sales are used as a measure of connectedness between two countries, as described previously.

The success variable examines whether the policy choices of top performers in health care, defined as countries with the lowest (bottom 10%) infant mortality each year, were imitated disproportionately. Infant mortality is used as the measure of health system success because the WHO has advocated for this as a measure of population health and made statistics widely available to researchers and policymakers over several decades.[68] Following Zachary Elkins, Andrew Guzman, and Beth Simmons, trade competitors are defined as countries that exported similar types of products.[69] Data come from the World Bank's World Development Indicators.[70] The position of the government on the left-right spectrum is modeled using Thomas Cusack's political "center of political gravity" concept, which is a weighted average of the positions of the party from which each cabinet minister comes, as reported in the work of Robert Franzese.[71]

Physician density is used as a proxy for the political strength of doctors here. In countries where doctors are scarce, their bargaining power increases and their ability to oppose programs that limit their professional autonomy and compensation possibilities increases as well.[72] Data on doctors per capita trace how many doctors are available per 1000 residents and come from 2006 OECD data. In this analysis, federalism is proxied by the number of federal regions in a country, and multiparty government is proxied by the number of parties in a government, using data from Robert Franzese.[73] Two additional domestic controls are included: the fraction of a country that is older than 65 years, because age might be a good proxy for preferences in health care, and the breadth of health coverage prior to the introduction of health care reform. While many theorists would expect that introducing an NHS would be easier if the country already had expansive health coverage, others might expect countries with relatively underdeveloped health care systems to have greater ease in introducing NHSs because medical interest groups should be weaker.[74]

Model I in Table 4.6 predicts whether a country introduced an NHS (1) or not (0). Model II only includes those variables that were ever statistically significant. In all models, standard errors are clustered by country. Of the domestic variables, three are statistically significant in the expected direction. The probability that a country will adopt an NHS is higher when a country has a left-wing government, few parties, and high prior coverage of the population. Somewhat surprisingly, countries with a federal structure are more likely to adopt an NHS than nonfederal countries. This is inconsistent with simple veto player theories, but consistent with the qualitative work of Maioni and Rico described earlier. A country's doctor density and population structure do not seem to matter. These findings are consistent with Huber's analysis of the determinants of cost-cutting in health care.[75] All three international diffusion variables are correctly signed and statistically significant. Countries exposed to news coverage from countries that have already adopted NHSs, countries whose trade competitors have adopted NHSs, and countries that perceive NHSs as successful in reducing infant mortality are more likely to introduce NHSs.

Because the size of logit coefficients cannot be interpreted directly, Figure 4.2 illustrates how much a shift from the 10th to the 90th percentile of each independent variable changes the probability that a country will adopt an NHS when all other variables are kept constant.[76] For example, a move from a country with a very left-wing government to a country with a very right-wing government, from the 10th to the 90th percentile of the partisan center of gravity index, corresponding to a move from 4.0 to 8.9, decreases a country's probability of introducing an NHS by about 68%.[77] A shift in the number of parties in government from one to four, a 10th to 90th percentile shift, decreases a country's

Table 4.6 **Predicting NHS Adoption**

	Expected sign	*Model I (n = 430)*	*Model II (n = 430)*
		Coefficient (std. error)	*Coefficient (std. error)*
Domestic influences			
Right-wing government	−	−1.69** (.74)	−.95** (.39)
Many parties	−	−1.78*** (.57)	−1.97** (.89)
Federalism	−	.36*** (.09)	.29** (.12)
Doctor density	+	−1.49 (1.10)	
Population over 65	+	−.46 (.38)	
Prior coverage	+	1.15*** (.33)	.83*** (.23)
International influences			
Imitation of countries in media	+	6.50*** (1.68)	8.98*** (2.36)
Policy success	+	5.00*** (1.79)	4.84** (1.89)
Competition	+	7.08*** (2.35)	4.41** (1.71)
Duration dependence			
Log (duration)		−1.28 (1.45)	−.71 (.67)
Constant		−107.73*** (30.54)	−81.64*** (13.63)

probability of introducing an NHS by about 61%. A shift from a unitary country to one with multiple federal regions, a 10th to 90th percentile shift, increases the probability of NHS adoption by 76%. A similar lag shift in the fraction of the population covered by health insurance in the prior year, from 30% to 100% coverage, increases the probability of NHS adoption by 75%. For the diffusion variables, a 10th to 90th percentile shift, or a shift from having 0% of a country's foreign newspapers coming from countries with an NHS to having 56% of these newspapers coming from countries with an NHS, leads to a 56% increase

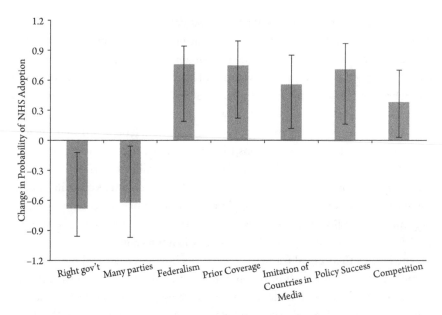

Figure 4.2 Predicting NHS Adoption: Shifts from the 10th to the 90th Percentile of Each Independent Variable

in the probability that an NHS will be adopted. A 10th to 90th percentile shift on NHS success, or moving from a point in time when none of the countries with the lowest infant mortality had an NHS to a point in time where all the countries with the lowest infant mortality had one, increases the chances of NHS adoption by 71%. A 10th to 90th percentile shift in one's trade competitors' choices, or shifting from 0% to 50% of trade competitors having an NHS, leads to a 38% increase in the probability of NHS adoption.

Additional specifications to test the robustness of these models were explored. First, duration dependence was entered into the model through different hazard functions. The specification of the hazard function did not change any of the substantive coefficients substantially. Second, the preexisting coverage variable was lagged for one, two, and three years, in case the expansion of coverage was jointly decided with the introduction of the NHS.[78] Again, results did not change substantially. Finally, the reported patterns do not depend on whether a narrower or a broader definition of an NHS is used.[79]

Conclusions

This chapter explains how radical reform in health policy occurs and attributes a critical role to international paradigms. Quantitative analyses of

OECD government decisions illustrate that governments were substantially more likely to adopt NHSs when the international environment was favorable, including when foreign countries disproportionately covered in the press had already adopted an NHS, when evidence of NHS success abroad was stronger, and when trade competitors had already adopted an NHS. Consistent with prior work on social policy, the ideological orientation of the governing coalition, the number of parties in the governing coalition, federalism, and the policy choices of prior administrations were found to be important predictors in the introduction of NHSs. More surprisingly, politically powerful doctors and older populations were not strong impediments. This chapter's contribution to the welfare state literature is to supplement these domestic accounts with an argument about how the positions of domestic actors with particular predispositions and interests shift in the presence of an international model.

The book's theoretical framework explains how international models shift domestic actors' choices. It posits that international models set the agenda for a diverse set of actors, not just for those favorably predisposed to a particular reform. Moreover, it emphasizes that electoral processes reinforce, rather than attenuate, elites' biases toward imitation of proximate and high-status countries. Chapters 3, 5, and 7 show how politicians use foreign models to win elections and persuade voters about the value of proposed legislation. This chapter used quantitative evidence of policy adoption from across OECD countries to go beyond campaign promises and legislative debates, illustrating that once in office, politicians in fact emulated the policy choices of countries that were rich, proximate, and familiar to voters.

The next chapter uses case study evidence from Greece and Spain to spell out how politicians use foreign models to appeal to voters in both their campaigns for reelection and in their efforts to pass important legislation. In these two late NHS adopters, medical associations were divided and did not forcefully oppose reforms that radically curtailed doctors' autonomy and income. Centrist and conservative parties also seriously considered Socialist proposals and debated international models extensively. For Socialist politicians, the existence of an international model assisted in the translation of a broad ideology into a concrete policy program and in prioritizing health care reform over other issues. Campaign documents, parliamentary debates, and other rhetoric targeted at the general public show elites' expectations that voters are favorably impressed by the imitation of foreign models. Politicians continuously referenced the choices of large and rich industrialized countries as well as the WHO's proposals. These data are analyzed next.

The introduction of NHSs is a critical case in many ways: the reform was materially enormous and conceptually radical, the international organization proposals were relatively "soft," and a key domestic constituency was initially hostile. If international models are powerful under these unfavorable circumstances, diffusion likely shapes a broad set of policy areas. In exploring the diffusion of family policies in chapter 5 and 6, I show how powerful diffusion can be when a more coherent international model is strongly promoted.

The proposed electoral mechanism of policy diffusion helps explain both the development of family policies and the development of health policies. There is no theoretical reason that makes this model particularly suitable to these two areas. Thus this empirical regularity suggests that the proposed electoral model may explain diffusion patterns in diverse fields.

In contrast, two other diffusion mechanisms examined here—learning from policy success and competition—appear to have a large influence in only a limited number of fields. While policy success is shown to influence the adoption of NHSs, policy success does not seem to shape the adoption of family policies studied in previous chapters. Lee and Strang argue that evidence of policy success does not influence subsequent policy adoption automatically. Rather, this happens only when evidence of success is connected with a theory that the particular policy should yield specific results.[80] In the health policy arena, success is relatively clearly defined by the WHO, and measures such as infant mortality have been widely available for decades. In contrast, in areas such as family policy, governments differ on fundamental goals, including whether a mother's participation in the workforce is desirable and whether governments should be involved in promoting larger or smaller families. The existence of a consensus on the goals of a policy and the ways to measure that policy might explain why policy success influences diffusion in some fields but not in others.

Additionally, trade competitors' choices shaped health policy patterns but were not influential in the spread of family policies. The difference in the costs of health care and family benefits may explain this. In OECD countries, health policy budgets are several times larger than family policy budgets. While firms may voice preferences against various regulations and taxes, threats of relocation may only prompt governments to act when the costs firms face are sizable.

Health Reforms in the United Kingdom, Spain, and Greece

In the late 1970s, in Italy, Greece, Spain, and Portugal, public social insurance systems provided health coverage to workers and their dependents alongside booming private health sectors. Then, in less than a decade's time, all four of these southern European countries switched tracks and legislated National Health Services (NHSs). This shift involved both an expansion of health care coverage and a radical reorganization of health care financing. In addition— and most controversially—these governments nationalized hospitals and clinics and moved doctors and nurses from the private to the public sector. This transformation is puzzling because governments typically amend social policies gradually, modifying expenditure levels at the margin rather than undertaking radical structural changes.[1]

The previous chapter explored reforms introducing NHSs across advanced industrialized countries. It illustrated that even a broadly defined and weakly promoted international model can influence national policy in a field with high monetary stakes and strong interest groups. As traditional political economy theories predict, I found that countries with left-wing governments and unified administrations were more likely to introduce NHSs. However, consistent with this book's theoretical claims, international models were also key factors in these transitions. More specifically, governments were substantially more likely to adopt NHSs when large, proximate countries covered in the media had already done so, when evidence of NHS success was stronger, and when trade competitors had adopted NHSs.

This chapter uses case study evidence to examine more closely the mechanisms through which international models influence domestic actors, focusing on Greece and Spain. In both Greece and Spain, Socialist politicians used international models to present their NHS proposals as mainstream and tried-and-true solutions to voters who might otherwise view these Socialist proposals as radical experiments. Socialist politicians won repeated elections by promising that they would modernize southern European societies, and offer their citizens the types of social benefits western Europeans already enjoyed. By presenting campaign documents, media accounts, legislative debates, and public opinion data, this chapter documents that international models facilitated the adoption of major domestic reforms through highly public and politicized processes. Experts were also important both in the design and the implementation of these reforms. That said, the account I present is entirely different from the dominant model in which experts take center stage and policy diffusion "unfolds largely inside the bureaucratic agencies of the state and is not driven in any direct way by electoral incentives and calculations."[2]

Health reform is a difficult test case for my theory, both because doctors stood to lose from the introduction of NHSs, and because the international health model was weak. As chapter 4 explains in more detail, while the World Health Organization (WHO) promoted universal coverage, equitable coverage, primary care, and prevention, its 1978 Alma-Ata Declaration did not explicitly endorse NHSs. Moreover, while many western European countries had introduced NHSs by the time Greece and Spain transitioned to democracy, many other European countries retained social-insurance-based health systems.

The diversity of European models on the question of health system financing and organization, and the silence of the WHO on this issue, allowed conservative opponents of NHSs to dilute the Socialists' message. However, while conservatives and Socialists disagreed on many points, including nationalization of the health sector, they both promised voters they would follow international and especially western European models. These were not empty campaign promises: center-right administrations in power in the late 1970s in both Greece and Spain prioritized important health reforms endorsed by the WHO in its 1978 Alma-Ata Declaration, including primary care and expanded coverage, and thus set the foundations for the introduction of NHSs by later Socialist administrations. In areas where international templates were clearer and more forcefully promoted, such as the family policies discussed in chapters 6 and 7, the influence of international templates was even stronger, and reforms that would otherwise generate controversy passed with very broad support.

The arguments developed and the foreign models referenced by diverse politicians all help support the proposed theory. Politicians in Greek and Spanish debates occasionally debated the success or failure of health policies abroad, but more frequently they simply promoted particular choices as modern and legitimate because they were endorsed by international organizations, notably the WHO, and large, rich, and proximate countries familiar to Greek and Spanish voters, notably Britain, France, and Germany. More distant countries with successful NHSs, such as the Scandinavian countries, were rarely mentioned. This happened even though Greek and Spanish Socialist leaders were very familiar with these countries' experiences. For example, Greek politician Andreas Papandreou had spent seven years in Sweden immediately prior to establishing the Greek Socialist Party in 1974. Similarly, politicians rarely made arguments about competition, and rarely referenced other southern European countries. For example, one might have expected Spanish politicians to point to Portugal or Greece, with recent transitions from social insurance to NHSs, as evidence of what countries at similar levels of development were doing or as evidence of what competitors in key export markets were doing.[3] Instead, politicians concentrated their public appeals on large, rich, and culturally proximate countries and international organizations.

In the case studies that follow, I first describe the political conditions preceding the reform to emphasize that international models allow late developers to introduce reforms under conditions that are less conducive to change than were the conditions in pioneering countries. Specifically, Britain, a pioneer, introduced an NHS only after its prior health care system had been discredited and a centralized health system had been test run during World War II. In contrast, Spain and Greece introduced major health reforms when they had functioning and extensive social insurance systems in place, and when budgetary conditions were challenging because of the oil crises of the 1970s. The fact that these reforms took place in the 1970s and 1980s, soon after both countries transitioned to democracy, is consistent with the proposed theory that democratic publics welcome foreign models. It is particularly telling that the centrist and conservative administrations that governed Greece and Spain in the late 1970s were receptive to international health care models that were Socialist in content. Whereas prior diffusion studies suggest that foreign models resonate only among actors predisposed to favor them,[4] I find that foreign models influenced diverse actors, including actors whose ideological predispositions and material interests conflicted with the content of the reform.

I continue to describe how Socialists in both Spain and Greece referenced international models frequently in their initial efforts to win office, in their efforts to justify legislative proposals once they came to power in the early 1980s, and in subsequent successful reelection campaigns. I then discuss the post-NHS debates in Greece and Spain to show that once the international paradigm had shifted away from nationalization and toward competition, this new conservative international paradigm quickly entered Spanish and Greek political debates, even though Socialist governments were still in power. Finally, I show that the Socialist administrations that introduced NHSs in Greece and Spain made no comparably radical reforms in other social policy areas.

Introducing an NHS in Britain

To highlight the importance of foreign models, I contrast developments in Spain and Greece, two late NHS adopters, with the politics of health reform in Britain, a pioneer in introducing an NHS. The adoption of an NHS in Britain is well studied and well understood. A radical crisis prompted a radical transformation. It took a near collapse of the health care system, followed by World War II, for Britain to introduce an NHS. To introduce a policy solution for the first time, government leaders need a deep crisis, a creative solution, strong supporters, and weak opposition.[5] In contrast, subsequent sections illustrate that the availability of foreign models permits late developers to introduce radical reforms under less favorable circumstances than those necessary to pioneer reforms; reforms can happen in late developers even in the face of a mild crisis, weak support, or strong opposition.

In 1948 the United Kingdom engaged in an unprecedented move. It created a free, comprehensive, and universal health service, from which all citizens, not just those who had made social insurance contributions, could benefit.[6] Many countries would follow in its footsteps. What differentiates Britain from other, later, adopters are the uniquely favorable circumstances under which it undertook the reform. First, the pre-NHS arrangements of health insurance and hospital care made interest groups, who were expected to oppose nationalization, both weaker and more likely to see the NHS as an improvement over the status quo. Second, timing was unusually advantageous. Wartime made the poor state of affairs particularly visible, demonstrated the administrative viability of a centralized health service, and created widespread political expectations of radical reform.

Britain's pre-war hospital system consisted of voluntary and municipal hospitals. Based on an unsustainable system of voluntary donations, hospitals were nearly bankrupt by the early 1940s.[7] As the social insurance system introduced in 1911 was limited to workers and excluded hospital care, mutual insurance societies dominated the insurance scene. Physicians received what they considered to be miserly payments from mutual insurers.[8]

The near collapse of the existing system prompted interest groups that would have otherwise opposed an NHS to accept and even call for radical change. When Aneurin Bevan became health minister in 1945, as part of a Labour Party government, he proposed a very radical measure—an NHS with nationalized hospitals and family doctors with basic salaries. To get the bill passed and implemented, Bevan first pitted specialists against general practitioners (GPs) and then ended up offering GPs financial increases they couldn't refuse.[9] Indeed, the British Medical Association had examined and supported the idea of having national health insurance extended to cover hospital care in various plans since 1930. In addition to the support of these interest groups, wartime health planning gave Britain the chance to test-drive a nationally organized health system. The Labour Party promised extensive social reform and won a landslide victory in 1945. In summary, the British NHS resulted from a confluence of extremely favorable conditions: a collapsing prewar health care system, World War II government promises for radical reform, World War II experiences with nationalized health care, and a landslide Labour Party victory.[10]

It is noteworthy that the promise for radical reform extended beyond health policy, as the Atlee administration made several major reforms besides the introduction of the NHS. Keynesian macroeconomic policies were coupled with universalist and expansionary approaches to social policy. Moreover, two other major pieces of social legislation were passed in the same year as the 1946 National Health Insurance Act: the National Insurance Act and the Industrial Injuries Act.[11] Two years later the same administration passed the National Assistance Act, repealed the poor laws, and introduced family allowances—a universal, categorical benefit for families with children.[12] Table 5.1 traces a series of health reforms that followed the establishment of the British NHS. First under the Conservatives and then under Labour, patient charges were introduced, withdrawn, and reintroduced, while Labour, under Wilson and before the second oil crisis, attempted to further reduce the number of paid beds. This period is characterized by minor reforms to the NHS and substantial similarities in both parties' policy choices, despite divergences in rhetoric.[13]

The shift away from socialized medicine also required uniquely favorable political conditions in the pioneering country. Major rethinking of the NHS only occurred under Thatcher, and even then, retrenchment was limited.[15] By the late 1980s, reforming the UK NHS was high on the public agenda; dissatisfaction with it had risen from 25% of the public in 1983 to 46% in 1989.[16] However, the British Medical Association was radically opposed to Thatcherite proposals. Thatcher, emboldened by her newly won third electoral victory and by her experiences in overcoming obstacles once thought insurmountable, was able to introduce market mechanisms into the British NHS.[17] In 1989 she organized GPs as fund holders, placing them, along with health authorities, as separate purchasers. She also set up semiautonomous hospitals as trusts to compete for purchaser funds along with directly managed and private health providers.[18] Once introduced in Britain, the purchaser/provider split immediately became a fashionable item among policymakers with substantially less radical ideological backgrounds, as later sections discuss.

Table 5.1 **Landmarks in UK Health Policy**[14]

	Pre-NHS events
1911	National Insurance Act introduces sickness insurance
1939	Emergency Medical Service set up
1942	Beveridge Report
1944	White Paper on Insurance, Health, and Full Employment
	Labour government (Atlee)
1946	National Insurance Act
	Industrial Injuries Act
	National Health Service Act
	Conservative government (Churchill)
1952	Prescription charges introduced
	Conservative government (Macmillan)
1962	Hospital Plan
	Labour government (Wilson)
1965	Prescription charges abolished
1966	Earnings-related supplements to sickness, employment, and widows benefit introduced
1968	Prescription charges reintroduced
1974	Phasing out of private beds from NHS
	Conservative government (Thatcher)
1986	Fowler Review of Social Security
1989	White Paper for Patients introduces purchaser/provider split
	Conservative government (Major)
1990	NHS and Community Care Act
1991	Citizens Charter
	Health of the Nation White Paper
	Labour government (Blair)
2000	NHS expenditures increased
2002	NHS expenditures further increased

Introducing Health Reforms in Southern Europe

Turning to southern Europe allows us to investigate how reform happens differently in late developers. When Spain, Italy, Greece, and Portugal introduced NHSs in the late 1970s and early 1980s, they already had functioning social insurance systems covering much of their population, and there was no widely perceived health crisis. Supporters of an NHS were making their first steps in the countries' political spheres: left-wing parties were just coming to power and labor unions were refounding themselves after long periods of underground activity. In contrast, powerful medical associations, which stood to lose from an NHS, were entrenched. Moreover, budgetary conditions were tight, because the oil crises of the 1970s had wreaked havoc on many European economies. Yet, NHS adoption in southern Europe was swift.

While the timing of health reforms is hard to explain on the basis of domestic conditions alone, this timing is consistent with the proposed theory of diffusion through electoral channels. The adoption of international health models happened shortly after the Greek, Spanish, and Portuguese transitions to democracy, and while the WHO's 1978 Alma-Ata Declaration, discussed in chapter 4, was still current. In contrast, an elite-driven diffusion model would have predicted extensive imitation of foreign models during periods of autocratic rule, when dictators are free to imitate foreigners and disregard domestic audiences.

The adoption of NHSs across southern European countries also helps identify what makes some countries particularly receptive to foreign models. For this task, a comparison of southern European countries to the U.S. case discussed in chapter 3 is useful. According to the informational theory I propose, foreign policy models can persuade uninformed voters that their leaders are pursuing desirable goals competently. Yet, voters in the United States have many substitute sources of good information. The Congressional Budget Office (CBO), credible think tanks, and world-leading academics produce valuable research on policy proposals. U.S. states often set their own path, making available an additional layer of policy experimentation that generates concrete data. In contrast, voters in Spain, and especially Greece, lack comparable sources of independent information domestically, and thus value foreign models more highly. Because neither country is as rich as the United States, government resources for policy innovation are more limited. Spain is a moderately sized country with a federal structure, but Spanish regions had limited powers over health policy at the time of NHS adoption. Greece is an even smaller country with no federal elements in its administration. For this reason, we should expect larger diffusion effects in southern Europe.

This book's theory provides a second reason to expect more diffusion in southern Europe than in the United States. According to the proposed theory, foreign policy models are most influential when they originate from proximate and rich countries, because these are covered disproportionately in the media and voters pay attention to them. Seen from the perspective of ordinary voters, the United States has few potential models. There are few countries at similar or higher levels of development, and some of these, notably Japan and Germany, are geographically and culturally distant. Instead, southern European countries have multiple neighbors with superior resources, and these are covered prominently in the southern European media. These countries share an outward-looking orientation, and a desire to modernize and be full participants in the European Community.[19] For these two reasons—the scarcity of credible domestic information and the prominence of foreign models—southern Europe responded more strongly to the NHS model than did the United States. In the United States, a universal health care model involving extensive private health care provision was adopted in 2010. In contrast, all southern European countries adopted NHSs in the late 1970s and early 1980s.

Variations within Spain and Greece allow me to test additional empirical implications of the proposed theory. Both countries experienced a succession of left and center-right governments in the 1970s and 1980s when the NHS model became internationally prominent. This variation allows one to examine the effects of foreign models over domestic actors with a range of ideological predispositions. Surprisingly, center-right governments in Spain and Greece seriously considered adopting the NHS model. The Italian case would illustrate this point even more strongly, as it is the only Organization for Economic Cooperation and Development (OECD) country that did not have a unified Socialist government in power when it introduced an NHS, but rather a coalition of ideologically diverse parties.[20] On the other hand, when parties with favorable ideological inclinations came to power, such as the Spanish and Greek Socialists, the international prominence of the NHS model pushed health care to the forefront of the reform agenda. Existing theories cannot predict whether left-wing governments will focus their attention on health care as opposed to other issue areas or whether left-wing parties will propose radical reorganizations rather than mere increases in expenditure. The record of southern European left-wing parties in other social policy areas is mixed at best;[21] radical health care reorganization is an anomaly.

Introducing Health Reforms in Spain

Unlike Britain's health care system, Spain's system at the time of reform was both stable and functional, preempting bottom-up demands for radical change. By the time of Francisco Franco's death in 1975, 82% of Spain's population had health coverage under an occupational social insurance system implemented nationwide in 1942 and extended thereafter.[22] Both experts and the general public were generally satisfied with health care in Spain.[23] Indeed, the recently legalized labor unions, the Confederación Sindical de Comisiones Obreras

(CCOO) and the Unión General de Trabajadores (UGT), were only seeking gradual improvements to extend the coverage and benefits of the existing social insurance system, while the main employers' organization, Confederación Española de Organizaciones Empresariales (CEOE), was calling for greater private administration within the existing system.[24] Economic conditions following the Spanish transition were tough: the oil crises of the 1970s slowed economic growth significantly, and this slow growth was coupled with high rates of inflation.[25] Conditions were not favorable for health policy reforms.

Yet, both centrist and Socialist administrations in the late 1970s and early 1980s introduced substantial reforms in the Spanish health care system that culminated with the introduction of an NHS by the Spanish Socialist Party (Partido Socialista Obrero Español [PSOE]) in 1986. These reforms met limited resistance from powerful domestic interest groups that accepted the rationale for reform in spite of the significant disadvantages they suffered. Instead, these groups sought secondary compromises. Reforms abroad and international organization proposals helped place health care high on the Spanish agenda and influenced the views of diverse actors on the shape and direction of appropriate measures. Spanish policymakers concentrated on the policy choices of high-status, proximate countries with linguistic and cultural connections. These were the countries politicians could reference to appeal to ordinary voters. In evaluating foreign models, Spanish policymakers also considered their success, but this consideration was secondary. Recall Table 4.5, which demonstrated the high correlation between references to foreign countries in the major Spanish paper, El País, and the unfamiliarity of Spanish citizens with other countries as captured in the Eurobarometer survey. This suggested that Spaniards had the most exposure to and greatest familiarity with France, Germany, Italy, and Britain. In addition, this showed that Spaniards had little exposure to and little familiarity with a number of countries, including Scandinavian countries and Greece. As discussed in later sections, Spanish politicians concentrated their campaigns and legislative references on rich western European countries familiar to voters.

Table 5.2 presents major developments in Spanish health policy. First, I present Spanish health reforms in the post-Franco period to outline how foreign models shaped the course of health policy in Spain. Next, I present more detailed evidence drawn from party platforms and parliamentary debates to indicate how foreign models mattered and which diffusion mechanisms influenced Spanish health policy. I also review available contemporary polls and show that Spanish Socialists won repeated elections because their campaigns to modernize Spain and introduce social programs resonated with voters, and despite significant concerns about the stagnant economy, high unemployment, and corruption. Then I present the positions taken by key interest groups.

Table 5.2 **Landmarks in Spanish Health Policy**[26]

	Pre-NHS Events
1900	Accidents at Work Act marks beginning of social insurance system
1942	Franco implements mandatory health insurance for industrial workers
1967	Basic Law on Social Security
	Centrist administrations
1978	National Institute for Health Care (INSALUD) is created shortly after Spain's democratic constitution, which includes the right to health
1981	Ministry of Health separated from Ministry of Labor
1981	Health care decentralization begins with the transfer of powers to Catalonia
	Socialist administrations
1984	Decree on Basic Health Structures (reform of primary care)
1986	General health law passed, creating NHS and covering all Spanish citizens
1989	General taxation becomes dominant source of health system funding
1991	"Abril Committee" proposes cost containment and organizational reforms
1992	Pilot programs created setting up explicit contracts with hospitals and prospective funding
1993	List of pharmaceuticals excluded from public financing published
1993	Free choice of general physicians and pediatricians, as piloted since 1984
1994	Agreement on the territorial financing of health care services
1995	Decree on health care services establishes what services NHS provides
1996	Free choice of specialist doctors
	Conservative administrations
1996	Decree on autonomy of management of health care institutions
	Decree on liberalization of pharmacy hours and pharmacy establishment
1997	Law of new forms of organization and management permits contracting out to private hospitals at the national level

(Continued)

Table 5.2 (**Continued**)

Conservative administrations	
1998	Government and pharmaceuticals industry reach agreement on cost containment measures
1999	Immigrants law, approved by opposition parties, grants substantial access to health care to adult immigrants (immigrant children's rights already effective)

Finally, I discuss post-NHS health reform efforts to show the continued UK influence on Spanish Socialists' thinking, even as the UK model shifted from Beveridge to Thatcher.

Health Reform Under a Center-Right Administration

Upon Spain's transition to democracy, a center-right administration led by the Unión de Centro Democrático (UCD) took power, governing from 1976 to 1982. Center-right governments do not typically prioritize universalist social policy, especially when faced with diverse economic and political challenges. However, the UCD government took action on health reform. First, the UCD administration declared that health care was a universal right and created a parliamentary committee on health reform, thus raising the status of this issue in the domestic political agenda. Next, it integrated diverse health services into a new Ministry of Health and Social Security, created a separate administrative organ for health, Instituto Nacional de la Salud (INSALUD), and began to devolve health authority to regional governments. The UCD government also created a new specialty training program for family and community medicine, a critical precondition for establishing a primary care system.[27]

While the UCD health reforms were modest in scope, the parliamentary debates on health care indicate that contemporary thinking was critically shaped by the experience of foreign countries, notably France, Germany, and the United Kingdom, and also that the proposals of the WHO had great legitimacy. In May 1980 the UCD minister of health and social security, Juan Rovira Tarazona, presented the outlines of the UCD's modest health reform proposals to parliament. At least half his speech was dedicated to a discussion of exchanges with the WHO and to the British, French, and

German health care models.[28] He first outlined that the administration had conferred with both domestic and foreign actors, and he detailed points of agreement between the various Spanish political parties. Then he stated that the disagreements that existed between the parties concerned three aspects of health reform: administration, financing, and civil society participation. In debating these points, he outlined two main alternatives: the British NHS on the one hand, and the French and German social insurance systems on the other. Regardless of whether the British or French/German models were most applicable, these references made clear that Spain's future lay in imitating large, rich western European countries rather than continuing with the status quo or examining other southern European countries that more closely resembled Spain. Rovira's discussion of the British NHS was particularly extensive, if narrow, in scope. He literally read multiple paragraphs from two articles identifying shortcomings of the UK NHS. This emphasis shows that policy success (or lack thereof) abroad was also a critical consideration.

In his speech to parliament, Rovira also made extensive references to exchanges between the administration and experts at the WHO. He noted that the WHO made detailed recommendations about reform in Spain and argued that the WHO would endorse the UCD proposals. For example, in arguing against health financing through general taxation, he noted: "In the conclusion of Alma-Ata in 1978 two types of financing are recognized, one based on taxes, and one based on social security. This latter form is explicitly mentioned. That is to say, it is not possible to affirm absolutely that financing via social security is inadequate, when it is mentioned at that meeting, and when they say that all countries should adopt the type of financing that best suits their condition."[29] Delegates from opposition parties contested this interpretation of the WHO's advice.

Both Rovira's testimony and the fact that it was contested indicate that Spanish policymakers of all political stripes expected voters to care about whether a proposal was consistent with the WHO's recommendations or not. Voters' desires that their country emulate international organization models thus contributed to policy diffusion: a vague and weakly promoted international model nonetheless prompted a center-right government to introduce moderate health reforms. If the WHO had spoken clearly and strongly in favor of an NHS, it seems likely that reforms would have gone significantly farther. We can only speculate on that counterfactual proposition. However, we can empirically investigate how a more receptive, Socialist audience would receive the same international models. The next section turns to this issue.

Health Reform Under Socialist Administrations

The Spanish Socialists made repeated public efforts to win office starting in 1976, and consistently promised to offer Spaniards the same social benefits western Europeans enjoyed, central among them being an NHS.[30] In December 1976, PSOE held its 27th Congress, its first post-dictatorship congress and the first to be held on Spanish soil since 1932. The 27th Congress' resolution on health care begins with a reference to the WHO's broad definition of health and continues with a commitment to socialize medicine and establish an NHS.[31]

Similarly, the 1977 PSOE manifesto declared: "We want to turn our country into a society similar to that of our neighbors in Europe, raising the standard of living of our fellow citizens, surpassing the limits of underdevelopment, to enter into a type of life proper for an industrial society of the European type."[32] The manifesto then listed health as one of several basic rights that it would strive to promote in the next legislature.[33] In its 1979 manifesto, the PSOE set the "developed countries of Western Europe" as their benchmark, and developed its promises to introduce "a National Health Service, that is administered through the autonomous communities in accordance with their specific health conditions."[34]

Similarly, in its 1982 manifesto, the PSOE lamented that European standards had not yet been reached: "Social security is currently insufficient and poorly administered. We spend little in comparison to countries in the European Economic Community, and spend the resources we do have poorly."[35] PSOE further promised: "We will progressively extend to all Spaniards the coverage of social security and health, within the framework of a National Health Service."[36]

Immediately after coming to power in 1983, the PSOE health ministry published the first outline of the planned reforms. Entitled *Política General del Ministerio de Sanidad y Consumo*, this document stands out for the absence of data regarding the Spanish health care system, although it had been recently amassed and analyzed by the Spanish civil service.[37] This document called for an integrated social health system, emphasizing prevention and primary care. "Primary care," "health promotion," "health education," "epidemiology," "working in groups," and "integrated health center," terms popular in the international literature but new to Spain, suddenly appeared in the main Spanish policy documents.[38] Spain introduced an important reform of primary care in 1984 "in concert with the principles of the Conference of Primary Care Alma-Ata."[39]

PSOE won reelection in 1986, following a campaign that highlighted the hope of joining the European Economic Community (EEC) and introducing western European social programs, and the difficult economic situation facing Spain. According to PSOE's 1986 manifesto, "the overall reform of Social Security, necessarily gradual, and the extension of benefits to all citizens in the form of minimum benefits, requires solidarity and efforts by all. In the coming years we will increase benefits to gradually approach the situation in the European Economic Community, making sure that the pace of this growth is consistent with the recovery and the revival of the Spanish economy."[40]

PSOE health minister Ernest Lluch introduced an NHS bill in 1986.[41] This involved universal coverage, public financing, mostly public management of service provision, and an emphasis on primary care. The key difference between the Spanish and British NHSs was that the Spanish system was to be substantially more decentralized. Echoing UCD minister Rovira, Lluch compared the French and German systems on the one hand and that of the United Kingdom on the other. Emphasizing considerations of policy success abroad, Lluch argued that NHSs had two advantages: more satisfactory health outcomes and lower costs.[42] With the support of the Communists and the main Basque and Catalan parties, PSOE passed the *Ley General de Sanidad* in April 1986.[43] This analysis suggests that while a Socialist government may have been necessary to carry out a radical reform, the terms of the debate were set by external models and shared by more conservative leaders.

Tables 5.3 and 5.4 tabulate references to foreign countries in the Spanish parliamentary debates introducing an NHS. The references reveal the Socialists' effort to portray their proposal as widely adopted, and thus as a vetted, mainstream choice. For example, Representative Palacios Alonso argued:

> Primary health care is both an integral part of a National Health System, and in fact constitutes the central function and principal nucleus of such as system ... These are not the words of Representative Marcelo Palacios, or of my Parliamentary Group, or of the Political Party to which I belong. They are the Alma-Ata Resolutions of 1978, signed by 70 ministers of 140 countries, and by the majority of health authorities of the world, through the WHO.[44]

Indeed, as Table 5.3 shows, the WHO, and in particular its Alma-Ata Declaration, tops the list of references to foreign sources. Moreover, every single one of these 27 references is positive. In the tables that follow, for both Spain and Greece, references are coded as positive if they refer positively to an international institution and call for following its advice, or if they refer positively to a foreign country and call for emulating its practices, whether or not the speaker desired to see an NHS in Spain. That is, the 27 positive references to the WHO indicated that no one disputed that Spain should follow

Table 5.3 **Spanish NHS Debate: References by Country and Attitude**

Country/region	Count	Positive	Negative	Mixed
WHO/Alma-Ata	27	27	0	0
United Kingdom	25	16	2	7
European countries	23	23	0	0
Italy	16	4	4	8
France	14	6	5	3
Germany	13	2	7	4
United States	13	6	6	1
Belgium	8	3	3	2
Developed countries	8	8	0	0
Sweden	5	3	0	2
Ireland	4	0	0	4
Luxembourg	4	1	0	3
Netherlands	4	2	0	2
Cuba	2	1	0	1
Soviet Union	2	0	1	1
Canada	1	1	0	0
Denmark	1	0	0	1
Greece	1	0	0	1
ILO	1	1	0	0
Poland	1	0	0	1
Underdeveloped countries	1	0	1	0
Total	174	104	29	41

WHO principles. For example, Representative Gorroño Arrizabalaga of the Basque Nationalist Party highlighted that "we all accept . . . the difficult yet beautiful challenge of the WHO, reflected in its proposition 'Health for All in the Year 2000.'"[45] However, there was debate on whether following WHO advice requires the introduction of an NHS or not. References to Britain are also frequent and more mixed, but mostly positive, and then come references to Europe. References to Portugal and Greece are scarce, even though fit and competitiveness considerations would have predicted such references. References to Sweden are also limited, even though Socialists were fully aware and supportive of the Swedish model.

As Table 5.4 shows, references to foreign sources are overwhelmingly positive, regardless of the political orientation of the speakers. No one disputed that Spain was a country on a path to joining developed countries in western

Europe and could draw useful lessons from abroad. Instead, the goal of the Conservatives was to highlight the diversity of foreign models in western Europe. In so doing, Conservatives sought to weaken the Socialists' claim that foreign countries' experiences justified the introduction of an NHS.

The overwhelmingly positive references hide the debate on which foreign models should be imitated and how exactly this should be done, with the Socialists advocating for NHSs such as the British system, and the Conservatives advocating for social security systems such as the French and German systems. However, they underscore the surprising agreement among both the Socialists and the Conservatives that western European benchmarks were appropriate because Spain was on its way to becoming a developed country. For example, to justify the expansion in health care spending, the Socialists claimed that Spain only spent 3.9% of GDP on health care, that the cutoff separating developing from developed countries was 4% of GDP, and that EEC countries spent 7.2%.[46] The Conservatives agreed with this reasoning, adding that "an appropriate health system for a developed country is one that devotes to such an important issue [health] more than five percent of the GDP."[47] However, they wanted to count both public and private expenditures, so as to cross the 5% threshold, and "give our health system . . . a spot among developed countries."[48]

By the 1989 campaign, PSOE was experiencing both the success and the first signs of problems with the NHS. PSOE sought to both specify its goals and justify its failures in comparison with other European states. According to the 1989 manifesto there was reason for celebration: "During our administration, we Socialists have made a significant effort to increase resources for the provision of public services. We have tried, in this way, to cover the large historical gap in social services between Spain and the other European Community countries."[49] However, not all was rosy, and foreign countries' experiences also helped PSOE account for difficulties. According to the 1989 manifesto, "as it happens in advanced nations, Spain is facing a rapid growth in demand for health services. This process results from the universalization of care to all citizens, the aging of the population, and also to the greater concern for health and physical wellbeing that a large majority of citizens now has. This set of circumstances requires us to make the best use of available resources."[50]

Despite difficulties that began to emerge, Spanish Socialists kept on winning reelection; they stayed in power continuously until 1996, despite an economic slowdown and significant concerns about corruption and crime.[51] This suggests that their campaigns and policies resonated strongly with voters. Socialist politicians themselves believed that there was widespread support for their efforts to modernize Spain in the image of western Europe. As José María

Maravall, a prominent Socialist politician and education minister from 1982 to 1988 put it:

> "Catching-up" with Western Europe, that is, the "normalization" of Spain by these comparative standards, was the main thrust of the reforms that the government of Felipe González launched from the end of 1982. "Catching up" with Western Europe meant joining the European Community, competing effectively with the other economies, and reaching their levels of satisfaction of social citizenship rights. In Spain, consensus over these goals was overwhelming.[52]

Available studies suggest PSOE leaders were correct to believe their vision of modernity, aimed at "catching up" with western Europe, was widely shared. The Spanish press covered developments in Europe in overwhelmingly positive tones; Europe was framed as a symbol of economic modernity and democratic stability.[53] Large majorities of Spaniards believed Spain belonged in Europe and should be part of the European Community at least since the 1970s.[54] Opinion polls also suggest that PSOE's redistributive agenda had broad support. For example, a national poll conducted in 1984, two years after PSOE took power, suggested that 87% of Spaniards believed that Spain would have fewer problems if people were treated more equally, while only 14% wanted the government "to offer fewer services, including such things as health and education, in order to reduce taxes."[55] Many factors likely contributed to PSOE's repeated electoral victories in the 1980s, the Socialists' "golden era."[56] Peter McDonough, Samuel Barnes, and Antonio López Pina concluded that what was legitimized in the 1980s in Spain was "a modicum of social as well as procedural fairness . . . consumer socialism for the cynical perhaps . . . driven as much by the imperative of bringing Spain up to speed with the European Community as by ideological precept."[57] In sum, the electoral strategy of benchmarking domestic policies against international ones was probably an effective way to reach Spanish voters.

Doctors and Spanish Health Policy Reforms

Spanish doctors, the key constituency expected to oppose government control over health care, were powerful but divided about these health reforms. In the 1970s, Spanish doctors were in a privileged material and political position. Doctors working in the public health system were permitted to supplement their income by treating patients privately, and as of 1983, more than 50% declared having an additional private sector job.[58] Politically, doctors were organized in a conservative medical association, the Organización Médica Colegial (OMC), whose power some observers characterized as "immense."[59] As late as 1977, doctors were able to use the state to introduce new measures to strengthen their professional power, notably a *numerus clausus* limiting entrance to medical schools.[60] Not surprisingly, the OMC, led by Ramiro Rivera, opposed the introduction of the NHS, as this model would have restricted doctors' ability to take on private clients.

What was surprising were divisions within the medical community. In 1979 more than 25% of Spanish doctors supported a fully socialized health system.[61] Consistent with diverse sociological accounts of the diffusion of innovations, the age distribution of NHS supporters was skewed: younger doctors were much more supportive of this health innovation than older ones.[62] The minority of doctors supportive of socialized medicine was very active, forming a variety of medical associations in competition with the established OMC and supporting PSOE government reforms. For example, the Spanish Society of Family and Community Medicine organized primary doctors to support the state in this key area. Indeed, young Socialist and Communist doctors began developing the first plans for an NHS as early as 1976.[63] While the OMC opposed the NHS, it ended up losing the battle, first to the government, then to competing medical associations, and finally internally. Ramiro Rivera, the OMC leader, was replaced after one term by a more accommodating successor.

Reforms Following the Introduction of an NHS

Reform efforts following the introduction of the Spanish NHS also show how the Spanish Socialists' proposals were heavily influenced by international developments. In 1991, 2 years after the Thatcher government had published "Working for Patients," and only 5 years after the PSOE had introduced the NHS in Spain, a PSOE government with an absolute majority in parliament created the Abril Committee to propose cost-containment measures. The Abril Committee proposed both managerial improvements and neoliberal reforms similar to those emphasized in the United Kingdom.[64] Some reforms were attempts to introduce competition into the public sector following the UK purchaser/provider split, while others aimed to improve management techniques by creating *sociedades públicas*, private not-for-profit groups resembling UK foundations and trusts.[65] Both the Swedish and UK reforms were mentioned in the text of the Abril Committee's reform proposals.[66] A final set of recommendations for increased copayments caused public outrage and prompted the Socialist government to try to distance itself from the proposals. However, many of the proposed cost-cutting and administrative reforms were introduced in subsequent years.[67] In summary, Spanish Socialists followed international paradigms both when they pointed in the direction of greater nationalization of health and when they pointed in the direction of market mechanisms. The informational model of policy diffusion helps to explain how both reforms could happen despite surprisingly unfavorable circumstances.

Introducing Health Reforms in Greece

Foreign templates were also critical to the development of health policy in Greece, and allowed Greece to introduce major reforms under inauspicious conditions. Whereas Spain was under Franco's rule continuously from 1939 to 1975, Greece was governed more or less democratically from 1949 until 1967 and then again from 1974 to the present.[68] Foreign ideas could thus trickle into domestic electoral politics more continuously than in Spain. Indeed, foreign models dominated discussions of health policy reforms in Greece, and we see Greek references to the UK NHS as early as 1949. In 1951, two years after the Greek civil war ended in 1949, a right-wing government introduced Law 1846, redefining social insurance. The introduction to this law references the Beveridge report in great detail, accepts the report's principles as guidance for the Greek reform, and highlights the UK practice of separating health from social insurance.[69] This is somewhat surprising given the strong anti-Communist political environment of the period—an environment where left-wing political activity was severely restricted. While Greek politicians favorably discussed the British NHS in the early 1950s, attempts to introduce an NHS in Greece in 1953 were quickly set aside as impossible to implement. The next large step in social insurance—the introduction of a noncontributory fund for farmers—occurred in 1961. Its most important provision for health care—rural health clinics—was based on the report of a former German agriculture minister.[70]

Following the collapse of the dictatorship in 1974, the conservative New Democracy Party won Greece's elections. It was a conservative government that first developed a plan for universal primary health care through a network of GP-like practitioners, but did not implement it. Later this plan became the basis for the Socialists' introduction of an NHS in the 1980s. As the international paradigms shifted away from centralization and toward market-oriented solutions in the 1990s, the same Socialist party (Panhellenic Socialist Movement [PASOK]) aimed to incorporate private initiatives in the system. Table 5.4 offers a historical overview of health reforms in Greece.

Throughout this period, domestic interest groups did not raise substantial opposition to legislative initiatives, as some were supportive of the governments'

Table 5.4 **Landmarks in Greek Health Policy**[71]

	Pre-NHS Measures
1922	Ministry of Hygiene and Social Welfare established
1928	Greek government invites WHO experts to prepare plan for reorganization of sanitary services and training of health personnel
1934	Social Insurance Fund for Urban Workers (IKA) established (offers medical treatment and lost wages to the insured and their dependents)
1953	Per diem reimbursement of hospitals by social insurance funds
1961	Establishment of noncontributory fund for farmers (OGA)
1970	(Dictatorship health minister) Patras Proposal calls for family doctor system, improved rural care, and single funding agency (never legislated).
	Conservative administrations
1976	National Planning Institute (KEPE) calls for transition to NHS via unification of insurance funds
1978–81	Health Minister Doxiadis tables major health reform proposal involving central and regional hospital planning and rural primary care network (proposal not discussed in parliament).
	Socialist administrations
1982	Ministry of Health separated from the Ministry of Social Insurance
1982	Central planning agency for health (KESY) created
1983	National Health Service introduced
1986	Restrictions placed on private hospitals
	Conservative administration
1992	New Democracy government introduces rhetoric of patients' rights and choice, cautiously raises restrictions on creation of private clinics, and authorizes NHS doctors to work part time in the private sector
	Socialist administrations (Simitis, prime minister since 1996)
1994	Restrictions on private health care provision reintroduced
1997	Health reform law (not implemented)
2000	Health for the Citizen Declaration (ambitious five-stage system reform)
2001	Decentralization of health system management Introduction of hospital managers

efforts, and others were internally divided. Instead, debates about the reforms, both at the drafting stage and also in campaigns and in parliamentary discussions, focused on other countries' experiences with NHSs. Policymakers at the drafting stage relied heavily on experts schooled in the United Kingdom, and experts played an important role at this early moment. However, politicians went on to select particular foreign models they would be able to sell to voters, and to campaign on promises to introduce western European social programs to Greece. Greek campaign documents and parliamentary debates support an emulation theory of diffusion: Greek politicians referenced the choices of large, "modern" European countries without showing systematic concern for evidence of policy success.

Recall from chapter 4 the high correlation between Greeks' familiarity with foreign countries and references to foreign countries in Οικονομικός Ταχυδρόμος, a prominent Greek newspaper of the 1970s. Both measures showed that Greeks were quite familiar with Germany, France, and Britain as well as with the United States and Italy. In contrast, Greeks appeared quite unfamiliar with Scandinavian countries, Spain, and Portugal. Subsequent public debates focused heavily on countries most familiar to ordinary Greeks.

Health Reform Proposals Under Conservative Administrations

When democracy was restored to Greece in 1974, the health system did not seem in need of immediate reform, although it faced some problems. Eighty-five percent of the population had health coverage through occupational schemes.[72] Additionally, a large private health sector covered significant gaps in public provision, at least for the better-off.

As in Spain, NHS proposals were first developed under a conservative administration. A right-wing New Democracy government took office immediately following the Greek transition to democracy in 1974 and won reelection in 1977. Spyros Doxiadis, the New Democracy health minister, had limited exposure to Greek politics; his prior career was in academic medicine in the United Kingdom and Sweden. He conducted an extensive study of foreign models and of contemporary Greek medicine and drafted a health reform bill. His advisors were primarily UK-trained doctors alongside some (U.S.- and UK-trained) health economists.[73] Although less radical than the NHS bill that was ultimately adopted, Doxiadis' proposal called for emphasis on primary care and prevention and for the establishment of a GP-like network of family physicians, consistent with the principles of the Alma-Ata Declaration. The conservative New Democracy party did not ultimately introduce Doxiadis's bill. However, both the draft bill and several of Doxiadis's advisors were consulted by the Socialist health minister Paraskevas Avgerinos. This permitted the Socialists to introduce a health reform bill only two years after coming to power.[74]

Health Reform Under Socialist Administrations

A Socialist landslide on October 18, 1981, allowed for the ultimate passage of the NHS in Greece in 1983. As in Spain, this was not an auspicious moment for major social reforms: there was no obvious health crisis, and economic performance was mediocre at best. Both Spain and Greece transitioned to democracy just as the era of Organization of Petroleum Exporting Countries (OPEC) price hikes and stagflation was beginning.[75]

References to health and other social reforms were central to the PASOK campaign, as were explicit connections between these proposals and the efforts of other European Socialist leaders. To give a sense of the campaign that preceded PASOK's 1981 victory, I present three images from pro-PASOK newspapers in the days immediately prior to the election. These newspaper images nicely encapsulate the theme of the book: that foreign models, in particular health and family models, diffused through very public election campaigns rather than through elite networks operating behind closed doors.

Figure 5.1 shows the front page of the pro-PASOK newspaper *Ta Néa* from Friday, October 16, 1981, two days before the elections that would bring PASOK to power. The headline reads: "Athens: A Mandate for Change for Mr. Papandreou." Below is a picture of the PASOK rally of the prior evening in Athens followed by a headline that reads, "The contract of PASOK with the People." The far left box explains "[t]he Socialism of PASOK" as follows: *"As regards economic and social structures, it is almost equivalent to the socialism of the French socialist movement.* It is based on planning, decentralization, self-determination, the active involvement of workers, farmers, of the people, in all decisions that concern them. *In the context of this socialism, there will be housing for every family, we will socialize Health and the Pharmaceuticals Industry, there will be a National Health Service, we will decentralize hospital coverage, and we will cover the country with a thick network of health centers."*[76]

Figure 5.2 is the front page of the pro-PASOK newspaper *Ta Néa* the day before the election. Prime ministerial candidate Andreas Papandreou is pictured next to Swedish Prime Minister Olof Palme. Palme's endorsement of PASOK and a discussion of ties between European Socialist movements follow in the text.

Figure 5.3 is from page 3 of the pro-PASOK newspaper *To Bήμα* from Sunday, October 18, election day. On the right is a cartoon of Papandreou crossing the finish line with a sign that reads: "Elections 1981." The headline of the column to the left of the cartoon reads: "Social Care." The article was written by Paraskevas Avgerinos. On October 18, 1981, Avgerinos issued his

Figure 5.1 Pro-PASOK Newspaper Front Page Two Days Before the 1981 Election

final plea to voters the morning before going to the polls. He was elected to parliament that day, and soon thereafter he was appointed health minister and introduced the Greek NHS. On election day, his page 3 plea stated:

> *In a properly organized society, social care is not charity, but an established right of every citizen that cannot be taken away. But in our country the duty of society for social care has been intentionally ignored by the Urban State and this space has been transformed into a field of exploitation and competition by private interests, separating Greeks into first and second class citizens.* What characterizes social care of governments to date is the amount of expenditure both for health and for social protection more generally. *In Greece, social expenditures for health represent 3.2 percent of GDP, which is 2–3 times lower from the equivalent percentage*

Figure 5.2 Pro-PASOK Newspaper Front Page One Day Before the 1981 Election

for other European countries. Our total expenditures for social care represent 14.8 percent of GDP, when the average for European Countries is 26.5 percent of GDP . . .

PASOK's program calls for special care for vulnerable population groups. A network of childcare facilities with correct staffing and

Figure 5.3 Pro-PASOK Newspaper the Day of the 1981 Election

functioning will be established throughout the country. The protection of maternity and the ratification of all international conventions that establish it as a social function will be among our main goals ...

Among the goals of the Movement is the socialization of the pharmaceuticals industry which will include in a nationalized system those production facilities that meet high standards. According to the World Health Organization, only 200 substances are considered basic therapeutic substances. In our country today there exist 11,000 substances in 26,000 forms. This creates confusion to the prescribing physician and to the pharmacist. The problem of too many drugs will find a solution with the establishment and implementation of the National Drugs Registry.

In summary, PASOK did not hide its plan to nationalize health care from the Greek public. Instead, in the days immediately before the 1981 elections, Greek Socialists focused their campaign efforts on selling their health and family proposals through comparisons with foreign models, inviting voters to benchmark their proposals against international standards. While many of these Socialist proposals called for an expansion of social benefits, Socialist leaders also made it clear to voters they planned to follow international standards that called for the curtailment of benefits by limiting the pharmaceuticals in circulation.

The Socialist PASOK party won national elections in 1981 and introduced the NHS law in 1983. The introductory report for the health care bill conveys a sense of destiny; it reads like a deterministic history where each step sets the scene for the next development. Yet, the history covered is not that of health care in Greece, but rather of social policy reforms in selected European countries. Indeed, Athanasios Fillipopoulos, the PASOK Member of Parliament (MP) introducing the law, creates a three-fold typology of health systems, classifying Greece in the progressive category of UK-type NHSs. The 1983 introductory report refers to certain measures as successes in other countries, such as the abolition of per patient fees so as to reduce doctors' incentives to oversupply their services (United Kingdom, Sweden, Italy, the United States)[77] and the gradual expansion of coverage to low-income patients (United Kingdom, Sweden, Germany, Denmark, France).[78] The 1983 introductory report also makes multiple references to the UK model that do not relate to the UK NHS's success, but rather to the fact that the United Kingdom had adopted this system.[79]

When the Greek NHS bill reached the parliament for consideration, references to foreign countries' policies were plentiful, and they included references to both the identity of prior NHS adopters and to the success or failure of these policies. The most frequently heard argument was that the adoption of an NHS constituted the way forward chosen by all modern countries; the status of model countries as "advanced" indicated that their policies were worthy of imitation.[80] The second argument, heard less often than the first, focused on the success of the UK NHS. Even when discussing UK NHS success, however, Greek Socialists cited measures of performance closely tied to its visibility, such as the number of publications that UK doctors had in international journals.[81]

The main opposition came from the conservative New Democracy party, while the Communists supported the law's principles and claimed it did not go far enough. In their opposition, many conservatives suggested that the NHS was no longer the international paradigm.[82] Others portrayed Greece as moving far beyond international best practice, claiming that both the United Kingdom and even some Communist countries now placed fewer restrictions on private medicine than those proposed by the Greek Socialists.[83] Conservatives also criticized the government for introducing an NHS without actually studying or providing adequate evidence for its success in the countries where it was introduced,[84] and disagreed with the government's interpretation of other countries' experiences.[85] Some conservatives referenced queues and delays in NHS systems abroad.[86] Still others centered their critique on the applicability of the NHS model to Greece, fearing the growth of a black market in health care provision.

The Communists tended to agree with the Socialists on basic principles. They criticized the conservatives for opposing the NHS as Communist, arguing that many market-oriented western countries had followed the model.[87] They called for strict controls on the private sector and for following Sweden's example of decentralizing health authority to local administrations. In summary, both proponents and opponents of the bill used foreign experiences with similar policies as their frame of reference. These references were of two types: references to the fact that particular rich, familiar, western democracies had adopted NHSs, and erratic evaluations of NHS successes and failures.

While the experiences of particular foreign countries were contested, the work of international organizations was more uniformly respected by the speakers. In this regard, Greek and Spanish politicians were very similar, as the earlier discussion indicated. Across party lines, speakers referred to principles enshrined in international conventions as undisputed policy goals. Several delegates cited the WHO's Alma-Ata Declaration.[88] Tables 5.6 and 5.7 tabulate references to foreign countries and international organizations in Greek parliamentary debates. As with the Spanish references discussed earlier, the vast majority of references to foreign countries' models are positive across party lines—even though the Conservative Party opposed the introduction of an NHS in Greece.

Table 5.5 **Greek NHS Debate: References by Country and Attitude**

Country/region	Count	Positive	Negative	Mixed
United Kingdom	48	32	14	2
European countries	42	31	7	4
All countries	24	20	2	2
United States	22	15	5	2
Sweden	19	11	7	1
France	18	13	4	1
Canada	13	11	1	1
Socialist countries	12	2	10	0
Western countries	11	8	3	0
Other countries	11	7	3	1
Germany	10	7	1	2
Italy	9	7	1	1
Romania	8	6	2	0
USSR	7	5	2	0
Bulgaria	5	5	0	0
Spain	5	5	0	0
WHO	5	5	0	0
Netherlands	4	4	0	0
Countries with NHS	3	3	0	0
Portugal	3	3	0	0
Underdeveloped countries	3	2	1	0
African countries	3	1	2	0
Hungary	2	2	0	0
International treaties	2	2	0	0
Poland	2	2	0	0
Cuba	2	1	1	0
Turkey	2	1	1	0
Albania	2	0	2	0
Totalitarian countries	2	0	2	0
Total*	318	218	83	17

*The following countries/regions received one reference only and are included in the totals but not listed in the table: Belgium, Denmark, East Germany, Israel, Norway, Switzerland, Yugoslavia, Argentina, Bangladesh, Chad, Chile, developing countries, the IMF, Iran, Kazakhstan, Mongolia, Saudi Arabia, South American Countries, and Syria.

Table 5.6 **Greek NHS Debate: References by Party and Attitude**

Party	Count	Positive	Negative	Mixed
Socialists	136	95	28	13
Conservatives	170	114	52	4
Communists	12	9	3	0
Total	318	218	83	17

The Socialists' appeals to Greek voters on the question of an NHS were very successful politically. Multiple polls show that Greek voters in 1983 and 1984 thought that health care and social insurance was the issue that the PASOK government handled best,[89] and in 1985 the government comfortably won reelection. However, significant problems with the Greek NHS emerged in later years, as the following discussion highlights.

Doctors and Greek Health Policy Reforms

When Greece introduced an NHS, doctors had a professional interest to preserve the status quo, and they had the political power to defend their interests. From 1934 onward, Greece had a social insurance health system: the Greek Medical Association had successfully lobbied so that patients could choose their doctors and doctors could work in both the private and public sectors.[90] Moreover, doctors participated directly in Greek politics, occupying about 10% of seats in parliament since the transition to democracy.[91]

Surprisingly, physicians did not use their power to block the NHS. Although a silent majority likely opposed the reforms, young doctors were striking from the late 1970s onward, seeking the establishment of an NHS.[92] At the time of the parliamentary debate on the NHS, the main medical associations had leaders with partisan ties to the PASOK government, and thus did not oppose the reform.[93] In light of this positioning, representatives affiliated with the Conservative Party won the leadership of medical associations by large margins.[94] However, the first strikes against the NHS occurred only a year after its passage and were relatively mild.

Following the 1985 elections, Health Minister Avgerinos was replaced by Giorgos Gennimatas, who was equally committed to implementing at least parts of the NHS legislation. He focused on reforming hospital care, but set aside plans for primary care in urban areas for a later date.[95] Medical association leaders continued to consult frequently and constructively with the Health Ministry for improved implementation of an NHS rather than mobilizing doctors to oppose the NHS as such.[96] Absent a clear international model of universal, publicly provided health care, Socialist doctors might have conceptualized their professional interests differently and battled the NHS more forcefully.

Reforms Following the Introduction of an NHS

Two major reform proposals were made under Socialist administrations in the 1990s and early 2000s, both reflecting the changing international paradigm. In 1993 Health Minister Dimitris Kremastinos invited a committee of foreign experts led by London School of Economics professor Abel Smith to report on how to reform Greek health policies. Not surprisingly, the committee recommended policies that were consistent with international best practice, albeit with a UK bias. Specifically, the committee recommended fund unification into a single-payer system, a purchaser/provider split, the expansion of capitation payments, outpatient practices, improvements in hospital management, emphasis on public health, and drug rationing.[97] In 2000 a new PASOK health minister, Alekos Papadopoulos, proposed an ambitious plan, "Health for the Citizen," with similar content.[98] Papadopoulos used two main models for this health reform: his team studied French and British decentralization efforts in health care and he drew from his own previous ministerial experience with the reorganization of local administration.[99]

Ultimately only minor reforms concerning decentralization and hospital managers were actually legislated. The argument made in introducing this bill was not the claim that decentralization suited Greece, but rather that "decentralization is the only European administrative model, and has been generally successful."[100] Indeed, the conservative New Democracy spokesperson, Athanassios Giannopoulos, accused PASOK Health Minister Papadopoulos of blindly adopting foreign models without any consideration of Greek particularities. More specifically, Giannopoulos accused the government of "downloading a bill from the Internet."[101] The Socialists proposed the introduction of per patient fees, and the conservatives critiqued this position as an arrangement that all other European countries avoid.[102]

In summary, Greek health debates followed international paradigms both when this meant a turn to socialized medicine and when the pendulum swung toward market-oriented reform. As in Spain, these debates focused on the WHO, and on the experiences of rich western European countries familiar to voters: Britain, France, and Germany. The tension between PASOK proposals in the 1980s and early 2000s was not lost on key participants in the debate. Avgerinos, the health minister who had introduced the NHS in 1983, explained this shift while serving as a Socialist MP in 2001 by noting a worldwide change in perceptions concerning the role of doctors in a health care system.[103]

Policy Reforms in Other Fields

Socialist parties in Greece and Spain introduced radical reform in an area where an international template was available, but they did not change the paradigm in other social policy fields, because large institutional reforms are challenging, especially in times of tight budgets. In his analysis of southern European Socialist parties' relative success across different policy areas, Hans Jürgen Puhle concludes that although these parties aimed to achieve four goals—democratization, Europeanization, modernization, and the creation of a modern welfare state—they were much more successful in achieving the first two than in fulfilling any redistributive aspirations.[104] This tension is particularly acute in the case of the Spanish PSOE, which was more restrained in overall expenditure increases than the Greek PASOK. In a 1998 review of PSOE's legacy, Juan Luis Rodríguez Vigil notes, "it is quite clear today that the health reform undertaken by the socialist governments took place more or less according to the PSOE 1982 manifesto. This distinguishes the health reform in a clear way from what occurred in other areas, where programmatic and electoral commitments were substantially modified as soon as the PSOE government took office."[105]

Conclusions

Introducing an NHS is a major reform: it typically involves an expansion in health care coverage, a redesign of health care financing, and, most controversially, greater direct government control over doctors and hospitals. In the late 1970s and early 1980s, all four southern European countries radically reformed their health systems, switching from Bismarckian social insurance systems to NHSs. This chapter presented the influence and significance of foreign models in bringing about these radical reforms by tracing the development of NHSs in three countries—Britain, a pioneer, Spain, and Greece, two late developers.

Radical conditions—World War II, an overwhelming Labour Party victory, and collapsing hospitals—were present when the UK NHS was pioneered. Greece and Spain, countries that implemented NHSs later, were able to profit from the pioneer experience and implement more radical reforms with greater ease. Late developers were able to convert established and stable occupational insurance systems into universal health services, to limit private medical practice, and to make these reforms under Socialist administrations that were coming to power for the first time.

This book's theoretical framework also explains how international models shift domestic actors' choices. It posits that international models set the agenda for a diverse set of actors, not just for those favorably predisposed to a particular reform. Moreover, it emphasizes that the electoral process reinforces, rather than attenuates, elite biases toward imitation of proximate and high status countries. Politicians favorably predisposed to the reform can reference the foreign model and signal to voters and other skeptical audiences that their preferred policy is not an outlandish, ill-thought-out experiment, but a vetted, competently designed, and mainstream solution. Negatively predisposed politicians and groups that stand to lose from the reform cannot ignore the proposal as easily as they could in the absence of the foreign model.

Case study evidence from Greece and Spain bears out these claims. In these two late developers, medical associations were divided and did not forcefully oppose reforms that radically curtailed doctors' autonomy and income. Centrist and conservative parties also seriously considered Socialist proposals and debated international models extensively. The existence of an international model helped Socialist politicians translate a broad ideology into a concrete policy program, prioritize health care reform over other more pressing issues, and persuade skeptical voters.

Party platforms, campaign promises, parliamentary debates, and other rhetoric targeted at the general public show elites' expectations that voters are favorably impressed by the imitation of foreign models. Politicians continuously referenced the choices of large and rich industrialized countries as well as the WHO's proposals. Some of these references related to policy success, but many emphasized the mere association of a particular policy alternative with a recognizable high status actor.

This book's contribution to the welfare state literature is to supplement domestic accounts with an argument about how the positions of domestic actors with particular predispositions and interests shift in the presence of an international model. The introduction of an NHS is in many ways a critical case: the reform is materially enormous and conceptually radical, the international organization proposals are relatively "soft," and a key domestic constituency is initially hostile. If international models are powerful under these unfavorable circumstances, diffusion likely shapes a broad set of policy areas. The next two chapters investigate how international models influenced family policy, a field with stronger international models and with interest groups that stood to benefit from these models.

Family Policy Diffusion Across OECD Countries

Family Policies: An Introduction

Across countries, men and women make very different decisions about when and how much to work, when and how to form families, and how to balance the two. Indicatively, while 74% of Danish women with a child under six are working, this fraction falls to 61% for American mothers, 51% for Italian mothers, and 33% for Hungarian mothers.[1] Families are becoming smaller in many advanced industrialized countries, while the gap between actual and desired family size, as reported in surveys, is growing.[2] The presence and nature of laws promoting work–family balance explain a large part of these patterns. For example, maternity leave laws can increase the employment rate of women of childbearing age by 7% to 9%.[3]

This chapter investigates the family policy choices of governments around the world, concentrating on advanced industrialized countries, and asks why different countries have chosen different laws. At present, a large majority of countries around the world have adopted family policies. More detailed data on developed countries indicates that these legal commitments are often backed by substantial resources. In 2001, Organization for Economic Cooperation and Development (OECD) countries spent about 2% of their gross domestic product (GDP), on average, directly for public family policies.[4] The two main subcategories of spending are family allowances and maternity leaves, and these are the policies studied in this chapter. Family allowances are in-kind and cash payments to families with children.[5] Leaves are regulations protecting working parents' jobs while parents take time off from work to care for newborns and young children. Maternity leaves are leaves that must be taken in the period surrounding the birth of the child; maternity leaves are typically paid.[6]

Analyzing family policy permits me to further develop and test my proposed theory of diffusion through democracy. I argue that policies spread across countries because voters benchmark their governments against countries with which they are familiar, that is, large, rich, and culturally proximate countries. This creates electoral incentives for politicians to borrow from these familiar countries' policies across diverse issue areas. Prior chapters have shown how national health policies are shaped by international influences. Turning to family policy allows me to test my theory in a different field, and to distinguish between patterns that are specific to one policy area and regularities that hold true across several policy fields.

Health policy represents a least-likely case for my proposed theory: international organizations' efforts to promote particular health policies were especially limited, and domestic interest group opposition was especially strong. In contrast, family policy is more typical of other social policy fields, such as unemployment policy, pensions, disability insurance, and antidiscrimination prohibitions. Family policy is typical both in the type of international organization activity it involves and in the structure of domestic interest groups. As described in chapter 4, the World Health Organization (WHO) only identified a broad goal for which all governments should strive—universal health coverage, with an emphasis on primary care. Unlike the WHO, the two international organizations involved in family policy, the European Union (EU) and the International Labour Organization (ILO), were much more specific in their policy advice; they did not advocate generally for government efforts to help women reconcile work and family. They also promoted desirable policy instruments—maternity leaves—and even identified parameters for the implementation of such policies—specific leave length and compensation rates.[7] Moreover, while the WHO efforts took the form of non-binding declarations, the ILO pushed for the ratification of legally binding conventions, and even asked countries that had not ratified these conventions to submit periodic reports. The EU had even stronger tools at its disposal—it promulgated legally binding directives, and can pursue legal action and fines against countries that do not implement the directives properly.[8]

International organization involvement in the regulation of maternity leaves is typical of international organization involvement in other social policy fields. The EU has dozens of directives on topics such as work hours, health and worker safety, and employment discrimination, among other areas.[9] The ILO has hundreds of conventions covering almost every risk workers face—from disability to unemployment to retirement and migration.[10] Studying international influences in family policy thus offers a springboard from which to generalize to other social policy issues.

Studying the field of family policy offers an additional methodological advantage: within-field variation. While maternity leaves have been the subject of substantial international organization efforts, there has been much less international activity in the field of family benefits: the ILO and EU have been constrained by their mandates to focus on family policy that intersects with employment. Studying both maternity leave and family benefits policy permits one to survey the field of family policy and to contrast policy areas that differ on the degree of international organization activity.

Additionally, domestic interest groups are structured differently in the family and health policy sectors, in ways that facilitate the diffusion of family policy models. Family policy debates typically pit unions, feminist groups, and left-wing parties, on the one hand, against employers, religious groups, and right-wing parties on the other. This is a typical configuration for debates on many social policy questions. This interest group configuration means that most international models have a high likelihood of being warmly received by at least one of the sides in the debate, and opposed by the other. In the case of family policy, we would expect material interests to lead unions and left-wing parties to support both maternity leaves and family benefits, and employers and right-wing parties to oppose these.[11] In contrast, in the area of health policy, no organized domestic group is eager to receive the foreign model; material considerations lead us to expect domestic opposition only. More specifically, one would expect the key organized interest group, medical doctors, to oppose the introduction of a National Health Service (NHS). NHSs can benefit broad and diverse constituencies, such as patients and taxpayers. But NHSs do not benefit organized labor more than social insurance-based systems do; indeed, some labor unions may prefer social insurance systems that reward their members with above average health care coverage. Thus no concentrated interest group exists to counterbalance the expected opposition of medical associations and to advocate for the domestic adoption of the NHS model.

To preview this chapter's findings, I find strong support for my theory of diffusion through democracy in cross-national regressions explaining national family policy choices across rich democracies. Governments mimic the policy choices of countries familiar to voters, and international organization influence is greatest in countries whose publics are internationally oriented. These findings are consistent with the findings reported in chapter 4 on health policy reforms across rich democracies. In both fields, governments mimic the policy choices of large, rich, and culturally proximate countries familiar to voters. However, in health policy, regression evidence suggests that emulation is one of several diffusion mechanisms operating alongside competition and learning from policy success. This chapter shows that in family policy, emulation of familiar countries is the main diffusion mechanism; competition and learning from policy success do not seem influential. Qualitative analyses in chapters 2, 5, and 7 confirm and help explain this pattern. In family policy, a dominant international model allowed advocates of maternity leave to reference the model without discussing its consequences, and left little space open for opposition groups. In health policy, a vaguely defined and weakly promulgated international model left much room for partisan debate about what worked and did not work in particular foreign countries.

As in health policy, international models are not the whole story: diverse domestic interest groups matter substantially. This chapter reports, consistent with a large literature on social policy, that domestic forces—notably strong labor unions, women in office, Christian parties, and demographic conditions—can explain part of the variation in national family policies. However, the availability of international models modifies the nature of domestic interest group conflict. This chapter shows that international models allowed late adopters of family leave to adopt this policy with substantially less domestic support, and significantly more domestic opposition, than early adopters. Qualitative analyses in chapters 5 and 7 explain how international models not only strengthen the hand of domestic advocates for a particular policy reform, but also change the views of expected opponents, notably medical associations in the case of national health services, and employers and conservative parties in the case of maternity leave.

International Organization Proposals

Two international organizations, the EU and the ILO, have sought to influence family policies in OECD countries. Both organizations' mandates authorize them to propose laws related to labor and employment issues: both organizations have proposed maternity leave laws. However, these international organizations' mandates do not cover fertility and poverty directly, therefore both organizations have been far less active in the area of family benefits. This chapter thus examines the diverse international influences on maternity leaves, and uses family benefits as a control policy area, to see how a similar field develops in the absence of international organization models.

The EU is a highly legalized regime: EU member states must pass national laws to comply with very detailed EU directives, and can be sued and fined when they fail to meet these obligations. On each of the dimensions of obligation, precision, and delegation, EU directives represent a much more legalized regime than ILO conventions.[12] The EU agreed on mandatory maternity leave for its members, which was to begin in 1994.[13] By that point, all EU member states had already adopted national maternity leave laws. This delay substantially limited the impact of the EU on maternity leave in OECD countries; the directive only changed the scope of the leave in a few member states.[14] Nonetheless, this study focuses on the period prior to 1994, both because this is when major reforms happened, and because it would be difficult to persuade a skeptic that any policy change after this date was not a consequence of the directive.[15]

The ILO is the United Nations (UN) agency focused on promoting labor rights. ILO member states can decide whether or not to ratify particular conventions, and are only obligated to put forth ILO conventions before parliament for ratification in a timely fashion.[16] In 1919 the ILO issued its Maternity Protection Convention (Convention 3), calling for a 12-week leave. This convention was updated in 1952; maternity leave was to be compensated at two-thirds of a woman's previous earnings. The Maternity Protection Convention was updated again in 2000 (Convention 183), extending maternity leave to 14 weeks and introducing other allowances.

The ILO did not promote family benefits until 1952, after many countries in the world had already adopted these. Moreover, it did so not so forcefully, through a separate convention, but only included these as part of ILO Convention 102, the Social Security Minimum Standards Convention. This convention references nine types of social benefits governments can offer: medical benefits, sickness benefits, unemployment benefits, old age benefits, employment injury benefits, maternity benefits, invalidity benefits, survivor benefits, and family allowances. To comply with this convention, countries must offer three of the nine benefits from this menu, and there is significant flexibility in how they provide these benefits. It is hard to see the impact of this late and limited effort to promote family benefits in the quantitative data that follow, although the more nuanced case studies in chapter 7 show some impact.

Surveying Global Adoption Patterns

This section presents global data concerning the adoption of maternity leave laws and family benefits programs. Mapping whether and when countries adopted these policies illustrates some global diffusion and some regional clustering. Inspecting the dates of adoption indicates that adoption rates for both maternity and family benefits display patterns suggestive of the diffusion of innovations. Graphing adoption rates by year illustrates a spike in maternity protection adoption rates immediately following the first ILO maternity convention, and an even sharper spike following the second ILO maternity convention—these patterns suggest an ILO impact on national decision making. Finally, this section presents some evidence that late adopters can implement more radical reforms with fewer domestic resources available than was the case for pioneers. This section displays global data graphically, rather than undertaking regression analyses, because data on appropriate controls are not available for most countries in the world for the period between 1880 and 1945. For a more systematic testing of the chapter's claims, regression analyses in the next section focus on OECD countries in the post–World War II period.

The great majority of developed countries have adopted some form of family benefits; even more countries around the world have adopted maternity and sickness insurance.[17] The maps in Figures 6.1 and 6.2 indicate adoption rates of maternity leave programs and family benefits programs, respectively. Lighter shades of grey indicate earlier adoption dates; black indicates that a country has not yet adopted the policy. Besides showing the prevalence of these policies around the world, the maps provide some first indication of clustering. That is, countries tend to be near countries with the same shade of grey, indicating that they adopted policies at approximately the same time. These maps suggest that maternity leave is more widespread than family benefits, and is almost universally offered. Comparing the two maps also suggests slightly less clustering in time and space in the family benefits field (compared to maternity leave); the map appears somewhat more checkered.[18]

The graphs in Figures 6.3 and 6.4 plot the cumulative adoptions of the two policies over time. In both graphs we see an S-shaped curve, although the data conform more closely to an S-shape in the case of maternity leaves. An S-shaped curve is indicative of diffusion. It results when innovations are first adopted hesitantly by community leaders, spread rapidly as their value is proven or as they become fashionable among more hesitant players, and finally display a slower adoption rate, as the fraction of the community that has yet to adopt may have strong reasons to oppose the proposed reform.

In Figure 6.4, thin black lines mark the first and second ILO Maternity Conventions. Spikes in adoptions following the first ILO convention in 1919, and especially in the year and immediate aftermath of the second ILO convention in 1952, suggest the ILO to be a possible influence.[19] The subsequent sections develop and test more specific hypotheses about international organization and cross-national influences on family policy development.

To examine the claim that late adopters can adopt a policy under less favorable conditions than pioneers, Figure 6.5 compares late and early adopters. The policies under study here were pioneered in the late 1800s. To find metrics comparable from this time period onward for a large sample of countries is challenging. Industrialization is a good general proxy for political conditions in the case of maternity leaves.

Industrial production, especially in its early days, posed particular risks to workers' health and life—in industry, workers were exposed to chemicals, prone to severe accidents, and were likely to be overworked to an extent unknown in agricultural settings.[20] Additionally, industrialization coincided

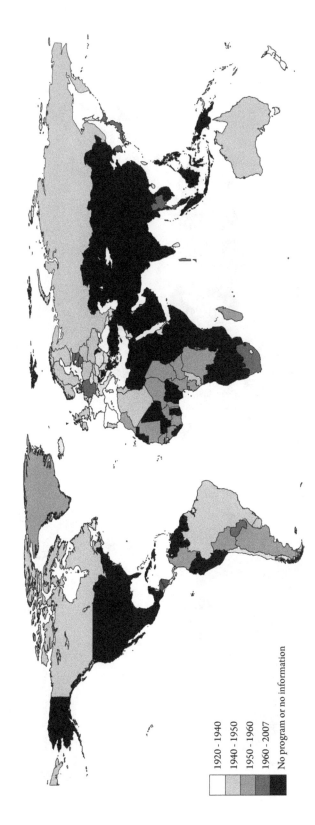

Figure 6.1 Adoption of Family Benefits Programs Around the World

1920 - 1940
1940 - 1950
1950 - 1960
1960 - 2007
No program or no information

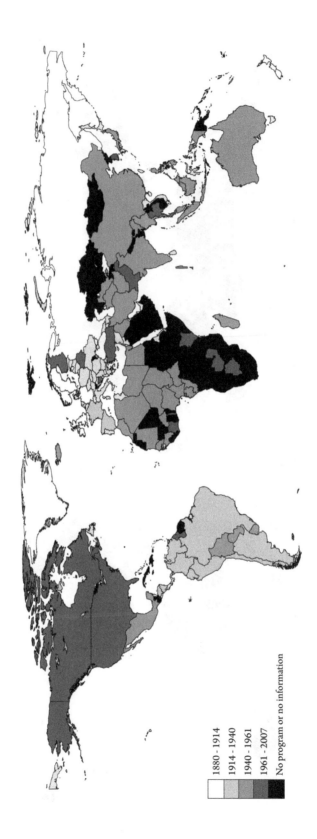

Figure 6.2 Adoption of Maternity/Sick Leave Programs Around the World

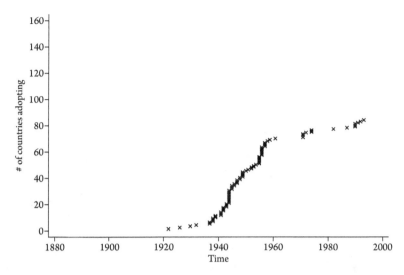

Figure 6.3 Cumulative Adoptions of Family Benefits Programs Around the World

in time with urbanization and the nonavailability of family arrangements to shelter workers from some of these risks.[21] With industrialization, the possibilities for worker mobilization and unionization increased as work was organized in larger units.[22] In short, the greater the fraction of a country's workforce employed by industry, the greater the problem of pregnant women at work is, and the more likely it is that workers will organize to push for regulation.[23]

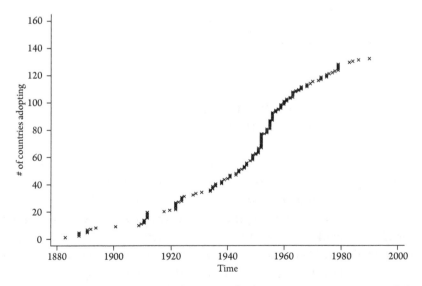

Figure 6.4 Cumulative Adoptions of Maternity/Sick Insurance Programs Around the World

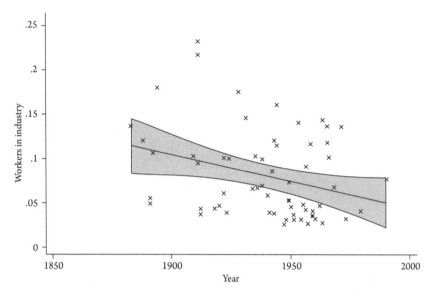

Figure 6.5 Industrialization at the Time Maternity/Sick Leave was Introduced

The graph in Figure 6.5 plots the date of introduction of maternity or sickness insurance. The data points represent the 63 countries in the world that have introduced such policies for which industrialization statistics are available.[24] The plot has a fitted values line, along with a 95% confidence interval (the lightly shaded area). The graph illustrates a negative and significant relationship: the later a maternity leave was introduced, the less industrialized the country in question was at the time. This claim concerning differences between pioneers and late adopters, along with the other diffusion claims, is tested more systematically below.

Maternity Leave Laws and Spending on Families Across Advanced Industrialized Countries

The prior section provided a first glance at global patterns. The sections that follow begin a more systematic analysis and examine how international influences shaped maternity leave laws and spending on family benefits across 18 OECD countries over 25 years. The countries are Australia, Austria, Belgium, Canada, Denmark, Finland, France, West Germany, Ireland, Italy, Japan, the Netherlands, New Zealand, Norway, Sweden, Switzerland, the United Kingdom, and the United States. The period is 1970 to 1994; 1994 is used as a cutoff because the EU-mandated maternity leave for its members started in this year.

Anne Gauthier and her research team have extensively compiled and examined comparative family policy data. The models that follow use these data: paid maternity leave is measured in weeks[25] and expenditures on family allowances are measured as a percentage of GDP.[26] Between 1970 and 1994, on average, OECD governments increased their efforts in the field of family policy; paid maternity leave increased from a median of 12 weeks in 1970 to 15 weeks in 1994; spending on family benefits increased from a median of 1% of GDP in 1970 to 1.5% in 1994. However, these averages hide substantial variation between and within countries over time. In the period under study, three OECD countries—New Zealand, Australia, and the United States—did not offer any paid maternity leave.[27] Similarly, in some years, Japan, New Zealand, and Switzerland spent less than 0.1% of GDP on family benefits. We also see substantial variation within countries over time; several OECD governments expanded the length of maternity leave at different points in time, while other administrations cut back these benefits, most notably in Italy and Norway in the mid-1980s. Within-country over-time variation in the value of family benefits is even more substantial; most countries under study had both administrations that expanded these benefits and administrations that made substantial cutbacks.

Whereas the introduction of NHSs studied in chapters 4 and 5 represented radical breaks with past policy, many of the family policy changes studied in this chapter and chapter 7 came about through incremental reform. Even these incremental changes, as chapter 7 illustrates, were important in electoral campaign messages, and garnered significant public attention.

International Influences on Domestic Law Reforms

Prior research on maternity leave laws, and on governments' social policy decisions more generally, focuses almost exclusively on domestic interest groups, such as labor unions, employer associations, left- and right-wing parties, and religious and feminist movements. This book argues that international developments are a key missing part of the story; foreign governments' choices and international organizations' proposals substantially influence national law reforms by providing voters with valuable information. The analyses that follow confirm that both the domestic and international environment significantly influence national law reforms.

To investigate the influence of international models, and to test diffusion theories, researchers create spatial lags. These represent the weighted average of the policy choices of a country's "neighbors." Researchers specify which countries are considered neighbors theoretically: for example, country A could be defined as country B's neighbor if it shares a border, competes in the same markets, or is covered heavily in country B's media. Researchers then test whether "neighboring" countries' choices are imitated disproportionately. To test the theory that governments imitate countries whose news voters follow disproportionately, the next section outlines what information reaches voters, and how the relevant spatial weight matrix was constructed. Subsequent sections outline how other international and domestic influences are examined, elaborate on the empirical strategy, and present results.

Media Coverage of Large, Rich, and Proximate Countries

Voters get information from television, radio, newspapers, and magazines, as well as other media: ideally, coverage data for each of these sources would be used. However, such data are not available in a cross-nationally comparable format for the time period under study (1970–1994). What is available in cross-nationally comparable format for the entire period and set of countries under study is foreign newspaper and magazine sales from each country in the sample to another country in the sample, and these data are used as a measure of media connectedness between two countries.[28] This is a new measure not found in the prior literature. For this reason, chapter 4 (on the diffusion of health policy across rich countries) explores its validity at length. That discussion shows that my measure of media connectedness correlates very highly with other available measures of media coverage from published studies. In chapter 4 I also show that this measure correlates very highly with measures of domestic press coverage of foreign countries, and with citizens' familiarity with particular foreign countries. These high correlations suggest that the spatial weights accurately identify countries with which citizens are likely to be most familiar.

Citizen Attentiveness to International Organization Messages

Whereas new measures are necessary to examine citizen attentiveness to particular foreign countries, the existing sociological literature provides a measure of citizen attentiveness to international organization messages. Sociologists of the world culture school have examined citizen participation in international nongovernmental organizations (INGOs), on the theory that countries whose citizens are involved in transnational groups are more attuned to global shifts. Prior research illustrates how global connectedness rises and falls over time, and how it varies by sector.[29] While sectoral data were only made available to researchers for a single year (1988), on the basis of these data, George Thomas and John Boli concluded that "world culture is heavily 'economic' in that not-for-profit bodies concerned with business and economic activity (industry and trade combined with tertiary economic organizations) account for about one-fourth of all active INGOs."[30] This suggests that policies directly related to the workplace might diffuse especially rapidly through this channel.

The citizen participation measure uses the number of INGOs to which a country's citizens belong.[31] For the regression models, countries are coded as either having large numbers of INGO memberships (1), if they fell in the top 20% of the sample, or not (0).[32]

A correlation between citizen participation in INGOs and policy outcomes when an international organization model existed (i.e., in maternity leaves), and the absence of such a correlation when no international organization model existed (i.e., in family benefits), is a probative, if indirect, test of international organization influence. If more detailed data on citizen participation in international labor law advocacy groups existed, this might help establish a particular pathway of influence. However, we would not know whether, in the absence of ILO proposals, these citizens would remain silent, or would have other motivations to advocate for labor laws with similar content.[33] Citizen participation is INGOs is more clearly exogenous to particular policy proposals.

Other International Influences: Competition, Learning from Success, and Ratification of International Agreements

This chapter also examines three other pathways of international influence highlighted in prior literature: country-to-country policy diffusion due to competition, country-to-country policy diffusion due to learning from policy success, and international organization influence through the ratification of international conventions. Much prior work emphasizes that firms are most likely to raise competitiveness considerations, and that elected leaders are directly concerned about evidence of policy success and about international legal obligations. Such factors might also be relevant to some voters. To be conservative, any observed evidence of diffusion through these pathways is credited to alternative theories rather than to the voter information model developed here.

Several recent studies have emphasized competition as a key driver of policy diffusion.[34] Labor regulation and worker benefits may influence firm (re) location decisions. Governments eager to attract firms, or fearful that firms will relocate to countries with less "burdensome" regulatory environments, may pay particular attention to the policy choices of countries with which they compete. Maternity leaves are labor regulations generally funded through taxes on labor; family benefits are often funded through general taxation and do not directly impact firms. Therefore countries might imitate competitors' choices disproportionately in setting maternity leave policy. Other scholars of comparative politics emphasize that governments do not imitate competitors' choices piecemeal, as it is sets of institutions, rather than individual policies, that drive national competitiveness.[35] Following the work of Zachary Elkins, Andrew Guzman, and Beth Simmons, trade competitors are defined as countries that exported similar types of products.[36] Whether trade competition shapes imitation in this field remains an open empirical question.

Learning from policy success is the theory that governments imitate policies when they receive evidence of policy success. The greater the consensus on what policy success means, the easier it is to measure success and attribute it to a particular policy, and the more widespread this information is, the more information exchanges should resemble learning. In the period examined here, maternity leaves were adopted to help women reconcile work and family. Politicians in many countries argued for maternity leaves primarily to allow women to join and stay in the workforce after having children, as chapters 3 and 7 show in greater detail. Countries are therefore coded as success models if they achieved high female labor market participation.[37] It is more difficult to evaluate whether family benefits programs are successful, because there is no consensus on what success means in this field: politicians pursued these for very diverse reasons in different countries and time periods. These objectives included reinforcing traditional views of the single-earner family, combating poverty, and increasing fertility. If politicians have complete information about policy successes, and the freedom and willingness to act on this information, we should expect to see the widespread imitation of successful policies. In contrast, if biased and fragmented information reaches voters, and if voters severely constrain politicians, we should expect more biased policy imitation patterns.

Additionally, international legal obligations could cause governments to adopt policies they would otherwise avoid. The ILO promulgated multiple maternity leave conventions, but did little to promote family benefits; the analysis below examines whether governments that ratified these conventions, and whether governments that ratified them early on, adopted more extensive leave policies domestically.[38] Interpreting ratification data requires great caution, because governments could decide on what policies to adopt based on domestic considerations alone, and only ratify international instruments as a step in carrying out these predetermined policies.[39]

Domestic Determinants of Family Policies

This section outlines the main political, economic, and demographic variables expected to shape family policy. The family policies examined here—maternity leave laws and state spending on families—consist of state-provided social benefits and state regulation of employment contracts. They are thus often analyzed as social policies, alongside measures on unemployment, sickness, or pension benefits.[40] The dominant theory in the social policy field—the power resources approach—identifies social democratic governments and organized labor as the forces for increased employment protection.[41] Thus we might expect trade unions and social democratic parties to support maternity leaves. In contrast, Christian democratic parties have often opposed paid maternity leave policies and other policies facilitating women's workforce participation in support of alternative policies that would permit mothers to stay at home with their children.[42] Unlike maternity leaves, cash benefits to families with children have been popular with parties across the political spectrum.[43] Following the work of Evelyne Huber and John Stephens, cumulative left cabinet seats from 1946 to the date of the observation were used as a measure of left-wing power, and the cumulative cabinet score for Protestant and Catholic parties of the right and center was used as a measure of Christian conservative power.[44] Union power was measured as the percentage of unionized workers in the labor force.[45]

Whether a country has women in government should also influence the family policies it adopts. Many studies across advanced industrialized countries report that women in parliament have different preferences from their male counterparts on women's issues and are more likely to support initiatives promoting family and labor issues.[46] The women-in-parliament variable also stands in as a proxy for general societal support for women's and family issues. Countries with women in power should have both higher family benefits and longer maternity leaves. The percentage of seats in parliament held by women is used to examine this hypothesis.[47]

Women's labor force participation, fertility, and unemployment levels could plausibly influence government willingness to carry out family policies at particular points in time, and are included as controls. Women's labor force participation was measured as the percentage of women age 15 to 64 years in the labor force.[48] Women's unemployment rates were also based on OECD data. Fertility data come from the U.S. census international database, as reported by Gauthier.[49] Because the causal relationships between family policy and these demographic and economic conditions could go in both directions, one should interpret these coefficients with particular care. All these variables are lagged by one year to mitigate this endogeneity concern.

Methods and Results

This section tests whether maternity leave laws and government spending on families in OECD countries are shaped by the choices of other countries covered in the news and by international organization templates. In addition, this section examines the determinants of family policy across OECD countries more generally. Pooled cross-sectional time series models predict maternity leave length and expenditures on family allowances, as described earlier. The data cover 18 OECD countries over 25 years. Estimating such models is challenging; the analysis below follows the work of Robert Franzese and Jude Hays.[50] The models estimated take the following form:

$$y = \varphi My + \rho Wy + X\beta + \varepsilon,$$

where y is the dependent variable (i.e., maternity leave length or spending on family benefits in each country each year); φMy is the first-order temporal lag: incremental policymaking characterizes family policy, and much of social policy more generally; and ρ is the spatial autoregressive coefficient, which captures the strength of the diffusion process. W is the spatial weight matrix. The elements of this matrix, $w_{i,j}$, reflect the degree of connectedness from unit j to unit i. As described previously, the researcher specifies this weight matrix and its elements reflect various relationships (e.g., whether countries i and j share a border, whether they export similar products, or whether country j is covered by country i's news media). Chapter 4 provides additional details on spatial weights.

Wy is the spatial lag. For each observation $y_{i,t}$, the corresponding element of Wy gives a sum of $y_{j,t-1}$ (neighbors' policies in the prior year), weighted by the degree of connectedness between the country and each neighbor. The theory of cross-national influence proposed above calls for this one-year lag for imitating neighboring countries' policies: governments' responses to developments abroad likely take a short period to materialize. In addition, this 1-year lag facilitates estimation.[51]

X is a matrix of observations of other independent variables, and β is a vector of coefficients. Because the independent variables discussed here do not capture all country-specific factors, the model also includes country-level fixed effects. ε is the vector of error terms.

A key challenge facing diffusion models generally is that unobserved shocks might generate contemporaneous changes in neighboring countries without any exchanges having occurred between them. Therefore specifications also include proxies for unobserved common shocks. Following the work of Olivier Blanchard and Justin Wolfers, dummies for particular years are included.[52]

It is also possible that common shocks are translated at different speeds by national institutions; notably, countries with many veto players may respond more slowly. Therefore some specifications include an interaction between five-year periods and a "constitutional structure veto points index"; this turns out not to be significant and is not included in the final specifications.[53]

To estimate these models, ordinary least squares regression with a spatial lag was used, as recommended by Franzese and Hays.[54] This could yield results that are biased, but alternative estimation strategies, such as spatial instrumental variable techniques, do not have superior properties for data sets of this size and moderate spatial correlations.[55] Moreover, simulations show that the size of any biases should be quite small. Indeed, because the spatial lag is temporally lagged, one might be more concerned about misspecification. If some policy diffusion occurs within the year of initial policy adoption, rather than in the subsequent year, as modeled here, these cross-national relationships will not be accounted for. Thus, if some governments respond to their neighbors rapidly, the reported effects might be smaller than the full diffusion effects.[56]

The regressions below examine how international and domestic factors shape OECD governments' choices in the field of maternity leave (Table 6.1) and family benefits (Table 6.2). The results support the hypotheses that governments are disproportionately likely to mimic countries whose news voters follow, and to follow international organization models more closely when citizens are active in INGOs. The results also confirm the centrality of diverse domestic political and socioeconomic correlates in the development of national family policies.

The analysis begins with models examining the role of domestic factors alone, following the comparative social policy literature, and continues by exploring the role of diverse international influences. In Tables 6.1 and 6.2, the first specification contains all potentially relevant domestic variables, the second specification contains domestic variables that turn out to be significant at any point, and subsequent specifications examine international diffusion mechanisms. The following discussion is based primarily on the final specifications containing all relevant domestic and international variables (Table 6.1, model VI; Table 6.2, model III) but also highlights any differences between specifications.[57]

The theoretical discussion presents three mechanisms of cross-national diffusion: governments may imitate trade competitors, governments may imitate top performers, and governments may imitate countries whose news citizens follow. The results show that only the last mechanism shapes family policy development. In the case of maternity leave, while the competition coefficient is positively signed, it is not statistically significant either when studied alone (model IV) or when studied alongside other diffusion

Table 6.1 **Models Predicting Maternity Leave Length**

	Model I Coefficient (SE)	Model II Coefficient (SE)	Model III Coefficient (SE)	Model IV Coefficient (SE)	Model V Coefficient (SE)	Model VI Coefficient (SE)
Temporal lag	.82*** (.027)	.85*** (.025)	.81*** (.027)	.81*** (.027)	.79*** (.028)	.79*** (.028)
Left cabinet	−.0049 (.053)	—	—	—	—	—
Conservative Christian cabinet	−.093 (.061)	−.091* (.053)	−.20*** (.061)	−.15** (.069)	−.17*** (.062)	−.14** (.069)
Unions	.094*** (.032)	.093*** (.031)	.12*** (.031)	.11*** (.031)	.087*** (.033)	.087*** (.033)
Women in parliament	.15*** (.047)	.13*** (.036)	.12*** (.036)	.11*** (.037)	.072* (.040)	.072* (.040)
Women in the workforce	−.048 (.034)	—	—	—	—	—
Female unemployment	−.059 (.058)	—	—	—	—	—
Many INGO memberships	—	—	1.08*** (.34)	1.18*** (.35)	.94*** (.35)	1.01*** (.36)
ILO convention ratification	—	—	.082** (.040)	.043 (.046)	.068* (.040)	.049 (.046)
Learning from success	—	—	.000044 (.024)	—	—	−.0037 (.024)
Imitating competitors	—	—	—	.12 (.074)	—	.062 (.078)
Imitating countries covered by the media	—	—	—	—	.16** (.065)	.14** (.069)
Year dummies	Yes	Yes	Yes	Yes	Yes	Yes
Period dummies × veto player index	Yes	No	No	No	No	No

(Continued)

Table 6.1 **Continued**

	Model I	Model II	Model III	Model IV	Model V	Model VI
	Coefficient (SE)	Coefficient (SE)	Coefficient (SE)	Coefficient (SE)	Coefficient (SE)	Coefficient (SE)
Country dummies	Yes	Yes	Yes	Yes	Yes	Yes
Constant	Yes	Yes	Yes	Yes	Yes	Yes
N	383	413	413	413	413	413

***Significant at the .01 level; **significant at the .05 level; *significant at the .10 level.
SE, standard error.

mechanisms (model VI). This result differs from prior literature; researchers have identified competition effects in several policy areas that directly or indirectly tax firms. Perhaps firms focus their lobbying efforts on policies more costly than maternity leaves; perhaps governments are less receptive to firm lobbying in policy fields that are visible and easily understood by the electorate. As the previous discussion indicates, competition to attract firms is not a plausible mechanism in the development of family benefits policies, as these are typically funded through general taxes and granted to workers and non-workers alike. The results also do not support the hypothesis of unbiased learning from policy success: countries that have the most women in employment each year are not disproportionately imitated across the OECD (Table 6.1, models III and VI). Using a broader measure of policy success—GDP per capita—similarly reveals no general unbiased imitation of top performers (results not shown). This finding is consistent with recent studies indicating that to the extent learning happens, it is severely biased.[58]

The results support the hypothesis that governments imitate countries that are covered disproportionately in the news. As described previously, foreign newspaper sales are used as spatial weights to characterize media relationships between country pairs; the regressions then test whether the policy choices of countries covered in the media are imitated disproportionately in countries receiving these news. The coefficients on this measure are significant and similar in size in all specifications (Table 6.1, models V and VI; Table 6.4, model III). The effect is moderate: for every week's increase in the leaves of countries whose news voters follow, a country increases its leave by about one day (Table 6.1, models V and VI). A similarly sized effect occurs in the family benefits area, where a one-unit increase in the spending of countries whose news is

Table 6.2 **Models Predicting Expenditures on Family Benefits**

	Model I	*Model II*	*Model III*
	Coefficient (SE)	*Coefficient (SE)*	*Coefficient (SE)*
Temporal lag	.86***	.85***	.87***
	(.030)	(.035)	(.035)
Left cabinet	.0088	—	—
	(.0085)		
Conservative Christian cabinet	−.013	−.018*	−.0099
	(.0087)	(.0094)	(.011)
Women in parliament	.0011	—	—
	(.0057)		
Total fertility rate	.10	.19**	.17*
	(.088)	(.096)	(.099)
Many INGO memberships	—	—	−.014
			(.069)
Emulation (foreign newspapers)	—	—	.15***
			(.056)
Year dummies	Yes	Yes	Yes
Period dummies × veto player index	Yes	No	No
Country dummies	Yes	Yes	Yes
Constant	Yes	Yes	Yes
N	374	408	408

***Significant at the .01 level; **significant at the .05 level; *significant at the .10 level.
SE, standard error.

followed increases domestic spending by about one-seventh (Table 6.2, model III). These effect size estimates are conservative. First, they assume a uniform one-unit shift in a country's neighbors' policies. If a country's neighbors shift their policies by one unit on average, but do so asymmetrically, effect sizes will change. If the more influential neighbors experience above-average changes, effect sizes will increase, and vice versa. More critically, these are short-run effects; larger effects unfold over time.[59]

The hypothesis that global norms influence national choices also finds support: both ratification of relevant ILO conventions and having a large number of INGOs correlate with increased maternity leave length. These findings should be interpreted with caution. As the large literature on international organizations has debated, a positive relationship between ratification and policy outcomes can either reflect the influence of international organizations or a prior interest of a government in the policy the international organization is promoting; moreover, the ratification finding does not reach conventional levels of significance in all specifications. However, qualitative analysis in chapter 7 leads me to believe that the reported ILO estimates could be overly conservative. This is because politicians in Greece and Spain first promised to follow international standards and ratify international maternity conventions during election campaigns, then made changes to national legislation, and only later ratified the relevant ILO conventions and reported this to the ILO.

The internationalist orientation of a country's citizens is more easily separable from particular policy proposals that might interest a government. As expected, countries with many INGOs have longer maternity leaves, but are no different in their family benefits policies. More specifically, countries with the most INGOs (top 20%) have maternity leaves that are about one week longer than those of other countries, but do not have different family benefits policies. This comparison between two family policies mitigates concern that an omitted variable correlated with a citizenry's internationalist orientation is driving the maternity leave results.

Domestic variables perform in the expected direction and generally support modified versions of the power resources thesis: conservative Christian cabinets impede, while unions and women in power facilitate, the development of maternity leave policy. These effects are sizable. Simulations show that moving from a country where conservative Christian parties have a limited role in government to a country where they play a substantial role (i.e., shifting from the 20th to the 80th percentile on the measure of conservative Christian cabinet strength used here) decreases paid maternity leave by almost four weeks. Relatedly, moving from a country with weak unions to one with strong unions, again a 20th to 80th percentile shift, increases maternity leave by approximately 2 weeks, as does moving from a country with few women in parliament to a country with many women in parliament (again a 20th to 80th percentile shift). Conservative Christian cabinets might also impede the development of family benefits (results not statistically significant) while fertility correlates positively with spending on family benefits.

To test whether politics are different in pioneer and late-adopter countries, model V was estimated separately on pioneer countries and on late adopters. These results are only summarized here; the full analyses are available from the author upon request.[60] Countries that adopted maternity leave before World War I, and thus before the 1919 ILO Maternity Convention and before an international maternity leave model was developed, were labeled pioneers; all others were late adopters.[61] This analysis supports the argument that strong domestic pressures are needed to bring about policy change the first time around, but that cross-national emulation, rather than domestic pressures, account for much of the policy development in late-adopter countries. More specifically, I find that coefficients on the main domestic political resources—religious cabinets, women in parliament, and unionized workers—were sizable in magnitude and statistically significant in the subsample of pioneer countries. In contrast, the coefficients on religious cabinets and women in parliament were much lower and statistically insignificant in the subsample of late adopters; the coefficient on unionization was statistically significant but smaller in magnitude for late adopters. Conversely, the coefficient on the spatial lag capturing emulation of familiar countries was very large and statistically significant for late-adopter countries; it was very small and statistically insignificant for pioneers.[62] In sum, in pioneer countries, policy adoption is explained mostly by domestic factors; in late-adopter countries, domestic factors play a much smaller role, and country-to-country emulation plays a much larger role.

Conclusions

This chapter's findings highlight that international organizations and country-to-country influences prove surprisingly powerful in explaining domestic family policy choices. More specifically, I find strong support for the central emulation mechanism proposed in this book: that governments mimic the policies of large, rich, and proximate foreign countries familiar to voters. Regressions predicting developments in maternity leave laws and government spending on families across advanced industrialized countries show that governments are more likely to imitate foreign countries whose news citizens follow. This diffusion mechanism helped explain both the development of family policies and the development of health policies described in chapter 4. There is no theoretical reason that makes emulation particularly suitable to these two areas. Thus this empirical regularity suggests that emulation may explain diffusion patterns in diverse fields. Additionally, this chapter reports that global norms, developed extensively through the ILO in the field of maternity leaves, shaped national choices: connectedness to the global system, measured by citizen involvement in INGOs, and ratification of ILO conventions were both linked to longer maternity leaves. Domestic forces, notably labor union protests, women in office, Christian parties, and demographic conditions can explain part of the variation in national family policies. However, domestic forces are particularly helpful in explaining the policy choices of early adopters; late adopters mimic international templates and adopt policies with far fewer domestic resources than pioneers.

7

Family Policy Development in Greece and Spain

Rich country governments use two main policy tools to redistribute significant resources toward families with children: family allowances and maternity leaves. Family allowances are cash and in-kind transfers to families with children. Maternity leaves are labor regulations protecting mothers' jobs around the time of the birth of a child, and are typically paid. Many rich countries also offer parental leaves, allowing both mothers and fathers time off from work to care for young children, but these are typically unpaid.

The previous chapter examined family policies across rich countries and used cross-country regressions to study how these policies are influenced by foreign models. This evidence supported the proposed theory of diffusion through democracy. The chapter reported that governments imitate the family policies of countries heavily covered in the national news media and familiar to voters and that international organization influence is greatest in countries whose publics are internationally oriented.

This chapter uses case study evidence to further explore the influence of foreign models on family policy developments. Case study evidence can document the mechanisms through which foreign models influence particular actors in the political system by presenting the views of voters, interest groups, and politicians. Analysis of the timing and content of reforms and of the rhetoric that accompanied policy change using primary and secondary sources highlights the centrality of foreign models to the development of family policy. This chapter employs multiple comparisons of such case studies: comparisons between the strength and coherence of international models, comparisons between countries' receptivity to foreign models during periods of democracy and autocracy, and comparisons between domestic politics in Spain and Greece.

Studying family policy allows me to compare the influence of different international templates within the same policy field. This chapter contrasts the strong influence of a maternity leave model that was developed early, defined precisely, and promoted forcefully by the International Labour Organization (ILO) with the more limited influence of a family allowance template that was developed much later, defined broadly, and promoted weakly. It is also helpful to contrast the strong efforts of the ILO to promote many workplace reforms with the weaker efforts of the World Health Organization (WHO) to promote the health care models discussed in chapters 4 and 5. While the WHO often limited itself to broad declarations and recommendations that were never legally binding, the ILO developed legally binding conventions, encouraged member states to become parties to these conventions, and monitored state progress even for states that chose not to join. The advantage of contrasting the two family policy reforms (maternity leaves and family allowances) is that important factors, such as the structure of domestic interest groups, are very similar in these two areas.

Nevertheless, the political processes of introducing and reforming maternity leave and family allowance policies were quite different in Greece and Spain depending on whether a strong international model existed. Greece and Spain adopted maternity leave policies very early—long before relevant domestic pressure groups developed—using the rhetoric of joining an international community. Later reforms occurred without much controversy because very diverse actors accepted the clear international template. In contrast, in the area of family allowances, where the international community offered a weaker template, Greece and Spain developed different policies and different groups subsequently fought over these forcefully. It is not unusual for different countries to develop different social policies or for social policy reforms to generate domestic controversy. After all, Spain is large and decentralized and the Catholic Church has played an important role in the development of its family policies. Conversely, Greece is a small and relatively homogeneous unitary state, and the Eastern Orthodox Church historically has taken a limited role in family policies.[1] What is striking about Greece and Spain is their very similar experiences with maternity leaves and the lack of domestic conflict on this issue within each country.

Studying family policy also allows me to contrast how receptive countries are to foreign models during periods of democracy versus during periods of autocracy. This comparison is possible because the ILO started promoting maternity leaves in 1919, the year it was founded, and both Greece and Spain have since experienced periods of democracy and periods of dictatorship.[2] Spain and Greece followed international templates closely in periods of democracy, whereas in periods of dictatorship they developed their own unconventional family policies. Family policy is not exceptional in this regard. This chapter also shows that Greece and Spain quickly ratified a broad range of ILO conventions on diverse labor issues during periods of democratic governance but were slower to adopt such conventions during periods of dictatorship. This pattern is consistent with the proposed theory that democracies often welcome international models. This is because ordinary citizens can use international models to benchmark their own government's policies and proposals.

Because I propose that democracies are very receptive to foreign models, in this chapter and in chapter 5 I focus on Spain and Greece in the late 1970s and early 1980s—the period immediately following their respective transitions to democracy. Studying this foundational period allows us to examine how political parties on both the left and the right positioned themselves on key social policy questions. While Socialists and conservatives differed on many social policy questions, they actively invoked foreign models in their campaigns and other public debates in both Greece and Spain. Despite stark partisan differences, they shared a belief that a particular vision of modernity would resonate with broad swaths of their electorates. This vision involved imitating rich western European countries and, moreover, doing so instead of imitating countries at similar levels of development in southern Europe, as theories of competition would predict.

Chapter 5 suggests that ideas from abroad not only influenced actors favorably predisposed to the international model, but also influenced expected opponents of the reform. More specifically, it shows that while Socialists actively campaigned to introduce National Health Services (NHSs) by referencing foreign models, conservatives who ultimately opposed the introduction of NHSs did not see the model's international pedigree as a negative. Instead, conservatives accepted that foreign models were relevant and persuasive, but contested how they should be interpreted and applied. This is even more striking in the area of family policy. In this field, conservatives were even more active in their use of foreign models and campaigned to expand some family programs by invoking international and European standards.

The evidence for these claims is organized in chronological order to create a clearer narrative. I begin with a discussion of maternity leave in Greece and Spain to show how both countries introduced maternity leave well before they industrialized, influenced by western European countries' policies and ILO conventions. I also show that they quickly adopted a broad range of other labor conventions developed by the ILO during periods of democratic governance. Next, I discuss the introduction of family allowances in these two countries and show how, in the absence of a clear international template, the countries diverged in their family allowance policies for much of the twentieth century. When the ILO belatedly and weakly started promoting family allowances in the early 1950s, Greece, a democracy at the time, responded. In contrast,

Spain, run by dictator Francisco Franco at the time, continued with its own highly unusual family policies.

Finally, I show how maternity leave was expanded in both countries following their transitions to democracy. Important reforms in maternity leave policy occurred before interest groups such as labor unions or feminist organizations started advocating for them in both countries. Instead, left-wing politicians promised voters that they would modernize their countries by adopting international and European maternity leave models, won repeated elections on these platforms, and faced limited opposition in introducing the relevant legislation. Conservative politicians who might have opposed well-compensated maternity leave because it benefits only working women, and thus discourages women from traditional homemaking roles, were silenced by the strong international model. Conversely, because the international template was much weaker in the area of family allowances, policy options were more heavily contested and the policies adopted in Greece and Spain were more varied.

Introducing Maternity Leaves in Greece and Spain: The Influence of the ILO

This section illustrates that Greece and Spain introduced paid maternity leave laws in the early 1920s and were strongly influenced to do so by international templates. Two important international milestones in family policy occurred in the late nineteenth and early twentieth centuries. First, the Berlin Conference of 1890 recommended a brief period of mandatory rest for working women around the time of childbirth. More importantly, in 1919, the ILO was founded in Washington, DC. That same year, the ILO promoted the eight-hour workday in its first convention, the adoption of unemployment insurance in its second convention, and twelve-week paid maternity leave in its third convention.

At the time they first introduced paid maternity leave laws, both Greece and Spain were constitutional monarchies with economies primarily based on agriculture. The timing of the introduction of maternity leaves was therefore striking because maternity leaves are labor regulations primarily designed to address the harsh conditions of factory work in industrialized economies. However, elected governments in both Greece and Spain introduced labor reforms before their countries industrialized and sought to anticipate and preempt demands from nascent labor unions by following international templates. This therefore supports my theoretical claim that foreign models allow late developers to introduce reforms earlier than we would otherwise expect. To retell this story I employ primary documents, but also rely heavily on unusually comprehensive and relevant secondary sources available for this period, such as Antonis Liakos' groundbreaking history of the influence of the ILO on Greek labor legislation in the interwar period.[3]

The model of policy development for late developers is quite different from the model followed by pioneers. For pioneers, a more standard domestic politics model applies: problems give rise to interest groups that in turn put pressure on politicians to adopt policies to solve these problems.[4] To demonstrate how policymaking occurs in pioneer countries, references to the British and French cases are useful. Census data from 1861 to 1911 reported that about 30% of British women were working, with 45% of these employed in industry and transport.[5] It took decades of labor and social activism for Britain to finally introduce a four-week unpaid maternity leave in 1891 and a paid maternity benefit in 1919.[6] Similarly, while French women's labor participation first exceeded 30% of the labor force in the 1860s, with about a third of these women working in industry and transport, it still took until 1913 for labor unions and social activists to successfully lobby for state-funded leaves.[7] In short, despite a sizable number of women in the workforce and extensive activism on behalf of maternity leave, it took decades of work to introduce reforms in pioneers such as England and France that industrialized early and pioneered maternity leave policies.

However, a much different process unfolded among late industrializers, as the Greek and Spanish experiences show. At the turn of the twentieth century, Greece was a predominantly agricultural country. According to the 1907 census, only 18% of the total population, and less than 3% of the female population, worked in industry.[8] Industrialization only took off in the mid-1920s, after 1.2 million refugees from Asia Minor arrived in a country of five million and dramatically increased its labor force.[9] Skilled workers' mutual help organizations surfaced in the 1870s, but the first modern labor union, the Greek Confederation of Labor, was not formed until 1918.[10] Furthermore, *The Ladies' Newspaper*, first issued in 1887, is considered the first evidence of Greek feminist activity, although its authors never used the term and shied away from the sensitive issue of political rights for women.[11]

Yet, as early as 1911, the Work Center of Athens presented a memorandum to the Greek parliament advocating for protective legislation for women and children. According to historians of this time period, "the center's memorandum took the existence of protective legislation for women and children in other countries as sufficient justification for its introduction into Greek society and assumed further debate was not necessary."[12] Parliament agreed and, in 1912 and 1913, introduced legislation protecting women and children who worked in industry. These laws did not create a right to paid maternity leave. Instead, they prohibited women and children from various types of work. For example, women were prohibited from work for eight weeks surrounding the birth of a child, among other things.[13]

Soon thereafter, in 1920, the Greek government ratified the Maternity Protection Convention introduced the previous year by the then newly founded ILO.[14] Under the leadership of Eleftherios Venizelos, the Greek government followed the international model and created a 12-week paid maternity leave for women.[15] In championing the legislation, Venizelos aimed to receive favorable international coverage for Greece's territorial ambitions and to anticipate and preempt the demands of the emerging labor movement.[16] While Greek feminists in the 1920s were divided on whether such legislation for women was desirable or unduly protectionist, some devoted their resources to writing to then ILO director Albert Thomas urging him to lobby the Greek government to improve women's wages and working conditions.[17] The subsequent introduction of the Greek Social Insurance Institute (IKA) in 1934 ensured the smooth administration and payment of this maternity leave allowance, which amounted to one-third of a woman's daily wage.[18] In summary, maternity leaves became available to Greek women prior to industrialization and prior to extensive labor union mobilization because a democratically elected Greek government followed foreign country and ILO models. Thus a desire to "reach the same level of civilization as the other civilized countries" helps explain Greek policymaking, whereas traditional domestic policymaking theories do not.[19]

The Spanish case is similar to the Greek one. Like Greece, Spain industrialized relatively late. In 1920 less than 22% of its workforce was employed in industry, although that figure conceals substantial regional variations.[20] A small and declining proportion of the workforce, less than 10% in 1920, was female, concentrated in agriculture and services.[21]

Despite this low overall industrialization and particularly low percentage of women in the industrial workforce, in 1900 and 1907, respectively, Spanish legislators followed norms introduced in 1890 at the first international conference on protective legislation in Berlin and passed three- and four-week "mandatory rest" periods for new mothers.[22] Soon after the 1919 Washington conference establishing the ILO and adopting the Maternity Leave Convention, Spain introduced paid maternity leave. Spanish legislation ratifying the Maternity Leave Convention and guaranteeing women 12 weeks of paid leave passed in July 1922.[23] In August 1923 a provisional fund to pay for this leave was set up.[24] As in Greece, Spanish participation in the first ILO conference in Washington, DC, is credited as a major motivating influence for the domestic legislation[25] and is mentioned prominently in the text of the law.

Fears of labor unrest were likely a contributor to the maternity leave legislation, as Spain had faced a crippling general strike in 1917. However, it is unclear that maternity leave was a prominent demand of the Spanish labor movement. Indeed, in later years, strikes in the more industrialized region of Catalonia focused on fighting maternity leave.[26] Single and widowed women, heavily represented in the workforce, thought it unfair that they had to contribute to social insurance funds benefiting mothers only.[27] Nevertheless, maternity leave grew solid roots in Spain. The military government of Primo de Rivera, which ruled Spain from September 1923 through January 1930, continued with the maternity leave scheme. In 1931, when Spain had entered its Second Republic period, a permanent scheme to insure women was implemented.[28]

These patterns were not limited to Spain and Greece. Interestingly, even a country like Sweden, considered the leader in family and work policies in the post–World War II period, was a late adopter of these policies in the late nineteenth and early twentieth centuries, as it industrialized relatively late. Sweden attended the first international conference on protective legislation in Berlin in 1890 and set up a parliamentary committee the following year "to consider to what extent the basic principles agreed upon at said conference ought to be applied in Sweden."[29] The committee found no immediate need for such reforms, as there were few women working in factories, even fewer returning to work less than four weeks after giving birth, and no complaints about the current policies. However, despite these factual findings, the domestic deliberations following the Berlin conference resulted in Sweden introducing its first law regulating the work of adult women in 1900. The law included four weeks of unpaid maternity leave "in accordance with the practice in other countries."[30]

This section has argued that foreign models allowed Greece and Spain to introduce maternity leaves well before domestic political demands and crises associated with industrialization made this essential. Elected leaders quickly imitated international models in an attempt to modernize their countries and diffuse possible future labor tensions. Is it possible that Greece and Spain adopted maternity leave policies because of, rather than in spite of, the limited need for such reforms at the time? Undoubtedly the immediate cost of maternity leave policies is low in agricultural societies. However, the Greek and Spanish governments in the 1920s ratified a large number of available conventions quickly.[31] These early conventions included ILO Convention 1, the convention establishing the eight-hour workday. The eight-hour workday was a central issue of labor conflict in early twentieth century with very substantial economic costs. This suggests that the breadth of ILO influence on both countries was substantial in multiple areas, not simply in maternity leave policy reform. The next section tests this claim more systematically.

Rapid Ratification of Many ILO Conventions in Periods of Democracy in Greece and Spain

While enthusiasm surrounding the establishment of the ILO was especially great in 1919, the organization continued to be influential in subsequent decades. This section studies ILO conventions systematically and illustrates that Greece and Spain were especially receptive to these conventions during periods of democratic governance. This is consistent with this book's thesis that democracy reinforces, rather than impedes, the diffusion of international models.

Since 1919, Greece and Spain have ratified dozens of ILO conventions on diverse labor standards, including all the conventions the ILO considers fundamental.[32] One way to conceptualize the ILO's power to give prominence to particular labor regulations and inspire governments to prioritize these is by studying conventions that countries ratified soon after they were adopted by the ILO.

As a first measure of the ILO's agenda-setting power, I study how many ILO conventions Greece and Spain ratified promptly, defined as conventions ratified within five years of their adoption by the ILO. ILO member states have an obligation to consider ratifying ILO conventions by putting them before their legislative bodies in a timely fashion.[33] However, ratifying any particular convention is not a legal obligation and likely requires significant support from domestic actors in addition to any push that comes from the international organization. This analysis does not include conventions that were ratified more than five years after they were adopted. For example, in Greece, the first Socialist administration elected in 1981 ratified many ILO conventions from the 1940s, 1950s, and 1960s. One way to interpret these late ratifications is as evidence of the continued relevance of the ILO. However, it is also plausible to argue that the government would have enacted the identical labor regulations absent the international organization's proposals. This question about whether ratification at any point in time should count as influence of the international organization has triggered heated debates in the international law and international relations literature.[34] To sidestep this issue, I focus on ratifications within the five-year window after the ILO conventions were adopted by the international organization, as it is more plausible to attribute these labor regulations, at least in part, to the agenda-setting power of the ILO.

This analysis suggests that Greece and Spain were very receptive to international standards during periods of democratic rule and somewhat less receptive to international standards during periods of autocratic rule. Between 1919 and 2011, Spain enjoyed 45 years of democratic rule, during which it ratified 42 ILO conventions promptly, or about one convention per year. In contrast, in its 43 years of autocratic rule, Spain ratified ILO conventions at a slower pace—it only ratified 25 ILO conventions promptly (i.e., within the five-year window after they were adopted). Greece, too, was more receptive to the ILO models during periods of democratic governance. During periods of democratic governance, Greece ratified approximately one ILO convention every 3 years, while during periods of autocratic rule, it ratified approximately one convention every 6 years. These patterns are consistent with this book's claims that democracies are receptive to foreign models and that foreign models are not necessarily imposed on unsuspecting citizens. Figure 7.1 presents these data in more detail.

To classify periods as democratic or autocratic, I used the Polity IV data set and standard political historiographies. It should be noted that several Greek and Spanish administrations in the 1920s and 1930s, as well as several Greek administrations in the 1950s and 1960s, are traditionally classified as democratic, a classification followed here, because they held regular elections and guaranteed important civil liberties. However, citizens of both countries did not enjoy full and stable democratic governance until the late 1970s.[35]

Introducing and Expanding Family Allowances in Greece and Spain

This section illustrates that, absent a clear international template for family allowances, Greece and Spain adopted their own somewhat idiosyncratic policies in the 1930s and 1940s. Once even a weak international template became available in the early 1950s, democratic administrations in Greece welcomed this. In contrast, Spain's dictator Francisco Franco continued with his own very unusual family allowances policies. Together, these claims further my central theoretical claim that international policy diffusion is consistent with domestic democracy and leads to the adoption of similar policies in countries that might otherwise follow divergent routes.

While the ILO developed detailed policies on maternity leaves in 1919, its first year of existence, and updated these policies in 1952 and 2000, equivalent templates were not available in the field of family allowances. The ILO did not mention family allowances in its conventions until 1952, long after many countries, including both Greece and Spain, first introduced these measures. Moreover, it only mentioned family allowances in a context of a broad convention on social security rather than a specific convention on this issue, as in the case of maternity leave. ILO Convention 102, the Social Security Minimum Standards Convention, mentions nine types of social benefits governments can offer: medical, sickness, unemployment, old age, employment injury,

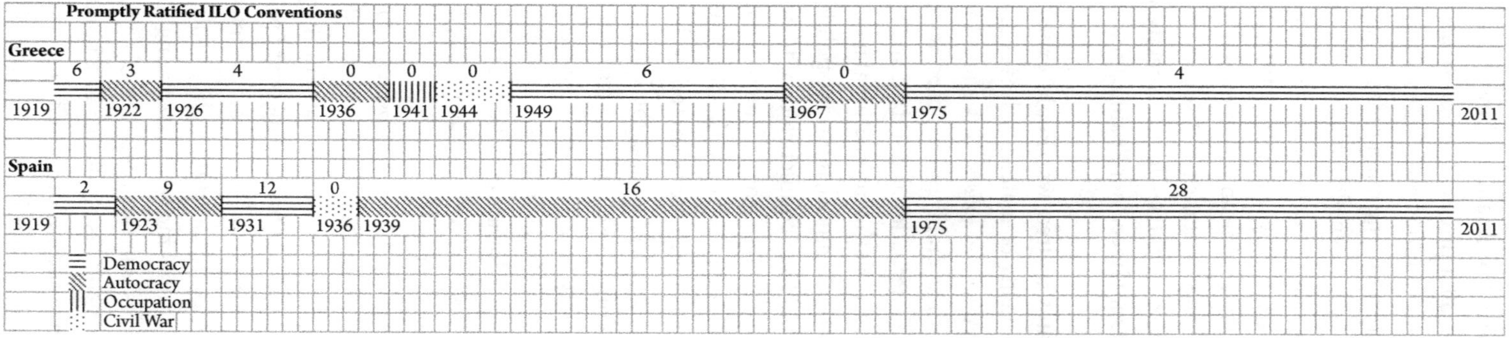

Figure 7.1 Promptly Ratified ILO Conventions

maternity, invalidity, survivor, and family allowances. To comply with this convention, countries must offer three of the nine benefits from this menu. In addition, the convention is flexible on how countries can structure the benefits they offer, allowing for all three of the main types of social benefit structures: universal benefits, means-tested benefits, and benefits based on social insurance contributions.[36] Greece was a democracy in 1952 and ratified this convention soon after it was adopted by the ILO in 1955. In contrast, Spain was an autocracy at the time, isolated from international institutions. It did not ratify this convention until after its transition to democracy in 1988.[37] Notably, in ratifying Convention 102, countries had to specify which three benefits they intend to offer.[38] Neither Greece nor Spain committed to offering family allowances.

If international templates matter, we should expect domestic policy to develop differently in the fields of maternity leaves and family allowances. Where a clear international model exists, this should mute domestic policy conflict. It should drive both favorably predisposed actors and negatively predisposed actors toward the international standard and lead to the adoption of domestic policies consistent with the international model. Conversely, in the absence of a strong international model, domestic politics should explain policy outcomes fully. We should see conflict-ridden domestic political debates and greater diversity in the policies different countries and different administrations ultimately adopt. This is in fact what the discussion that follows shows. The influence of the ILO was much more limited in the area of family allowances than in the area of maternity leave, as the ILO convention mentioning family allowances—Convention 102—arrived late and was not very specific. ILO Convention 102 was only occasionally referenced by advocates for family allowances during policy debates in Greece and Spain and had a limited impact in the design of family allowances policy in these countries. Its impact on Greece was greater because Greece was a democracy when this convention was adopted, while Spain was not.

Spain first introduced family allowances policies for families with many children under the Miguel Primo de Rivera dictatorship (1923–1930), but these were relatively modest.[39] Subsequently, family policy was radically revised soon after Franco solidified his control over Spain. The early decades of the Franco dictatorship were periods of almost complete international isolation for Spain. In 1942 Franco made family policy central to his social efforts and introduced the Plus Familial measure. According to this measure, a percentage of industrial workers' salaries (between 5% and 25%) was collected and redistributed among coworkers according to a point system, with points given for a dependent spouse and children.[40] Civil servants became recipients of equivalent family policy programs in 1954.[41] Additional family allowances, such as supplements for families with many children,[42] were also introduced, along with prizes and other symbolic awards for especially prolific parents. These policies helped promote conservative understandings of the family consistent with Francoist ideology. For example, the size of the benefits increased substantially when women chose to leave the workforce and stay at home; the father, rather than the mother, could claim the benefits; and only children born following a Catholic wedding were eligible.[43] However, these measures also served as important antipoverty measures. Meil Landwerlin estimates that, in total, direct spending on families constituted more than 50% of Spanish social security expenditures through the 1960s.[44] In sum, under an internationally isolated dictatorship, Spain developed extensive family allowances programs, but these were highly idiosyncratic in form and reflected the Franco regime's very conservative ideology.

In the later years of the Franco dictatorship, Spain developed ties with foreign countries and international organizations and undertook major economic and social policy reforms. Spain was accepted as a member of the United Nations (UN) in 1955 and joined other international bodies soon thereafter. In 1963 Spain's modern social insurance laws were introduced and family policy was reformed, including eliminating the Plus Familial. Family allowances remained, but per child amounts became the same regardless of birth order. A 1964 tax reform cut some of the tax benefits for families with many children. By Franco's death in 1975, family allowances represented only 1% of Spain's gross domestic product (GDP).[45] This more limited role of family allowances in a social insurance system put Spain in line with other European countries. In addition, as mentioned earlier, it is in this second part of the Franco dictatorship that Spain showed some receptivity to international standards by ratifying several ILO conventions.

Greece's experience with family allowances was quite different from Spain's. In the 1930s and 1940s, a variety of laws conferring small regulatory advantages to families with many children were passed. The most important of these was Law 1910/1944, which, among other provisions, set up charitable funds for impoverished large families.[46] Unlike in contemporary Spain, these benefits were of limited economic significance. They also did not reflect Franco's highly conservative understanding of the family. Under the Greek benefits legislation, working women, women with illegitimate children, and single women were not treated less favorably than other women. Notably, Greece introduced the first extensive system of family allowances in the 1950s—only after the ILO had proposed its weak model; the country ratified ILO Convention 102 in 1955, three years after it was adopted. As mentioned above, by ratifying this convention, Greece did not commit to offering family allowances as specified by Convention 102; rather, it only considered extending benefits in this field over time. In fact, Greece inserted family allowances into its social insurance system in 1958, following ILO proposals and domestic advocacy. Throughout the late 1950s, private sector workers had lobbied in favor of family allowances and other workplace benefits by claiming that Greek workers had less favorable working terms than workers in other European countries.[47] Under Law 3868/1958, implemented by Royal Decree 23/1959, family allowances were made available to many categories of private sector salaried employees.[48]

In summary, Spain and Greece developed different family benefits' policies in the 1930s and 1940s, in the absence of a clear international template. After the ILO started promoting family benefits in the 1950s, Greece, a democracy at the time, was receptive to this template. In contrast, Spain, ruled by the isolated Franco dictatorship, developed its own idiosyncratic system of benefits. Because family allowances were a flagship policy of the Franco regime, they were highly stigmatized in Spain following its transition to democracy. In posttransition Greece, they did not carry the same stigma because family allowances were not strongly associated with the Colonels' dictatorship that governed Greece from 1967 to 1974.

Maternity Leaves Following Greece and Spain's Transitions to Democracy

Following their transitions to democracy in the late 1970s and 1980s, both Greece and Spain used international models to expand their maternity and parental leave policies. Both extended the length of paid maternity leaves, expanded the number of workers who were eligible to qualify for such leaves, and introduced new parental leaves available to both men and women. The introduction of these reforms is consistent with the proposed theory of diffusion through democracy, which suggests that democratic regimes will be receptive to international models and politicians will highlight international models in an effort to persuade skeptical voters that their policies are mainstream and competently designed.

In the late 1970s and 1980s, the Greek and Spanish Socialist parties (Panhellenic Socialist Movement [PASOK] and Partido Socialista Obrero Español [PSOE], respectively) promised to modernize Greece and Spain and to offer benefits comparable to those available in rich western European countries, as chapter 5 describes. Both parties won repeated electoral victories on these platforms and introduced major reforms before Greek and Spanish civil society groups had a chance to organize and formulate these types of demands from the bottom up. Specific international templates, in the form of ILO conventions, were central to debates to introduce these laws. Greek and Spanish politicians had no legal obligation to reform their maternity and parental leaves deriving from ILO membership. They had a choice about whether to ratify particular ILO conventions, and often first reformed a domestic social policy and then ratified the relevant convention. However, the persuasive power of these international templates was significant, so Socialist politicians referenced international standards in diverse public forums to persuade voters of the wisdom of their policies.

Very clear international templates in the area of maternity leaves also influenced conservative politicians. In both Spain and Greece, domestic debate was muted and these leave expansions were relatively uncontroversial. Maternity leaves are sometimes opposed by conservative politicians because they are regulations that burden employers and confer benefits on working women, thus encouraging women to work outside the home. Nevertheless, in Greece and Spain, politicians from all political stripes accepted the normative legitimacy of the international templates the ILO offered and did not object to the progressive vision of women's workforce participation that maternity and parental leaves reflected. Conversely, as the subsequent section explains, there was heated debate in the area of family allowances where the international standards were less clear.

I concentrate on reforms in the 1970s and 1980s because this is the era when critical reforms happened in Spain and Greece and because the international environment in this field changed in the 1990s. In the 1990s, the European Union (EU) introduced binding directives in the areas of maternity and parental leaves. While ILO members can choose to ratify or not ratify particular conventions, EU member states have a legal obligation to introduce national legislation to comply with all EU directives addressed to them. In practice, EU member states typically meet their obligations, although national laws are often introduced after substantial delays.[49] However, EU directives are often adopted late, after most member states have already introduced related national laws. This was the case with directives on maternity and parental leaves. Because the ILO started promoting maternity leaves in the 1910s, while the EU started promoting them in the 1990s, the ILO, an organization with far fewer legal tools and economic resources at its disposal than the EU, had a far greater influence on Greek and Spanish policy.

These reforms cannot easily be explained by bottom-up pressures from organized interest groups alone. The reforms were introduced at a time when fewer than half of Spanish and Greek women worked. Labor unions did not take an interest in gender equality or family policy during this period but joined the debate later on.[50] Feminists in Greece and Spain were quite active in the 1980s, but they prioritized questions such as divorce and abortion, steering clear of topics that implicated women's responsibilities as homemakers. In the 1990s, feminists in both Greece and Spain were able to shape family policy more directly by creating women's secretariats and institutes, but these were built and gained influence after the reforms studied here.[51] In Spain, family organizations had negligible impact on policymaking because they had few members and were organized at the local or regional level, and thus lacked suitable national representation.[52] In Greece, they were somewhat more organized, but their impact on policy formulation was weak.[53] Similarly, there is little evidence that preschool teachers or other care providers were organized in ways to influence political debates.[54] The subsequent sections illustrate that despite limited bottom-up pressures for immediate reform, both Greece and Spain extended maternity and parental leaves soon after their transitions to democracy, following international templates.

These circumstances were much less favorable than those necessary to introduce such reforms for the first time. Indicatively, when Sweden pioneered parental leave in 1974 by making 6 months of leave available to either parent in addition to maternity leave, it had had decades of social democratic government in power, the policy was supported by the country's main trade union, and two-thirds of Swedish women were participating in the labor market.[55]

Expanding Maternity Leaves and Introducing Parental Leaves in Greece

In Greece, important reforms in family policy happened in the early 1980s under the first Socialist administration governing Greece from 1981 to 1985. Statutory maternity leave was extended to 12 weeks in 1982, when Greece ratified ILO Convention 103. In accordance with this 1952 ILO convention, Greek law made the last 6 weeks of the leave obligatory, placing a limitation on women's choices that upset some feminists. Additionally, parental leave was first introduced in 1984. This legislation is considered a milestone for Greek policy because it also provided a number of other benefits to working parents, including the requirement that large firms offer onsite child care facilities.[56] Initially, three months of unpaid leave were offered to each parent, during which the worker's post would be reserved. This right is nontransferable, to encourage fathers to take up some child care duties. At first the law only covered private sector workers in large firms, but the law's coverage was subsequently greatly expanded. The details of the passage of the law are discussed below, but it is important to note that feminists and labor unions were focused on very different matters in 1984 in Greece.[57] Instead, Socialists campaigned by promising Greek women that they would soon enjoy the same rights that women in other Western countries enjoyed. In addition, the ILO convention on workers with family responsibilities, Convention 156, was used as a backdrop and standard reference in parliamentary debates.[58] Greece ratified the ILO convention in 1988 and further expanded parental leave benefits to cover public sector workers.

Reaching Western standards of gender equality and offering benefits to working women were important themes of Greece's 1981 campaign that brought the Socialist PASOK party to power. To present one such example, Figure 7.2 shows the front page of the pro-PASOK newspaper *To Βήμα* from September 22, 1981. It covers a major speech on gender equality that candidate Andreas Papandreou offered on September 21, 1981, less than a month before his landslide victory. Important reforms promised in this speech, in many other speeches during the campaign, and in the PASOK manifesto included civil weddings, legal abortions, nondiscrimination in the workplace, expansion of leaves for parents, and increased child care facilities. To justify these reforms, Papandreou's speech highlighted, and the front-page article in *To Βήμα* repeated, that the position of Greek women was very disappointing

Figure 7.2 Front Page of *To Βήμα* on September 22, 1981, Covering a Papandreou Speech Focused on Gender Equality

relative to the position of women in other Western countries. Other leading Socialists also justified their reforms by reference to international standards. For example, Figure 5.3 in chapter 5 and the accompanying text presents the promises Paraskevas Avgerinos made on election day, October 18, 1981. Paraskevas Avgerinos was a prominent PASOK member who became the first PASOK minister for health and social welfare. His prominently placed statement not only justified the introduction of health reform by reference to the other Western countries and to the WHO, but it also clarified that PASOK would focus on working women, ratify all the relevant international conventions that protect motherhood, and expand child care facilities.[59]

Parliamentary discussion of Greece's laws on maternity and parental leaves took place very smoothly, even though many other PASOK proposals generated great controversy. The ratification of ILO Convention 103 on maternity protection in 1982, which extended maternity leave to 12 weeks, occurred without parliamentary debate. In 1984 an important bill introducing parental leave and other measures to reconcile work and family responsibilities described above also prompted limited discussion.[60] Speakers from all parties supported the principle of giving parents leave, arguing that parental leave was a universally accepted measure enshrined in ILO Convention 156.[61] The ILO adopted Convention 156 on Workers with Family Responsibilities in 1981, but Greece had not ratified this convention at the time of the 1984 debates. Consensus among all parties was very surprising given the contentious nature of Greek political debate, and speakers for the governing Socialists went as far as to commend the conservative opposition for their support.[62] All proposed amendments, from left and right alike, favored extending the leave program. Making the leave compensated, extending its length, and broadening the bill's coverage to include more workers were the common suggestions.[63] Opposition delegates criticized the government's decision to limit the bill's ambit to private sector employees by repeatedly invoking ILO Convention 156, which does not make any such distinction.[64] The government representatives also viewed ILO Convention 156 as an implicit standard, soon to be reached.[65] They assured the parliament that the bill's provisions were in accordance with ILO Convention 156, at least with regard to public sector employees, and that extension of the convention's protection to the remaining employee groups was imminent.[66]

What is missing from these debates is just as illustrative as the focus on ILO conventions. First, the debate clearly indicates that interest groups had no input on the bill. The Communist Party spokesperson, Diamantis Mavrodoglou, complained that neither the main labor confederation, General Confederation of Greek Workers (GSEE), nor other unions were consulted.[67] The conservative spokesperson, Efrosini Spentzari, asked why the public sector union, Civil Servants' Confederation (ADEDY), did not protest its exclusion from the leave.[68] She also condemned women's groups' lack of interest in family policy.[69] Second, unlike in the family policy debates where delegates lined up to discuss their constituents' difficulties, debates on maternity leave contained fewer references to problems working women in Greece already faced. These debates suggest that Greece introduced maternity leave earlier than it would have in the absence of foreign models, well before working women, labor unions, and feminists demanded these reforms. The availability of foreign models allowed favorably inclined Socialist politicians to bring gender equality reforms to the agenda early on. And the influence of these models was not limited to favorably inclined Socialist politicians, but extended to conservative leaders who might otherwise have opposed reforms facilitating women's work outside the home.

Expanding Maternity Leaves and Introducing Parental Leaves in Spain

Spain followed a similar trajectory to Greece, expanding paid maternity leaves and introducing unpaid parental leaves in line with international templates as it transitioned to democracy. Spain expanded maternity leave from 12 to 14 weeks, first temporarily through Law 16/1976 and then permanently through Law 8/1980,[70] and it expanded maternity leave once more to 16 weeks through Law 3/1989.[71] In 1989 Spain also introduced unpaid child care leaves, which allowed both parents to take up to a year of leave and then return to their previous jobs.

From the first election campaign onward, the Spanish Socialist party PSOE promised that it would introduce rights and benefits already available to citizens of Spain's richer European neighbors. Chapter 5 explains how PSOE made such appeals to promote its health reform efforts. PSOE also prioritized gender equality as an important goal in each of its electoral manifestos. For example, in its 1977 manifesto, PSOE campaigned for "a type of life proper for an industrial society of the European type,"[72] a life that includes "the full equality of rights for women."[73] The Socialists made similar appeals in their 1979 and 1982 manifestos.

After coming to power in 1982, PSOE claimed credit for narrowing the distance between Spain and richer western European countries and sought reelection to fully close this gap. In 1986, after four years in power, PSOE's manifesto stated that "today, the Spanish citizen enjoys a system of rights and liberties comparable to that of any Western European country."[74] However, according to the manifesto, while PSOE had made significant progress toward "a fairer society for women," more legal and social modernization was needed to make Spain's situation "comparable to the situation of countries in the European community." PSOE also promised to expand social security benefits and improve working hours, following the lead of European Economic Community (EEC) countries. Again, PSOE offered a message of partial but still incomplete progress in its 1989 manifesto:

> Today, Spanish women enjoy equality rights that are comparable to those women enjoy in the more advanced European countries. Nevertheless, there are still obstacles to their full and equal participation in work, culture and politics. For many women, it is still difficult to reconcile professional life and family, to access jobs considered masculine or positions of responsibility and decisions.[75]

While PSOE took credit for trying "to cover the large historical gap in social services between Spain and the other European Community countries,"[76] it promised further reforms to close this gap more completely.

These promises to expand maternity leave following European and international standards were also central to debates in parliament introducing the relevant legislation. To illustrate this point, I discuss the introduction of Law 3/1989.[77] I focus on this law both because it was a very significant law for working women in Spain, and because, by 1989, Spanish legislation was in many ways very similar to that of many European countries. It is thus interesting to note that Spanish politicians not only referenced European and international standards when Spain was far behind, but they continued to reference foreign models as Spanish legislation became more protective of working women than the European average in some respects. Perhaps the most significant reform introduced by Law 3/1989 was an extension of paid maternity leave to 16 weeks and 18 weeks in the case of mothers with multiple births. This reform, according to the text of the law, was intended to allow for sufficient attention to the health of the mother and to the betterment of her relationship with the child, "following the recommendations of the World Health Organization."[78] The law also made the last six weeks of maternity leave, following the birth of the child, mandatory, in accordance with Spain's obligations under ILO Convention 103.[79] Other provisions of the law created unpaid child care leave for both parents, and allowed workers to challenge sexual harassment in the workplace. It is striking how quickly sexual harassment laws spread from their first introduction in the United States in 1980, through guidelines of the Equal Employment Opportunity Commission (EEOC), to much of Europe soon thereafter.[80] In the case of Spain, other scholars have noted that it was possible to pass sexual harassment legislation relatively early because of the "strong social and political support for integrating Spain into the groups of economically developed and politically democratic countries ... because the matter was already regulated in the countries Spain sought to emulate."[81]

Manuel Chaves González, then PSOE labor minister, who later rose to become PSOE chairman, introduced Law 3/1989 to parliament by making repeated references to international organizations and foreign countries. He noted that equality of opportunity for men and women was a fundamental principle of the EEC, and discussed both the EU treaty and more specific European legislative proposals.[82] However, he explained that Spain was already in compliance with its EU obligations.[83] He argued that the proposed legislation, which "implemented the Socialists' electoral commitments," expanded maternity leave following other international organization recommendations.[84] Chaves noted that "the World Health Organization favored extending maternity leave as much as possible."[85] He noted that other aspects of the legislation were consistent with ILO standards, such as the fact that 6 weeks of that leave were made obligatory, and that the leave could be transferred to the father in case of the mother's death.[86] He celebrated the fact that the proposed legislation would put Spain "at the same level of the European Economic Community that are most advanced on this subject, like France and Denmark, and ahead of the majority of European countries that continue to offer maximum leaves of 14 weeks."[87] Another important theme in Chaves' speech concerned Spanish women's growing participation in the labor market. He noted that Spanish women's participation had just reached 32.8% in 1998, a number that is "still low if compared to the European median."[88] The fact that comparatively few Spanish women were working, and thus in need of leave, suggests that once more the Spanish government used international models to anticipate bottom-up demands, introducing legislation earlier than we would otherwise expect in order to ensure electoral victories.

Many members of parliament, both from the governing Socialists and from minority regional parties, echoed these themes. For example, representative Rafael Hinojosa i Lusena explained that he and other members of the Catalan minority supported the law even though it was imperfect because "it is a progressive law that brings us closer to Europe."[89] Some conservative delegates disagreed with the law, but even these did not take issue with the fact that international comparisons were appropriate benchmarks. For example, Celia Villalobos Talero argued not against leave in general, but rather that it was best that Spain offer the same level of benefits as most other European countries, meaning 14 weeks of paid maternity leave rather than 16 weeks.[90] At the end of the day, however, the law passed easily with very broad support from multiple parties.[91]

In summary, soon after transitioning to democracy, Greece and Spain expanded their maternity and parental leave programs in very similar ways and following clear international templates. These maternity leave reforms formed part of both Socialist parties' broader agendas to modernize their countries and offer benefits similar to those offered in other rich western European countries. This agenda, and the messaging used to promote it, were very popular among voters, as evidenced by repeated Socialist Party victories in both countries throughout the 1980s and much of the 1990s. Moreover, strong international models allowed maternity leave reforms to be placed on both countries' agendas early on, before well-organized domestic interest groups built bottom-up demands for such reforms. It is very possible that, absent these international models, other pressing needs for economic and political reform would have taken priority. Strong international models also allowed these reforms to pass without great political controversy. Absent these clear international templates, might Greek and Spanish conservatives have put up greater opposition to reforms that encouraged women to participate in the workforce? How might maternity leave policy have developed in the absence of a strong international model? The next section looks to the development of family allowances to answer this question.

Family Allowances Following the Transition to Democracy in Greece and Spain

Family allowances developed quite differently from maternity leaves following the transition to democracy in Greece and Spain, in part because there was no strong international template in this field. In the absence of a strong international template, and without intense bottom-up demands, family allowances were not placed high on the policy agenda of either country in the 1970s and 1980s. Additionally, the limited reforms that were made were quite different in the two countries. In Greece, there were modest expansions in benefits, while in Spain there were some cutbacks and controversy because family allowances were closely associated with the discredited Franco regime.

As I explain below, all of this is consistent with the prior literature. I present it here in part to create a counterfactual scenario for a policy that is similar to maternity and parental leaves, but lacked a forceful international template. No two policy areas are identical, but, as chapter 6 explains, maternity leave and family allowances have important similarities, as they both benefit families with young children and impose comparable costs on the state budget. The family benefits counterfactual can help highlight how striking the influence of a clear, forcefully promoted international template in the area of maternity and parental leave was. This international leave model promoted by the ILO enabled maternity and parental leave to be prioritized, to be reformed consistently in two different countries, and to generate little controversy. That being said, while family allowances were ultimately not expanded in Spain in the 1970s and 1980s, conservative politicians campaigned to introduce these reforms and partially succeeded many years later. I present these campaign promises here to show how Spanish conservatives used international and European references to try to dissociate family allowances from the Franco dictatorship and to reframe these benefits as appropriate for a modern democracy. As major reforms did not happen in either country in the period studied here, this section is brief. For more comprehensive histories of the domestic politics of family policies in southern European countries, Manuela Naldini as well as Ussel and Meil Landwerlin provide excellent introductions.[92]

Absent a clear international template and without strong bottom-up pressure from labor unions, feminists, and profamily associations, the expansion of family allowances did not become a priority item on either Greece or Spain's national agenda. This is not surprising. In the wake of the 1970s oil crises, the two fledgling democracies had dozens of other economic and political issues to resolve, including guaranteeing civil rights and civil liberties, setting up democratic institutions, and battling very high levels of inflation.[93] What is surprising is that amidst the many pressures these posttransition governments faced, they prioritized maternity and parental leaves. This is because Greek and Spanish politicians presented such reforms as key components of what modern European countries should offer.

In contrast, reforms in the area of family allowances were not only minor, but were also very different in the two countries. Socialists in Greece expanded family allowances somewhat through Law 1346/83. This law introduced an additional benefit for the third child of certain categories of workers covered by specific social insurance funds. Conversely, the most important family benefit reform in Spain, Law 26/1985, explicitly eliminated many unusual benefits available during the Franco era for dependent spouses and very large families. This law "adapted the Spanish legislation to the standard practice in the EEC," but preserved important benefits for dependent children that were also available in many European countries.[94] While explicit reforms in this area were limited, in both countries high rates of inflation eroded the value of family allowances throughout the 1980s.

The divergent trajectories of Greece and Spain are not surprising. In the absence of a strong international template, and given the diverse domestic political pressures, we have no expectation that countries will move in lockstep. However, the difference in Greek and Spanish responses to family allowances puts into perspective their very similar reforms in the area of maternity and parental leave.

Following Spain's transition to democracy, debates on the question of family policy were tainted by the Franco regime's choices. It did not help matters that Manuel Fraga, the Conservative Party leader for much of the 1980s, had previously held important ministerial posts under Franco. To dissociate family allowances from their Francoist past and present them as appropriate for modern democracies, conservative politicians referenced diverse available European and international standards, as none of these spoke forcefully on their preferred policy. While Spanish Socialists and conservatives disagreed on whether family benefits should be extended, it is important to note that both campaigned on the promise of bringing Spain closer to Europe, a promise that included modernizing Spain's welfare state. In their 1977 manifesto, the conservatives promised "an advanced social policy", "along the lines of modern conservative, centrist, and populist parties, that offer many services in all European countries."[95] They called for family allowances to be increased, given the rising cost of goods, and for special benefits to be given to very large families.[96]

Conservatives repeated these themes in subsequent manifestos. For example, in their 1982 manifesto, the party called for greater benefits to be given to stay-at-home wives following "the resolution of the Committee of Ministers of the Council of Europe and its Parliamentary Assembly."[97] In their 1986 manifesto, conservatives said "it was especially necessary to reform family allowances offered through the Social Security System, to ensure that they are not merely symbolic, and increase their quantity to the levels of benefits available in other countries of the European Community,"[98] and also emphasized that it was important "to amend Spanish legislation to conform with European legislation (Directive 79/7 of November 19, 1978) to avoid sex discrimination in Social Security matters, in both the receipt of benefits and in annulment, separation, and divorce proceedings."[99] These campaign promises show that the conservatives were no different from the Socialists in using diverse international references to present their preferred proposals as mainstream and well designed to voters who might otherwise be concerned that these were radical and ill-thought-out experiments.

Similarly, delegates of the Conservative Party, as well as occasionally the Catalans and the center-right party Centro Democrático y Social, tried to raise the issue of family allowances in parliament, but they did so relatively infrequently and without much success. The entirety of parliamentary questions and proposals on the topic of family allowances in the 1978–1989 period took up just a page and a half.[100] But even in the small space dedicated to the topic, references to ILO Convention 102 were an important element in this questioning.[101] Because the governing Socialists saw family allowances as a remnant of the Franco regime, and because there was no strong international template to emulate, the governing Socialist Party did not respond positively to this line of discussion. As late as 1989, when conservative delegates asked the governing Socialists to develop a coordinated policy to protect families, Social Affairs

Minister Mathilde Fernandez replied that it was best not to protect families as such, but instead their individual members. Moreover, she argued that there was not one family, but different classes of families, because it is in the family where social stratification can be most clearly seen.[102]

In summary, in the absence of a strong international template for family allowances, there was significant partisan controversy over the direction of reforms in this policy area. This contrasts sharply with the area of maternity and parental leave, where a strong international template allowed conservatives, Socialists, and Communists alike to quickly agree on appropriate reforms.

Conclusions

The case studies presented in this chapter have shown how elected leaders incorporate foreign models into their policymaking processes, focusing on politicians' efforts to use foreign models to legitimate their preferred policies by persuading voters that they are mainstream and well designed. Spain and Greece developed policies very differently in the case of maternity and parental leaves, where clear foreign templates were available starting in 1919, than in the case of family allowances, where less clear international templates were developed much later.

In the case of leaves, strong international models led democratically elected administrations in both Greece and Spain to first introduce maternity leaves in the early 1920s, anticipating voter demands and preempting labor union protests. Following both countries' return to democracy in the late 1970s, political leaders and citizens on both the right and left disagreed on many social policy questions, but agreed that they should modernize their countries following international and European standards. Therefore the availability of clear international models on questions of maternity and parental leaves helped mainstream policies that promoted gender equality that might have otherwise been controversial in these conservative societies. Socialists in Greece and Spain successfully campaigned for gender equality generally and for leaves to help working women in particular, and conservatives never seriously challenged these reform proposals. Policy debates took the form of the approval, adaptation, and extension of foreign models.

In the case of family allowances, where international organization proposals were developed later and templates were less clear, domestic reform efforts proved controversial, and Greece and Spain pursued different reforms. Most interestingly, influenced by the centrality of family policy under Franco, Spanish Socialists understood family allowances as backwards and singled out this social policy area for cuts. Conservative politicians who sought to expand family allowances tried to legitimate their reform proposals by referencing European and international standards, but were unsuccessful in their efforts in the 1970s and 1980s.

Finally, we have seen that the influence of international models is great in many other areas of labor and social reforms. Greece and Spain quickly ratified a large number of ILO conventions, especially under democratic administrations. Chapters 4 and 5 showed how international models influenced health policy reform. The next chapter, chapter 8, concludes by discussing the implications of these findings for international organizations and domestic reform advocates.

8

Conclusions and Implications

This book bridges two large literatures: the literature on international diffusion and the literature on domestic policymaking. Earlier theories of policy diffusion in international and comparative law, international relations, and organizational sociology focus on political elites; they emphasize interactions within networks of experts, national bureaucrats, and politicians. In these accounts, decision-makers travel to international meetings, exchange ideas with their foreign colleagues, and then bring international models home. However, these accounts are in tension with literatures on domestic policymaking in democratic states. These literatures on domestic policymaking stress that elected leaders are very responsive to domestic constituencies. Elected leaders are not free to bring home new ideas from international meetings if these ideas displease core domestic audiences essential for winning reelection.

This book provides a different explanation for how ideas from abroad enter the domestic policymaking sphere. I argue that domestic democratic politics and international diffusion are not antithetical, but often reinforce one another. Democracy facilitates the diffusion of international norms, because voters can and do use international standards as benchmarks against which to judge domestic proposals. Politicians have electoral incentives to imitate international models, to signal to voters that their policy proposals are not ill-thought-out experiments, but mainstream, vetted, and well-designed solutions.

My theory begins with domestic politics: voters are often uncertain about their elected leaders and their policy proposals. Voters often worry that a new proposal may not work, or may only benefit a specific interest group. Information that a familiar foreign country has already adopted this law, or that a prominent international organization recommends it, can reassure voters that the proposal is not an untested experiment or a radical choice. Politicians, in turn, anticipate positive voter responses to certain international models and design and present their reform proposals accordingly.

When elected politicians, rather than technocrats, make key decisions, different models spread around the world. Technocrats, who do not depend on voters for reelection, can review the policies of diverse countries. Politicians can only choose among the models adopted by large, rich, and culturally proximate countries, because these countries alone are familiar to voters. Only such references to familiar countries help politicians signal that their proposals are competently designed and mainstream. Technocrats can carefully consider policy successes and failures separately in each issue area. Politicians often must rely on crude signals about the fact that prior adopters of a policy are generally successful countries. This is because politicians cannot easily convey detailed information to voters, and must instead communicate simple information that is easy to verify and hard to contest. Relatedly, while technocrats benefit from a diversity of foreign models to figure out what works best, politicians are better off when a single international model prevails, as this sends a simple, clear signal to voters. Chapters 1 and 2 spell out these theoretical points in greater detail.

To document these claims empirically, and offer evidence that international models influence outcomes in high-stakes domestic debates, this book focuses on social policy, a field in which well-organized domestic interest groups fight over large sums of money and debate fundamental values. I contrast two areas of social policy: health policy and family policy. Health policy is an area where international institutions such as the World Health Organization (WHO) have only made limited efforts to define and spread detailed templates, and where powerful domestic interest groups—medical associations and pharmaceuticals groups—stood to lose from these templates. Nevertheless, even under these inauspicious conditions, international models facilitated the adoption of major health reforms in several countries. Family policy is a field where international bodies such as the International Labour Organization (ILO) defined highly specific templates early on and made extensive efforts to promote these. These clear international templates spread rapidly around the world and minimized domestic conflict over potentially controversial family policy reforms.

To substantiate these claims, this book combines three types of empirical evidence: public opinion experiments to show that voters indeed respond favorably to information from abroad, case study evidence to show that politicians incorporate particular foreign models in their electoral campaigns and legislative debates, and cross-national regressions to show that international models influence policy adoption and implementation. Chapter 3 demonstrates that information about international models changes voters' attitudes on social policy debates. Even U.S. voters, traditionally thought to believe in American exceptionalism, are more likely to favor the adoption of a policy when told that other countries have already adopted it, especially when they hear that the United Nations (UN) recommends this policy for all countries. Consistent with my theory, people with limited information and doubts about their government's choices respond especially strongly to endorsements from abroad. This evidence corroborates a fundamental premise of my argument: that international models can increase voter support for important reforms.

International models' power to sway voters' views is important to politicians, who can garner support by anticipating and shaping voter reactions to information from abroad. Chapters 3, 5, and 7 illustrate how politicians rely on international models to make their argument for reform, providing case studies from the United States, Spain, and Greece. In all three countries, politicians of all political stripes referred to foreign models frequently in public debates, including election campaigns and discussions on major legislative proposals. Whether they supported or opposed a given proposal, leaders from right- and left-wing parties referenced the same few large, rich, and culturally proximate countries familiar to voters in their attempts to win public support for their position. They ignored models from less familiar countries, even when these were especially successful or closely matched politicians' ideological preferences.

The U.S. case study illustrates the pattern of references to foreign models that my theory predicts. American politicians debating health and family reforms focused heavily on Canada, a relatively large and culturally similar U.S. neighbor with which American voters are familiar. Examples from family policy debates in the early 1990s are even more telling. In these debates, American politicians referenced Germany and Japan with great frequency. Neither Germany nor Japan is particularly successful in the field of family policy. However, both countries' rapid growth in the late 1980s and early 1990s made them especially relevant to American voters.

In smaller and less powerful democracies than the United States, politicians' references to international models are more central to election campaigns. These references also focus heavily on large, rich, and culturally proximate countries familiar to voters. In Greece and Spain, politicians campaigned by promising their citizens that they would soon enjoy benefits comparable to those of richer western European countries and repeatedly referenced Britain, France, and Germany in both health and family policy debates. They ignored reforms in other southern European countries, even though these countries had similar institutional structures and similar levels of development. In addition, Socialist politicians made few references to Scandinavian countries and conservative politicians made few references to the United States, even though these countries' choices more closely reflected their ideological leanings. Finally, politicians of all stripes made repeated references to international standards, especially WHO recommendations and ILO conventions, including conventions their countries had not ratified.

The above references illustrate international models' key role in electoral campaigns and legislative debates, but their influence extends beyond rhetoric. Politicians also drew on international models to formulate the policies that were eventually adopted. Cross-national regressions allow me to study the policy choices of dozens of Organization for Economic Cooperation and Development (OECD) countries over several decades and to assess the importance of international factors while controlling for diverse domestic forces. The evidence presented in chapter 4 shows that governments were substantially more likely to adopt National Health Services (NHSs) when the international environment was favorable, namely when foreign countries disproportionately covered in the media had already adopted an NHS, when evidence of NHS success abroad was stronger, and when trade competitors had already adopted an NHS. In the area of family policy, countries extended their maternity leave policies and expanded their spending on family benefits following similar reforms in countries prominently covered in the media. In addition, the ILO was very successful in shaping national maternity leave policies, not only in countries that had ratified its conventions, but also in countries whose citizens were very involved in international nongovernmental organizations (NGOs).

Patterns of diffusion in family and health policy differ in one important respect, consistent with the proposed theory. In the area of maternity and parental leaves, a single international model was developed and forcefully promoted by the ILO for decades. As a result, countries around the world swiftly adopted the international model without much controversy. The existence of a single, clearly promoted international model limited opposition to a policy that might otherwise have upset conservatives, because it conferred benefits only on working women and excluded women who stayed at home. In contrast, the diffusion of health policies shows a more varied landscape with some policies spreading more widely than others. Broad goals endorsed by the WHO, such as universal coverage and primary care, were readily adopted by rich democracies. However, on questions of health financing and organization, where diverse international models persisted, debates arose about which international model was best, limiting each model's ultimate reach. Even in this case, however, Socialist governments used foreign models to dispel concerns that the nationalization of the health sector was a radical experiment and succeeded in introducing NHSs under unlikely circumstances across southern European countries.

This book looks beyond the traditional enforcement mechanisms of international law to explore a novel pathway through which international law and nonlegal instruments can lead to domestic reforms. Traditionally, international law and international relations scholarship has emphasized the efforts of *foreign* actors. For example, in these traditional enforcement mechanisms, international organizations can allocate funds on condition that governments comply with international agreements, and foreign states can choose to cooperate only when other states keep their commitments.[1]

I show how proponents of reform can mobilize *domestic* support from ordinary voters and local politicians, and thus build on a growing literature on the importance of domestic constituencies.[2] By putting together blueprints for reforms, international bodies can provide voters with useful informational signals and politicians with strong backing for change. Diffusion through democracy can also reinforce traditional mechanisms of compliance, where these are operative. It is likely most useful in those cases where the availability of traditional mechanisms of compliance are limited, because reforms have very large domestic consequences for the target state but very small impacts for actors outside its borders. Critical issues like human rights, democracy, and economic development have only an indirect impact on the lives of foreigners. As a result, foreign governments, and thus international organizations, often have limited resources to promote these important goals abroad.[3] In these fields, building up domestic constituencies may be the only realistically available strategy for lasting reform. The sections that follow explore some important implications for the design of international organizations and transnational advocacy efforts, to explain how to enhance their legitimacy and efficacy.

Implications for the Legitimacy of International Organizations and Transnational Advocacy Efforts

An important critique of international bodies is that they face a democratic deficit.[4] Many worry that international organizations often supplant domestic democracy by imposing the policy views of outsiders on unwilling domestic publics. Jed Rubenfeld writes, "[i]nternational law is antidemocratic. The existing international governance organizations are famous for their undemocratic opacity, remoteness from popular or representative politics, elitism, and unaccountability. International governance institutions and their officers tend to be bureaucratic, diplomatic, technocratic—everything but democratic."[5] Jack Goldsmith and Daryl Levinson describe "a deep strain of U.S. political thought [that] portrays international law as an illegitimate attempt by democratically unaccountable foreigners to interfere with the legitimate self-governance of democratic majorities at home."[6] Conservative voices concentrate on how human rights and environmental regimes are antidemocratic[7]

while progressive critics focus on the democratic shortcomings of international trade and finance regimes.[8]

The democracy critique surfaces with particular force in debates about
transgovernmental networks, governance through soft law, and the spread of
norms and best practices. Many legal scholars consider norm diffusion particularly threatening to democracy because procedural safeguards that "domes-
ticate" and "democratize" hard international law, such as treaty ratification,
are not usually employed in the context of soft law.[9] Anne Marie Slaughter
warns that

> [when] a regulatory agency would reach out on its own account to
> its foreign counterparts, even in an effort to solve common prob-
> lems[, this] raises the possibilities not only of policy collusion,
> whereby transgovernmental support can be marshaled against
> domestic bureaucratic opponents, but also of the removal of issues
> from the domestic political sphere through deliberate technocratic
> de-politicization.[10]

There are no easy answers to the democratic deficit question. Scholars who
defend diffusion through technocracy do so in two ways, both of them indirect. First, the spread of international norms and international regulation is
portrayed as a necessary evil, necessary because criminals and corporations
operate across borders. If criminals and corporations can move profits, pollution, or arms across borders, then regulators must necessarily expand their
reach beyond the nation-state and coordinate their activities, even at the
expense of democracy.[11]

The second defense relies on a distinction between democracy and majori-
tarianism. Like domestic courts, international organizations must sometimes
invalidate majoritarian decisions to ensure that a majority does not become
tyrannical. In these accounts, domestic courts and international organizations
are democratic because they help guarantee fundamental societal values and
long-term stability in the face of fickle electorates. Slaughter reconciles transnational networks with democracy by proposing a new theory of "disaggregated
democracy" based on "anti-majoritarian rationales, deliberative politics, and
self-actualization through networks."[12] Robert Keohane, Stephen Macedo, and
Andrew Moravcik similarly argue that international organizations can improve
domestic democracy by guaranteeing minority rights, combating special interests, and expanding deliberation.[13] Eyal Benvenisti extends the domestic justifications for antimajoritarian judicial power to transnational judicial cooperation.[14]

These defenses are significant but indirect. They presume that international
and foreign influences constrain the flexibility of electoral majorities to adopt

their preferred laws. My theory challenges this presumption head-on. Rather than constraining the electorate, references to foreign government choices and international organization proposals can help voters evaluate domestic reform proposals and dispel concerns that these proposals represent untested experiments or reflect the ideals of political extremes. Thus ideas from abroad do not distract politicians from the concerns of their electorates, but instead help build a national electoral majority behind particular policy proposals. By connecting references to foreign laws and international organization proposals to majoritarian values, this theory offers a direct response to criticisms of foreign laws and international organizations' recommendations as undemocratic.

However, this is not the end of the debate. An important question that remains is whether diffusion through democracy leads to the adoption of the best possible policies. On this question, my conclusions are more mixed. Important literatures in constitutional law and also in law and economics highlight that we should not look indiscriminately around the world and treat models from any country on any subject matter in the same way. These literatures suggest criteria for optimizing the selection of foreign laws worthy of imitation. Diverse theories propose examining laws from countries with shared legal heritage,[15] laws that proved successful on the ground,[16] laws on questions that rely more heavily on factual rather than moral determinations,[17] or laws that are the product of independent deliberation at the national level.[18]

Optimal diffusion and actual diffusion through democracy share some features. Countries with a shared legal heritage, identified as appropriate templates by some constitutional theorists, are often heavily covered in the national media and thus become familiar to voters, as my theory suggests. Moreover, many wealthy countries, which tend to be covered disproportionately by the media, also tend to follow extensive domestic deliberation processes, a feature lauded by other constitutional theorists. Similarly, in practice, international organizations base their recommendations on diverse inputs and tend to reflect policies already adopted by key members and often by a wider circle of countries as well. Thus international organization recommendations magnify the influence of rich countries' choices.

While optimal and actual diffusion processes share important features, the fit is far from perfect. To start, many rich countries that capture media attention are not democracies. Moreover, there exist additional systematic problems with diffusion through democracy. Laws spread through democratic processes not necessarily because they were successful on the ground, but because the countries promoting them are rich and culturally proximate. While these countries are likely to have formulated many good laws, in a particular policy area, the best choice may come from elsewhere. The emphasis on the laws of wealthy developed countries, while useful for their peer countries, is particularly problematic for developing countries. As developing countries' leaders seek to leapfrog ahead and promise their constituents rapid progress, they may only study rich countries' choices, overlook excellent templates from other countries at similar levels of development facing similar problems,[19] and adopt templates that are unlikely to work in their home countries.[20]

Another potential drawback of diffusion through democratic processes, which is shared by diffusion processes more generally, is that it constrains the space for experimentation. Diverse theorists have critiqued uniformity in national laws, let alone regional or global models. Some have called for decentralizing decision-making to the lowest government level that can fully internalize externalities, in the hope that like-minded people will sort themselves into small homogeneous groups and better realize their preferences.[21] Other theorists have praised experimentation and decentralized decision-making to allow for direct citizen participation and local monitoring.[22] My account of policy diffusion suggests that, whatever the normative merits and costs of experimentation, the scope for such experimentation is constrained in practice. As a law starts to spread and gains the endorsement of international organizations, it becomes increasingly appealing for local politicians and their electorates. A thumb on the scale in favor of an internationally dominant alternative may discourage experimentation with other alternatives.

Designing Effective International Organizations and Transnational Advocacy Efforts

International law, international norms, and trans-border advocacy influence state behavior through a variety of mechanisms. This book has examined one such pathway — diffusion through democracy — and broadened our theoretical and empirical understanding of its working. I have argued that this mechanism can be employed effectively and influence state behavior in a variety of contexts. If I'm right, this has implications for a broad range of institutional design debates, such as the use of legally binding and non-binding international instruments, membership in international organizations, and rhetorical strategies for transnational advocacy. The subsequent pages outline a few such institutional design implications, to show that we may want to revisit central debates in international law and international relations.

One important choice that international organizations and NGOs face is whether to design international instruments that involve binding obligations for states[23] or focus instead on creating soft law and non-binding norms.[24] International organizations that once concentrated on the development and ratification of binding legal texts now focus many of their energies on developing soft law and non-legal templates.[25] Networks of government regulators proliferate and make the spread of information a central component of their work.[26] Nongovernmental organizations concentrate on spreading best practices and on developing indicators, and on naming and shaming poor performers.[27]

The proliferation of such non-binding instruments is puzzling, because many international lawyers and scholars assume that binding international law has a much greater impact on state behavior than non-binding norms.[28] These commentators emphasize two benefits specific to binding international law. First, that only violations of binding international law can trigger direct sanctions and harsh reputational consequences.[29] Second, that legal formalities associated with hard law create moral legitimacy and "exert a pull towards compliance."[30] Even advocates of soft law often value non-binding agreements only as a precursor to legally binding accords.[31]

My argument emphasizes a third mechanism: the informational content of international law. Hard law, soft law, as well as certain forms of non-law (such as foreign states' practices), can all effectively convey information. These informational effects are very large because principal-agent problems are inherent in representative democracies—voters must decide whether to reelect politicians or not based on limited information. As a result, the limited information that reaches voters, rather than the more extensive information that reaches policy experts and leaders, shapes national legal reforms.

While hard law, soft law, and non-law can all effectively convey information, they are not equally costly to develop. Binding multilateral agreements are difficult to adopt because supermajorities are necessary in many international institutions. Moreover, many states must then overcome domestic ratification hurdles.[32] As a consequence, hard law agreements develop more slowly and are narrower in scope than soft law agreements could have been.[33] The case of international maternity leave illustrates the significant costs in negotiating agreements that bind many countries. Even though maternity leave proposals have been debated internationally since the 1910s, EU countries could not agree on a binding directive until after they had all adopted national maternity leave laws in the 1990s. In the case of global health, the absence of hard law is even more striking—since its establishment in 1948, the WHO has promulgated a single binding agreement, the 2009 Framework Convention on Tobacco Control.[34] However, this apparent shortage of binding agreements does not make the WHO ineffective at promoting norms internationally. As described in chapters 3 and 4, the 1978 Alma-Ata Declaration facilitated systemwide reforms toward primary care in many countries. While legally binding tools have important distinctive advantages, the proposed informational theory explains why non-binding instruments can have a much larger influence on state behavior than previously believed.

Another set of implications concerns the design of international institutions. An important debate for international organizations is how to set membership standards.[35] Many argue that membership in an international organization should depend on countries' performance in particular issue areas. For example, membership in human rights regimes should be conditional on whether a country meets minimum human rights standards, membership in environmental regimes should be conditional on minimum environmental standards, and membership in trade regimes should be conditional on minimum trade openness standards.[36] In contrast, others argue that broader membership—perhaps universal membership—would more effectively acculturate states into conforming to internationally legitimate forms of behavior.[37]

The proposed theory suggests that a different standard may be appropriate. It may be important to include all democracies as members, even democracies that are currently poor performers on the issues of greatest interest to international organization. This is because, in democracies, electoral mechanisms can encourage politicians to adopt international standards once voters become aware of these. In turn, membership in an international regime is likely to increase voters' familiarity with the policies espoused by the regime and thus help build pressure on politicians to adopt these. Other empirical work also supports the idea that non-binding international law can spread more quickly among democracies than non-democracies.[38]

Another set of implications concerns who international organizations and transnational networks should address. Diffusion through democracy suggests that international organizations and advocates should make greater efforts to spread their messages directly to citizens. Some scholars take the contrary position, arguing that international organizations will be most effective in persuading leaders in "less politicized and more insulated, private settings."[39] Similarly, some argue that the small size and professional composition of expert committees increases socialization by creating an atmosphere that facilitates deliberation.[40] More pragmatically, even when international organizations are in theory committed to transparency, they rarely devote substantial resources to spreading information to citizens. The ILO stands out from other international organizations in the types of efforts it has put in place to spread its messages widely. Typically citizens and international organizations are linked through national governments. In contrast, in the ILO, nongovernmental bodies play a much greater direct role. Nongovernmental bodies from each state, specifically employer and labor union delegations, vote on conventions and file formal complaints when governments violate these.[41] The ILO monitors and reports on whether states conform with ratified conventions, unratified conventions, and even with ILO recommendations.[42] It is likely that these mechanisms help explain why principles enunciated in ILO conventions and recommendations are adopted widely, even though many conventions have few ratifications.[43]

The proposed theory also has implications about the issues activists should prioritize and the methods they should employ as they seek to spread norms across countries. The theory of diffusion through democracy suggests that international models are most effective as benchmarks in fields where voters face high uncertainty, and cannot easily tell whether politicians are proposing effective solutions that will benefit the public at large. In contrast, transnational advocates sometimes prefer to focus their efforts on policies that are clearly correct. For example, human rights activists often challenge clear-cut violations of civil and political rights, and ignore social and economic rights, on the assumption their efforts will be less effective on issues that involve deep trade-offs.[44] In contrast, this book illustrates that spreading information to voters about how foreign countries solve social and economic problems can bring about major change by improving the electoral fortunes of domestic leaders advocating for similar proposals.[45] Relatedly, many transnational advocates seek out sympathetic audiences, whereas the proposed theory suggests that the biggest opinion shifts happen among persons who are initially skeptical. Finally, I have argued that when there exists international consensus on a single model, the rhetorical power of foreign models is at its apex. Reform advocates should thus frame their proposals in general terms, to be able to credibly claim that global consensus exists, while reform opponents will be more successful by moving to a lower level of generality, and highlighting diversity abroad.

These first illustrations about international institution design and transnational advocacy are intended to open up conversations and avenues for further research. This book has argued that international norms are not in tension with domestic democracy and that international norms can spread especially quickly through domestic political processes. If this theory is correct, much good can result from the efforts of international organizations and transnational advocates to develop and promote non-binding international instruments, to include all democratic states in international regimes, to directly engage citizens, and to broaden the range of issues on which they advocate. However, major challenges remain, as diffusion through democracy is an imperfect process, and only one among a variety of tools international organizations and transnational advocates have at their disposal. Identifying how to combine diffusion through democracy with other tools remains an important open question. Finding a way to recover some of the advantages of diffusion through technocracy, especially the attention experts can pay to how different models succeed or fail in different contexts, will likely be a critical first step towards the answer.

ACRONYM TABLE

EU	European Union
ILO	International Labour Organization
IMF	International Monetary Fund
INGOs	International Non-Government Organizations
OECD	Organization for Economic Cooperation and Development
UN	United Nations
WHO	World Health Organization
NHS	National Health Service

NOTES

Chapter 1

1. See, among many others, Beth Simmons, Frank Dobbin & Geoffrey Garrett, *The Global Diffusion of Public Policies*, 33 Ann. Rev. Soc. 449 (2007); Ryan Goodman & Derek Jinks, *How to Influence States: Socialization and International Human Rights Law*, 54 Duke L.J. 621 (2004) [hereinafter Goodman & Jinks, *Socialization*]; Ryan Goodman & Derek Jinks, Socializing States: Promoting Human Rights Through International Law (2013) [hereinafter Goodman & Jinks, Socializing States]; Derek Jinks, *The Translation of Global Human Rights Norms: The Empirical Dimension*, 41 Tex. Int'l L.J. 415 (2006); Erik Voeten, *Borrowing and Non-Borrowing Among International Courts*, 39 J. Legal Stud. 547 (2010); Karen Alter, *The Global Spread of European Style International Courts*, 35 West. Eur. Pol. 135 (2012); Mary Dudziak, Exporting American Dreams: Thurgood Marshall's African Journey (2008); Karen Alter & Lawrence Helfer, *Nature or Nurture: Lawmaking in the European Court of Justice and the Andean Tribunal of Justice*, 64 Int'l Org. 563 (2010). *But see*, Pierre Verdier, *Transnational Regulatory Networks and Their Limits*, 34 Yale J. Int'l L. 113 (2009) (arguing that the promise of transnational regulatory networks has been overstated).

2. See, e.g., Anne Marie Slaughter, A New World Order (2004); Kurt Weyland, Bounded Rationality and Policy Diffusion: Social Sector Reform in Latin America (2007) (emphasizing the role of experts in spreading pension reforms); Kal Raustiala, *The Architecture of International Cooperation: Transgovernmental Networks and the Future of International Law*, 43 Va. J. Int'l L. 1 (2002) (clarifying the functions of transgovernmental networks); Harold Hongju Koh, *Bringing International Law Home*, 35 Hous. L. Rev. 623, 651–53 (1998) (emphasizing the role of bureaucratic compliance procedures); David Zaring, *Informal Procedure, Hard and Soft, in International Administration*, 5 Chi. J. Int'l L. 547 (2005) (identifying "domestic bureaucracies" as "the primary impetus" of the internationalization of regulation); Vicki C. Jackson, *Constitutional Comparisons: Convergence, Resistance, Engagement*, 119 Harv. L. Rev. 109 (2005).

3. See, e.g., Michael N. Bartnett & Martha Finemore, *The Politics, Power and Pathologies of International Organizations*, 53 Int'l Org. 699, 713 (1999) (stating that officials in international organizations "are the 'missionaries' of our time. Armed with a notion of progress, an idea of how to create the better life, and some understanding of the conversion process, many IO elites have as their stated purpose a desire to shape state practices by establishing, articulating, and transmitting norms that define what constitutes acceptable and legitimate state behavior.").

4. Weyland 2007, *supra* note 2, at 13.

5. Kenneth Anderson, *Foreign Law and the U.S. Constitution*, 131 Pol'y Rev. 33 (2005). For a discussion on the universalism of this exceptionalist rhetoric, see Anu Bradford & Eric Posner, *Universal Exceptionalism in International Law*, 52 Harv. Int'l L.J. 3 (2011). For discussions of how the United States received foreign models in earlier eras, see Daniel T. Rogers, Atlantic Crossings: Social Politics in a Progressive Age (1998) (presenting social policy exchanges between American and European progressives at the turn of the century) and Mary Dudziak, Cold War Civil Rights: Race and the Image of American Democracy (2000) (outlining how Cold War politics shaped domestic civil rights initiatives).

6. Bruce Bender and John R. Lott Jr., *Legislator Voting and Shirking: A Critical Review of the Public Choice*, 87 Pub. Choice 67 (1996); Paul Burnstein, *The Impact of Public Opinion on Public Policy*, 56 Pol. Sci. Q. 29 (2003); Bingham G. Powell, *Political Representation in Comparative Politics*, 7 Ann. Rev. Pol. Sci. 273 (2004).

7. *Cf.* Jackson, *supra* note 2, 116–18 (2005) (suggesting that examining the views of decision-makers whose choices have real-world consequences will yield more information than will abstract theoretical discussions).

8. Fabrizio Gilardi, Katharina Füglister & Stéphane Luyet, *Learning and the Conditional Diffusion of Health-Care Cost-Sharing Policies in Europe*, working paper (July 29, 2010) (*available at* http://www.fabriziogilardi.org/resources/papers/refprice_july2010.pdf).

9. *See, e.g.*, Goodman & Jinks, *Socialization, supra* note 1; Goodman & Jinks, Socializing States, *supra* note 1. Large literatures in sociology and political science emphasize that proximate countries mimic each other's policies without explaining why this is so; chapter 2 discusses these literatures.

10. See, among others, Jack Goldsmith & Eric Posner, The Limits of International Law 91–100 (2005) (outlining why states sometimes prefer treaties and at other times use non-legal agreements); Andrew T. Guzman & Timothy L. Meyer, *International Soft Law*, 2 J. Legal Analysis 171 (2010) (presenting a theoretical framework on how states choose between hard and soft law in the international arena); Jacob E. Gersen & Eric Posner, *Soft Law: Lessons from Congressional Practice*, 61 Stan. L. Rev. 573 (2008) (presenting a theoretical framework on the influence of soft law domestically); Anna di Robilant, *Genealogies of Soft Law*, 54 Am. J. Comp. L. 499 (2006) (outlining the historical uses of soft law); Kenneth W. Abbott & Duncan Snidal, *Hard and Soft Law in International Legal Governance*, 54 Int'l Org. 421 (2000); Commitment and Compliance: The Role of Non-Binding Norms in the International Legal System (Dinah Shelton ed., 2000) (presenting case studies on the effects of soft international law in human rights, trade, finance, the environment and arms control).

11. John S. Odell, *Case Study Methods in International Political Economy*, 2 Int'l Stud. Perspectives 161, 165 (2001).

12. For 2007, the most recent year available, the figure was 47.41%. *OECD Factbook 2010*, at http://www.oecd.org/els/social/expenditure.

13. *But see* Sarah Brooks, *Interdependent and Domestic Foundations of Policy Change: The Diffusion of Pension Privatization Around the World*, 40 Int'l Stud. Q. 273 (2005); Fabrizio Gilardi, et al., *Learning from Others: The Diffusion of Hospital Financing Reforms in OECD Countries*, 42 Comp. Pol. Stud. 549 (2009); Detlef Jahn, *Globalization as "Galton's Problem": The Missing Link in the Analysis of Diffusion Patterns in Welfare State Development*, 60 Int'l Org. 401 (2006).

14. Gøsta Esping-Andersen, Three Worlds of Welfare Capitalism (1990).

15. Data are drawn from the U.S. Social Security Administration, *Social Security Programs Throughout the World* (1999), *at* http://www.ssa.gov/policy/docs/progdesc/ssptw/ (last visited Apr. 10, 2007).

16. *See, e.g.*, Catherine R. Albiston, Rights on Leave: Institutional Inequality and the Mobilization of the Family and Medical Leave Act (2010); Kimberly Morgan, Working Mothers and the Welfare State: Religion and the Politics of Work-Family Policies in Western Europe and the United States (2006); Gillian Lester, *A Defense of Paid Family Leave*, 28 Harv. J. L. & Gender 1 (2005).

17. *See* Laurence R. Helfer, *Monitoring Compliance with Un-ratified Treaties: The ILO Experience,* 71 LAW. & CONTEMP. PROBS. 195 (2008); Laurence R. Helfer, *Understanding Change in International Organizations: Globalization and Innovation in the ILO,* 59 VAND. L. REV. 649 (2006).

18. On the tradeoffs between hard and soft law, and related institutional design questions, see Kenneth W. Abbott et al., *The Concept of Legalization,* 54 INT'L ORG. 401 (2000); Kenneth W. Abbott & Duncan Snidal, *Hard and Soft Law in International Legal Governance,* 54 INT'L ORG. 421 (2000); Kenneth W. Abbott & Duncan Snidal, *Why States Act Through Formal International Organizations,* 42 J. CONFLICT RESOL. 3 (1998); Laurence R. Helfer, *Overlegalizing Human Rights: International Relations Theory and the Commonwealth Caribbean Backlash Against Human Rights Regimes,* 102 COLUM. L. REV. 1832 (2002); Karen Alter, *Delegating to International Courts: Self-Binding vs. Other-Binding Delegation,* 71 LAW & CONTEMP. PROBS. 37 (2008); Oona Hathaway & Scott Shapiro, *Outcasting: Enforcement in Domestic and International Law,* 121 YALE L.J. 252 (2011) (outcasting involves denying the disobedient the benefits of social cooperation and membership).

Chapter 2

1. For useful overviews of the political science and sociology literatures, see Frank Dobbin et al., *The Global Diffusion of Public Policies,* 33 ANN. REV. SOC. 449 (2007); Ryan Goodman & Derek Jinks, *How to Influence States: Socialization and International Human Rights Law,* 54 DUKE L.J. 621 (2004) [hereinafter Goodman & Jinks, *Socialization*]; RYAN GOODMAN & DEREK JINKS, SOCIALIZING STATES: PROMOTING HUMAN RIGHTS THROUGH INTERNATIONAL LAW (2013).

2. *See, e.g.,* David Law & Mila Versteeg, *The Evolution and Ideology of Global Constitutionalism,* 99 CAL. L. REV. 1163 (2011); Tom Ginsburg et al., *Commitment and Diffusion: How and Why National Constitutions Incorporate International Law,* 28 ILL. L. REV. 201 (2008).

3. *See, e.g.,* Holger Spamann, *Contemporary Legal Transplants: Legal Families and the Diffusion of Corporate Law,* 2009 BYU L. REV. 1813 (2010); Hideki Kanda & Curtis J. Milhaupt, *Re-Examining Legal Transplants: The Director's Fiduciary Duty in Japanese Corporate Law,* 51 AM. J. COMP. L. 887 (2003). *See also* Daniel Berkowitz, Katharina Pistor, & Jean-Francois Richard, *Economic Development, Legality, and the Transplant Effect,* 47 EUR. ECON. REV. 165 (2003).

4. *See, e.g.,* Máximo Langer, *Revolution in Latin American Criminal Procedure: Diffusion of Legal Ideas from the Periphery,* 55 AM. J. COMP. L. 617 (2007); Máximo Langer, *From Legal Transplants to Legal Translations: The Globalization of Plea Bargaining and the Americanization Thesis in Criminal Procedure,* 45 HARV. INT'L L.J. 1 (2004).

5. *See, e.g.,* David John Frank et al., *Environmentalism as a Global Institution,* 65 AM. SOC. REV. 122 (2000).

6. *See, e.g.,* Katerina Linos, *Diffusion through Democracy,* 55 AM. J. POL. SCI. 678 (2011).

7. *See, e.g.,* Bruno de Witte, *New Institutions for Promoting Equality in Europe: Legal Transfers, National Bricolage and European Governance,* 60 AM. J. COMP. L. 49 (2012).

8. *See, e.g.,* Karen J. Alter et al., *Transplanting the European Court of Justice: The Experience of the Andean Tribunal of Justice,* 60 AM. J. COMP. L. 1 (2012).

9. Still others argue that states adopt certain laws when international organizations make this a condition for membership or money. The discussion below explains why conditionality works differently from the diffusion mechanisms explored in greater detail in this book.

10. Zachary Elkins, Andrew Guzman & Beth Simmons, *Competing for Capital: The Diffusion of Bilateral Investment Treaties, 1960–2000,* 60 INT'L ORG. 811 (2006).

11. JOHN STOPFORD, SUSAN STRANGE & JOHN HEALEY, RIVAL STATES, RIVAL FIRMS: COMPETITION FOR WORLD MARKET SHARES (1993); KENICHI OHMAE, THE BORDERLESS WORLD: POWER AND STRATEGY IN THE INTERLINKED ECONOMY (1999).

12. Kil Chang Lee & David Strang, *The International Diffusion of Public Sector Downsizing*, 60 INT'L ORG. 883 (2006).

13. Fabrizio Gilardi, Katharina Füglister & Stéphane Luyet, *Learning and the Conditional Diffusion of Health-Care Cost-Sharing Policies in Europe* (July 29, 2010) (working paper) (*available at* http://www.fabriziogilardi.org/resources/papers/refprice_july2010.pdf).

14. See, among many others, John W. Meyer & Brian Rowan, *Institutionalized Organizations: Formal Structure as Myth and Ceremony*, 83 AM. J. SOC. 340 (1977); Paul J. Di Maggio & Walter W. Powell, *The Iron Cage Revisited: Institutional Isomorphism and Collective Rationality in Organizational Fields*, 48 AM. SOC. REV. 147 (1983).

15. Martha Finnemore, *International Organizations as Teachers of Norms: The United Nations Educational, Scientific and Cultural Organization and Science Policy*, 47 INT'L ORG. 565 (1993); Martha Finnemore, *Norms, Culture and World Politics: Insights From Sociology's Institutionalism*, 50 INT'L ORG. 325 (1996).

16. Abhijit V. Banerjee, *A Simple Model of Herd Behavior*, 107 Q. J. ECON. 797, 798 (1992); Sushil Bikhchandani, David Hirshleifer & Ivo Welch, *A Theory of Fads, Fashion, Custom and Cultural Change as Informational Cascades*, 100 J. POL. ECON. 992 (1992).

17. Kurt Weyland *Theories of Policy Diffusion: Lessons from Latin American Pension Reform*, 57 WORLD POL. 262, 283 (2005) [hereinafter Weyland 2005].

18. Beth Simmons, *Compliance with International Agreements*, 1 ANN. REV. POL. SCI. 75 (1998).

19. For critical reviews, see, among others, ALAN WATSON, LEGAL TRANSPLANTS: AN APPROACH TO COMPARATIVE LAW (1974); ALAN WATSON, COMPARATIVE LAW: LAW, REALITY AND SOCIETY (2007); Duncan Kennedy, *Three Globalizations of Law and Legal Thought, in* THE NEW LAW AND ECONOMIC DEVELOPMENT 19 (David M. Trubek & Alvaro Santos eds., 2006).

20. Michele Graziadei, *Legal Transplants and the Frontiers of Legal Knowledge*, 10 THEOR. INQ. LAW 695 (2009) ("further progress in the field requires the development of a clearer picture of what prompts individual action leading to a transplant.").

21. For a recent review of this literature, see Didem Buhari-Gulmez, *Stanford School on Sociological Institutionalism: A Global Cultural Approach*, 4 INT'L POL. SOC. 253 (2010).

22. John W. Meyer, *The Changing Cultural Content of the Nation-State: A World Society Perspective, in* STATE/CULTURE: STATE FORMATION AFTER THE CULTURAL TURN 137 (G. Steinmetz ed., 1999).

23. Harold Hongju Koh, *Internationalization Through Socialization*, 54 DUKE L.J. 975, 977 (2005).

24. For a review of this literature see Dobbin, Simmons, & Garrett, *supra* note 1. For the critique echoed above, see Jamie Peck, *Geographies of Policy: From Transfer-Diffusion to Mobility-Mutation*, PROG. HUMAN GEOG. 5 (2011) ("Diffusion studies...had merely inferred—essentially from patterns in policy adoption data—how and why particular policies were traveling, with the result that 'we know almost nothing about the process by which such policy transfer occurs'"). For a related critique, see also David Marsh & J.C. Sharman, *Policy Diffusion and Policy Transfer*, 30 POL. STUD. 269, 274–75 (2009).

25. ANNE MARIE SLAUGHTER, A NEW WORLD ORDER (2004).

26. Michael Mintrom, *Policy Entrepreneurs and the Diffusion of Innovation*, 41 AM. J. POL. SCI. 738 (1997); Michael Mintrom & Phillipa Norman, *Policy Entrepreneurship and Policy Change*, 37 POL. STUD. J. 649 (2009).

27. Weyland 2005, *supra* note 17; KURT WEYLAND, BOUNDED RATIONALITY AND POLICY DIFFUSION: SOCIAL SECTOR REFORM IN LATIN AMERICA (2007) [hereinafter WEYLAND 2007].

28. For studies of how lawyers develop and spread ideas within countries, see Lauren B. Edelman, *Legal Environments and Organizational Governance: The Expansion of Due Process in the American Workplace*, 95 AM. J. SOC. 1531 (1990). For an understanding of how accountants do this, see Stephen J. Mezias, *An Institutional Model of Organizational Practice: Financial Reporting at the Fortune 200*, 35 ADM. SCI. Q. 431 (1990). For studies of how professional groups spread ideas across countries, see generally Peter M. Haas, *Introduction: Epistemic Communities and International Policy Coordination*, 46

INT'L ORG. 1 (1992). *See also* Albert O. Hirschman, *How the Keynesian Revolution Was Exported from the United States, and Other Comments, in* POLITICAL POWER OF ECONOMIC IDEAS: KEYNESIANISM ACROSS NATIONS 347–50 (Peter A. Hall ed., 1989) (describing how U.S. economists were critical in the diffusion of Keynesian policies in a great variety of countries).

29. WEYLAND 2007, *supra* note 27, at 13.
30. Bruce Bender & John R. Lott, Jr., *Legislator Voting and Shirking: A Critical Review of the Public Choice,* 87 PUB. CHOICE 67 (1996); Paul Burnstein, *The Impact of Public Opinion on Public Policy,* 56 POL. SCI. Q. 29 (2003); Bingham G. Powell, *Political Representation in Comparative Politics,* 7 ANN. REV. POL. SCI. 273 (2004).
31. *See, e.g.,* DOUGLASS ARNOLD, THE LOGIC OF CONGRESSIONAL ACTION (1990); Larry M. Bartells, *The Study of Electoral Behavior, in* OXFORD HANDBOOK OF AMERICAN ELECTIONS AND POLITICAL BEHAVIOR (Jan E. Leighley, ed., 2008).
32. Imbeau, Pétri & Lamari conduct a meta-analysis of cross-national quantitative studies that examine the influence of the left on different facets of public policy; of the 693 parameter estimates they review, a large majority concern the influence of the left on redistributive politics. Louis Imbeau, Francois Pétri & Moktar Lamari, *Left-Right Party Ideology and Government Policies: A Meta-Analysis,* 40 EUR. J. POL. RES. 1, 18 (2001). Specifically, 288 examine the role of the left in promoting particular social policies, 119 examine the role of the left in total government spending, and 42 study the influence of partisanship on the progressivity of taxes.
33. Douglas A. Hibbs, Jr., *Political Parties and Macroeconomic Policy,* 71 AM. POL. SCI. REV. 1467 (1977). Hibbs' study is the second most-cited piece in the American Political Science Review's 100 year history, only following Bachrach and Baratz' "Two Faces of Power" (1962). Lee Sigelman, *The American Political Science Review Citation Classics,* 100 AM. POL. SCI. REV 667, 670 (2006).
34. The power resources thesis emphasizes the role of organized labor in the development of modern welfare states. *See, e.g.,* Walter Korpi, *Power, Politics, and State Autonomy in the Development of Social Citizenship,* 54 AM. SOC. REV. 309 (1989); GØSTA ESPING-ANDERSEN, THREE WORLDS OF WELFARE CAPITALISM (1990); EVELYNE HUBER & JOHN STEPHENS, DEVELOPMENT AND CRISIS OF THE WELFARE STATE: PARTIES AND POLICIES IN GLOBAL MARKETS (2001); David Bradley, Evelyne Huber, Stephanie Moller, Francois Nielsen, & John D. Stephens, *Distribution and Redistribution in Post-Industrial Democracies,* 55 WORLD POL. 193 (2003).
35. *See generally* Jonas Pontusson & Peter Swenson, *Labor Markets, Production Strategies, and Wage Bargaining Institutions—The Swedish Employer Offensive in Comparative Perspective,* 29 COMP. POL. STUD. 223 (1996); Peter Swenson, *Arranged Alliance: Business Interests in the New Deal,* 25 POL. & SOC. 66 (1997); Isabela Mares, *The Sources of Business Interest in Social Insurance: Sectoral versus National Differences,* 55 WORLD POL. 229 (2003).
36. *See generally* Margarita Estévez Abe, Torben Iversen & David Soskice, *Social Protection and the Formation of Skills: A Reinterpretation of the Welfare State, in* VARIETIES OF CAPITALISM: THE INSTITUTIONAL FOUNDATIONS OF COMPARATIVE ADVANTAGE (Peter Hall & David Soskice eds., 2001); Torben Iversen & David Soskice, *An Asset Theory of Social Policy Preferences,* 95 AM. POL. SCI. REV. 875 (2001) [hereinafter Iversen & Soskice 2001].
37. Peter Hall & Rosemary Taylor, *Political Science and the Three New Institutionalisms,* 44 POL. STUD. 936 (1996).
38. *See, e.g.,* George Tsebelis, *Conditional Agenda-Setting and Decisionmaking Inside the European Parliament,* 1 J. LEGAL STUD. 65 (1995); ELLEN M. IMMERGUT, HEALTH POLITICS: INTERESTS AND INSTITUTIONS IN WESTERN EUROPE (1992).
39. *See, e.g.,* PAUL PIERSON, DISMANTLING THE WELFARE STATE? REAGAN, THATCHER, AND THE POLITICS OF RETRENCHMENT (1994); Paul Pierson, *Increasing Returns, Path Dependence, and the Study of Politics,* 94 AM. POL. SCI. REV. 251 (2000); Katerina Linos, *Path Dependence in Discrimination Law,* 35 YALE J. INT'L L. 116 (2011).
40. *See, e.g.,* HALL & SOSKICE, *supra* note 36.

41. Allan H. Meltzer & Scott F. Richard, *A Rational Theory of the Size of Government*, 89 J. POL. ECON. 914 (1981), Iversen & Soskice 2001, *supra* note 36, and K.O. Moene & M. Wallerstein, *Earnings Inequality and Welfare Spending*, 55 WORLD POL. 485 (2003) examine how welfare policy changes when voters are interested not only in redistribution but also in insurance. TORSTEN PERSSON & GUIDO TABELLINI, POLITICAL ECONOMICS: EXPLAINING ECONOMIC POLICY (2000), chapters 2 and 3, provide a more complete review of this research tradition.

42. Moene & Wallerstein, *supra* note 41; Roland Benabou, *Inequality and Growth, in* NBER MACROECONOMICS ANNUAL 1996 (Ben Bernanke & Julio Rotemberg eds., 1996); Roberto Perotti, *Income Distribution and Investment*, 38 EUR. ECON. REV. 827 (1994); Roberto Perotti, *Growth, Income Distribution, and Democracy: What the Data Say*, 1 J. ECON. GROWTH 149 (1996).

43. *See, e.g.*, Mark Armstrong & Steffen Huck, *Behavioral Economics as Applied to Firms: A Primer*, 6 COMP. POL. INT'L 3 (2010); J. R. Meszaros, *Preventive Choices: Organizations' Heuristics, Decision Processes and Catastrophic Risks*, 36 J. MANAGEMENT STUD. 977 (1999).

44. *See, e.g.*, Donald Wittman, *Candidate Motivation: A Synthesis*, 77 AM. POL. SCI. REV. 142, 142 (1983).

45. ANNABELLE MOHAMMADI ET AL., FOREIGN NEWS IN THE MEDIA: INTERNATIONAL REPORTING IN 29 COUNTRIES 34–37 (1987).

46. MOHAMMADI ET AL., *supra* note 45, at 34–37.

47. The proposition that media coverage focuses on rich and proximate foreign countries is supported in many studies of newspaper, newsmagazine, and television content analysis. *See, e.g.*, Robert Buckman, *How 8 Weekly Newsmagazines Covered Elections in 6 Countries*, 70 JOURNALISM Q. 780 (1993); Tsan Kuo Chang, Pamela Schoemaker & Nancy Brendlinger, *Determinants of International News Coverage in the U.S. Media*, 14 COMM. RES. 396 (1987); K. Swain, *Proximity and Power Factors in Western Coverage of the Sub-Saharan AIDS Crisis*, 80 JOURNALISM & MASS COMM. Q. 145 (2003); MOHAMMADI ET AL., *supra* note 45; Robert Stevenson, *Mapping the News of the World, in* A DIFFERENT KIND OF HORSE RACE: ESSAYS HONORING RICHARD F. CARTER 17 (Brenda Dervin & Steven Chaffee eds., 2003); Howard Ramos, James Ron & Oskar Thoms, *Shaping the Northern Media's Human Rights Coverage, 1986–2000*, 44 J. PEACE RES. 385 (1998).

48. LISBETH CLAUSEN, GLOBAL NEWS PRODUCTION (2003); Stevenson, *supra* note 47.

49. Hiromi Cho & Stephen Lacy, *International Conflict Coverage in Japanese Local Daily Newspapers*, 77 JOURNALISM & MASS COMM. Q. 830 (2000); Folker Hanusch, *Valuing Those Close to Us: A Comparison of German and Australian Quality Newspapers' Reporting of Death in Foreign News*, 9 JOURNALISM STUD. 341 (2008).

50. Susanne Janssen, *Foreign Literatures in National Media: Comparing the International Focus of Literary Coverage in Europe and the United States, 1955–2005*, 44 ARCADIA 352 (2009); Susanne Janssen, Giselinde Kuipers & Marc Verboord, *Cultural Globalization and Arts Journalism: The International Orientation of Arts and Culture Coverage in Dutch, French, Germany and U.S. Newspapers, 1955 to 2005*, 73 AM. SOC. REV. 719 (2008).

51. *See* Jason Barabas & Jennifer Jerit, *Estimating the Causal Effects of Media Coverage on Policy-Specific Knowledge*, 53 AM. J. POL. SCI. 73 (2009).

52. *See, e.g.*, THE CHICAGO COUNCIL ON FOREIGN RELATIONS, GLOBAL VIEWS 2004: AMERICAN PUBLIC OPINION AND FOREIGN POLICY 17 (2004). This poll did not ask about feelings toward Canada.

53. *See, e.g.*, THE CHICAGO COUNCIL ON FOREIGN RELATIONS, *supra* note 52.

54. PSOE, PSOE MANIFESTO (1977).

55. Bill Clinton, first general election presidential debate (Oct. 11, 1992) (transcript *available at* http://www.presidency.ucsb.edu/ws/index.php?pid=21605#axzz1jw8vSJML) (introducing the Family and Medical Leave Act) (emphasis added).

56. Bill Clinton, first general election presidential debate (Oct. 11, 1992) (transcript *available at* http://www.presidency.ucsb.edu/ws/index.php?pid=21605#axzz1jw8vSJML) (introducing his health reform proposal) (emphasis added).

57. For more thoughts on how voters make trade-offs between competent leadership and leadership that closely reflects their values, see Justin Fox & Kenneth W. Shotts, *Delegates or Trustees? A Theory of Political Accountability*, 71 J. POL. 1225 (2009).

58. This quote comes from debates surrounding the Health Security Act of 1993, in which Congressman John Conyers (D-MI) argued: "Germany enacted national health insurance in 1883. Britain in 1948. Japan in 1962. Canada in 1985. It is time for America to do the same in 1993. This American Health Security Act preserves the strengths of our existing health care system, while adopting the most successful tried-and-true features from Canada, Japan, and Europe. Unlike other proposals, this plan is not an experiment." 139 CONG. REC. 4130, 4132 (1993).

59. In an important study of the diffusion of the Children's Health Insurance Program across U.S. states, Craig Volden reports that reform success in other U.S. states influenced legislators more than administrators, while the emulation of neighboring states was not an important factor for the diffusion of the innovations he studied. Craig Volden, *States as Policy Laboratories: Emulating Success in the Children's Health Insurance Program*, 50 AM. J. POL. SCI. 294, 307–10 (2006). The health insurance innovations Volden studied share some similarities with the health insurance innovations this book studies in chapters 4 and 5. The most important similarity is that in both fields, it is possible to define success and find acceptable tools to measure it. Chapters 4 and 5 elaborate on this theme, and explain why success played a greater role in the diffusion of health care reforms as compared with family reforms, a field in which there was no agreement on how to conceptualize and measure policy success. However, there also exist critical differences between the two studies. Volden studied very recent reforms in a federal country in which many citizens follow media that cover the entire nation and publicize developments in one state to citizens of other states. This book studies the global diffusion of reforms; global media is still very limited, and most citizens get their information about reforms abroad from national media. Moreover, the reforms studied here occurred in historical periods where much less information about policy success was collected and disseminated.

60. Compare Vicki C. Jackson, *Constitutional Comparisons: Convergence, Resistance, Engagement*, 119 HARV. L. REV. 109, 116–18 (2005) (suggesting that more information can be gleaned from the views of decision-makers whose choices have real-world consequences, than from more abstract theoretical discussions).

61. See, for example, the statement of representative Palacios Alonso: "'Primary health care is both an integral part of a National Health System, and in fact constitutes the central function and principal nucleus of such as system'... These are not the words of Representative Marcelo Palacios, or of my Parliamentary Group, or of the Political Party to which I belong. They are the Alma-Ata Resolutions of 1978, signed by 70 Ministers of 140 countries, and by the majority of health authorities of the world, through the World Health Organization" (338 Diario de Sesiones del Congreso de los Diputados 35, daily ed., Oct. 8, 1985). The Spanish adoption of a National Health Service is discussed in detail in chapter 4.

62. For example, in debates preceding the adoption of the 1993 Family and Medical Leave Act, Representative Olympia Snowe (R-ME) argued: "Until recently the United States was alone among industrialized nations, with that well-known center of enlightened government, South Africa, in lacking a family leave policy. Now even South Africa has adopted a more progressive policy than we have, leaving us in shameful isolation." 136 Cong. Rec. 9822, 9877 (1990). For more extensive discussion of the Adoption of the Family and Medical Leave Act in the United States, see *infra* Chapter 3, and Katerina Linos, *Diffusion through Democracy*, 55 AM. J. POL. SCI. 678 (2011).

63. *See, e.g.*, Jonathan Baron, Nicole Y. Altman, & Stephan Kroll, *Approval Voting and Parochialism*, 49 J. CONFLICT RES. 895 (2005).

64. For example, in arguing against health financing through general taxation, Unión de Centro Democrático (UCD) health minister Juan Rovira Tarazona noted: "In the conclusion of Alma-Ata in 1978 two types of financing are recognized, one based on taxes, and one based on social security. This last form is explicitly mentioned. That is to say, it is not possible to affirm absolutely that financing via social security is inadequate, when

it is mentioned at that meeting, and when they say that all countries should adopt the type of financing that best suits their condition." (86 Diario de Sesiones del Congreso de los Diputados 5711, daily ed., May 6, 1980).

65. See *infra* chapter 3 for more discussion of U.S. health reform efforts.

66. See *infra* chapter 3.

67. This is especially true for general elections. At other stages of the process, for example during primaries, politicians may focus more on core voters. For further discussions of the impact of swing and core voters on policy outcomes, see Avinash Dixit & John Londregan, *The Determinants of Success of Special Interests in Redistributive Politics*, 58 J. Pol. 1132 (1996).

68. American University News, *Transcript of discussion between U.S. Supreme Court justices Antonin Scalia and Stephen Breyer, AU Washington College of Law* (Jan. 13, 2005), *available at* http://domino.american.edu/AU/media/mediarel.nsf/1D265343BDC218978 5256B810071F238/1F2F7DC4757FD01E85256F890068E6E0?OpenDocument. *See also* Antonin Scalia, *Commentary*, 40 St. Louis U. L.J. 1122 (1996) (stating that judges "are not some international priesthood empowered to impose upon our free and independent citizens supra-national values that contradict their own").

69. Kenneth Anderson, *Foreign Law and the U.S. Constitution*, 131 Pol'y Rev. 33 (2005)

70. Steven Calabresi, *"A Shining City on a Hill": American Exceptionalism and the Supreme Court*, 86 B.U. L. Rev. 1335 (2006).

71. Richard Posner asserts that "[t]o cite foreign law as authority is to flirt with the discredited...idea of a universal natural law; or to suppose fantastically that the world's judges constitute a single, elite community of wisdom and conscience." *No Thanks, We Already Have Our Own Laws*, Legal Aff. July–August (2004): 40, *available at* http://www.legalaffairs.org/issues/July-August-2004/feature_posner_julaug04.msp. John McGinniss calls foreign borrowing the "aristocratic element of a mixed regime." John O. McGinniss, *Foreign to Our Constitution*, 100 Nw. U. L. Rev. 325 (2006). *See also* Anu Bradford & Eric A. Posner, *Universal Exceptionalism in International Law*, 52 Harv. Int'l L.J. 1 (2011).

72. *See, e.g.*, Slaughter, *supra* note 25 (identifying transgovernmental networks as central to international governance); Kal Raustiala, *The Architecture of International Cooperation: Transgovernmental Networks and the Future of International Law*, 43 Va. J. Int'l L. 1 (2002) (clarifying the functions of transgovernmental networks); Harold Hongju Koh, *Bringing International Law Home*, 35 Hous. L. Rev. 651–53 (1998) (emphasizing the role of bureaucratic compliance procedures); David Zaring, *Informal Procedure, Hard and Soft, in International Administration*, 5 Chi. J. Int'l L., 547 (2005) (identifying "domestic bureaucracies" as "the primary impetus" of the internationalization of regulation).

73. *See, e.g.*, Erik Voeten, *Borrowing and Non-Borrowing Among International Courts*, 39 J. Leg. Stud. 457, 552 (2010) (noting how the role of ideology as a motivating force for the use of external sources is frequently suggested in the U.S. context); Jacob Foster, *Constitutional Interpretation: Lessons from South Africa*, U.S.F. L. Rev. 79, 130–31 (2010) (noting "the argument that foreign law is misused by liberal jurists to move the law in a more substantively liberal direction" in the United States).

74. *See generally*, James N. Druckman, *On the Limits of Framing Effects: Who Can Frame?* 63 J. Pol. 1041 (2001).

75. *See* Jessica L. Weeks, *Autocratic Audience Costs: Regime Type and Signaling Resolve*, 62 Int'l Org. 35, 46 (2008).

76. *See generally* Giovanni Sartori, Parties and Party Systems: A Framework for Analysis (1976); Arend Lijphart, Democracy in Plural Societies: A Comparative Exploration (1977).

77. *See, e.g.*, Barry Friedman, The Will of the People: How Public Opinion Has Influenced the Supreme Court and Shaped the Meaning of the Constitution (2009); Christopher Casillas, Peter Enns & Patrick Wohlfarth, *How Public Opinion Constrains the U.S. Supreme Court*, 55 Am. J. Pol. Sci. 74 (2011).

78. *See generally* Alan M. Jacobs, Governing for the Long Term (2011) (discussing how politicians' short time horizons differ from many social policies' longer horizons).

79. For an extensive discussion of decoupling, see Goodman & Jinks, *Socialization, supra* note 1.
80. *See* Edward Mansfield, Helen Milner & Peter Rosendorff, *Why Democracies Cooperate More: Electoral Control and International Trade Agreements*, 56 INT'L ORG. 477 (2002).
81. *See* Xinyuan Dai, *Why Comply? The Domestic Constituency Mechanism*, 59 INT'L ORG. 363 (2005).
82. Songying Fang, *The Informational Role of International Institutions and Domestic Politics*, 52 AM. J. POL. SCI. 304 (2008).
83. Timothy Besley & Anne Case, *Incumbent Behavior: Vote-Seeking, Tax-Setting, and Yardstick Competition*, 85 AM. ECON. REV. 25 (1995). The key difference between the model proposed here and yardstick competition models developed for the U.S. federal context concerns the way in which neighboring states are defined. Besley and Case and many other scholars of the diffusion of innovations across U.S. states define neighboring states in a simple geographic sense. This is a useful shorthand in the case of federations, in which states that border one another share many cultural traits, often fall in the same media market, and allow citizens to cross borders easily and frequently. However, this same simple model of neighboring states does not work well for country-to-country diffusion. Many countries border countries that are culturally, politically, and economically dissimilar. When this happens, national media do not simply focus on geographic neighbors, but on large, rich, and culturally proximate countries, as discussed above and documented empirically in chapter 4.
84. *Cf.* David S. Scharfstein & Jeremy C. Stein, *Herd Behavior and Investment*, 3 AM. ECON. REV. 465 (1990). A large literature in financial economics is based on a 1990 model by Scharfstein and Stein that assumes that incompetent leaders must make decisions based on public information alone, but competent leaders have additional private signals about the desirability of an action and that these signals are perfectly correlated. In such a setup, borrowing occurs because when a decision-maker makes a different choice from a prior decision-maker, he signals that at least one of them is incompetent, and thus decreases his own probability of being perceived as competent. Extensions to the Scharfstein and Stein model indicate that when competent politicians' signals are correlated imperfectly, borrowing occurs nonetheless, but the weaker the correlation, the weaker the borrowing tendency. *See, e.g.,* John R. Graham *Herding Among Investment Newsletters: Theory and Evidence*, 54 J. FIN. 237 (1999). When competent leaders' signals are uncorrelated, emulation can still occur, but the mechanism differs—it is no longer based on the principal-agent dynamic whereby politicians seek to improve their reputation and their reelection chances. *See* Marco Ottaviani & Peter Sørensen, *Herd Behavior and Investment: Comment*, 90 AM. ECON. REV. 695 (2000); Scharfstein & Stein 2000. If politicians do not seek reelection alone, but instead seek some mix of reelection and public policy outcomes, emulation weakens.
85. Borrowing might be especially strong when foreign governments make unexpected decisions, when, for example, left-leaning governments introduce reforms associated with right-wing ideology, such as cutting corporate tax rates. *See* Nathaniel M. Jensen & René Lindstädt, *Learning Right and Learning From the Left: Diffusion of Corporate Tax Policy Across Borders*, 45 COMP. POL. STUD. 283 (2012).
86. Countries adopt policies continuously; the early/late developer dichotomy is just a conceptual shorthand.

Chapter 3

1. Support for the UN in other Organization for Economic Cooperation and Development (OECD) countries in which the Pew Survey was conducted in 2007 is as follows: Japan 51%, United States 55%, Britain 64%, France 67%, Germany 67%, Spain 70%, Canada 70%, Italy 75%, and Sweden 84%. For comparability, respondents who answered "don't know," an option only available in some countries, are excluded in calculating these percentages.

2. *See* Chicago Council on Foreign Relations, Global Views 2004: American Public Opinion and Foreign Policy 50–53 (2004).

3. Charles H. Blake & Jessica R. Adolino, *The Enactment of National Health Insurance: A Boolean Analysis of Twenty Advanced Industrial Countries*, 26 J. Health Pol. Pol'y & L. 679, 702 (2001).

4. For a more extensive discussion of the literature on how politicians use polls, see generally John G. Geer, From Tea Leaves to Opinion Polls: A Theory of Democratic Leadership (1996).

5. Michael Tomz, *Domestic Audience Costs in International Relations: An Experimental Approach*, 61 Int'l Org. 821, 837 (2007).

6. Knowledge Networks administered the survey. To construct a representative sample, Knowledge Networks uses random-digit dialing and address-based sampling methods to select participants and create a panel that is representative of the entire U.S. population. Once selected, respondents answer questionnaires online. Households are provided with Internet access and hardware if necessary. Households that already have Internet access receive incentive points, redeemable for cash, for completing their surveys. In both experiments, the response rate exceeded 60%. Prior research confirms that the Knowledge Networks sample is not only representative as regards demographic variables reported in the Current Population Survey, but also closely matches more specialized surveys recording interest in politics. *See* Michael Tomz, *Domestic Audience Costs in International Relations: An Experimental Approach*, 61 Int'l Org. 821, 837 (2007).

7. *See, e.g.*, Chicago Council on Foreign Relations, *supra* note 2, at 35 ("Despite the findings that Americans support giving many international organizations greater powers, overall feelings toward them are mixed. This is probably related to feelings about their performance as distinguished from the desirability of their function").

8. The exact question asked was: "As you may know, the members of the UN General Assembly have agreed on a set of principles called the Universal Declaration of Human Rights. Some people say the United Nations should actively promote such human rights principles in member states. Others say this is improper interference in a country's internal affairs and human rights should be left to each country. Do you think the UN should or should not actively promote human rights in member states?" (2008 worldpublicopinion.org poll, cited in Council on Foreign Relations, Public Opinion on Global Issues: A Web-based Digest of Polling from Around the World 88, Worldpublicopinion.org (Nov. 2009), http://www.worldpublicopinion.org/pipa/digests.php#aw (follow "read the full report" under "Public Opinion on Global Issues"). Many other questions on human rights promotion garner an even higher level of public opinion support.

9. The exact question asked by the Chicago Council on Global Affairs in 2007 was: "Overall, do you think that countries that are part of international trade agreements should or should not be required to maintain minimum standards for working conditions?". The Chicago Council on Global Affairs & Worldpublicopinion.org, Trade and Labor Environmental Standards: March 2007, worldpublicopinion.org (Mar. 2007), http://www.worldpublicopinion.org/pipa/articles/btglobalizationtradera/334.php?nid=&id=&pnt=334&lb=btgl (click "questionnaire").

10. *See, e.g.*, Chicago Council on Foreign Relations, *supra* note 2.

11. *Id.*

12. Zachary Elkins, *Micro-level Foundations of Diffusion Theory: Experimental Evidence* 29 (Aug. 2010) (paper presented at the meeting of the American Political Science Association).

13. *See e.g.*, Steven Calabresi, *"A Shining City on a Hill": American Exceptionalism and the Supreme Court*, 86 B.U. L. Rev. 1335 (2006) (contrasting the culture of the "lawyerly elite," who eagerly borrow from abroad, with "another culture among ordinary Americans that holds that Americans are a special people, in a special land, on a special mission."). Chapter 2 presents and discusses these claims in greater detail.

14. Cross-tabulations of the data show statistically significant responses across diverse groups. These cross-tabulations are not included in the manuscript, but they are available from the author upon request.

15. Michael Tomz, Jason Wittenberg, & Gary King, CLARIFY: Software for Interpreting and Presenting Statistical Results, version 2.1. Available at (http://gking.harvard.edu).

16. Respondents were classified as Republicans or not based on a 7-point scale. The vast majority of respondents supported or at least leaned toward either the Democratic or the Republican party. The few people who did not lean toward either party are grouped with the Democrats for all the analyses; this does not influence the results.

17. *See, e.g.,* Erik Voeten, *Borrowing and Non-Borrowing Among International Courts,* 39 J. LEGAL STUD. 457, 552 (2010) ("The role of ideology as a motivating force for the use of external sources is frequently suggested in the U.S. context"); Jacob Foster, *Constitutional Interpretation: Lessons from South Africa,* U.S.F. L. REV. 79, 130–31 (2010) (noting "the argument that foreign law is misused by liberal jurists to move the law in a more substantively liberal direction" in the United States).

18. Joseph Grieco, Christopher Gelpi, Jason Reifler & Peter D. Feaver, *Let's Get a Second Opinion: International Institutions and American Public Support for War,* 55 INT'L STUD. Q. 563 (2011).

19. *See* Dennis Chong & James N. Druckman, *Framing Theory,* ANN. REV. POL. SCI. 103, 106 (2001).

20. *See generally* James Druckman, *On the Limits of Framing Effects,* 63 J. POL. 1041 (2001).

21. *See,* Dennis Chong & James N. Druckman, *Framing Public Opinion in Competitive Democracies,* 101 AM. POL. SCI. REV. 637 (2007).

22. *See* Jason Barabas & Jennifer Jerit, *Are Survey Experiments Externally Valid?,* 104 AM. POL. SCI. REV. 226, 226 (2010); Donald Kinder, *Curmudgeonly Advice,* 57 J. COMM. 155, 157 (2007).

23. For a careful discussion of the normative concerns underpinning maternity leave proposals, *see* Gillian Lester, *A Defense of Paid Family Leave,* 28 HARV. J.L. & GENDER 1 (2005). *See also* CATHERINE R. ALBISTON, RIGHTS ON LEAVE: INSTITUTIONAL INEQUALITY AND THE MOBILIZATION OF THE FAMILY AND MEDICAL LEAVE ACT (2010) (discussing the implementation of the Act); KIMBERLY MORGAN, WORKING MOTHERS AND THE WELFARE STATE: RELIGION AND THE POLITICS OF WORK-FAMILY POLICIES IN WESTERN EUROPE AND THE UNITED STATES (2006) (discussing maternity leave debates across European countries).

24. Prior experimental research suggests that contestation is a somewhat effective strategy. When voters are first presented with an endorsement and then presented with information pointing in the opposite direction, the effect of the endorsement declines in magnitude but remains positive. *See* Chong & Druckman, *Framing Public Opinion, supra* note 19. It seems plausible that Republicans questioned how foreign models worked abroad to reduce the effectiveness of the foreign endorsement.

25. Box Office Mojo, http://www.boxofficemojo.com/movies/?page=main&id=sicko.htm (only domestic sales included in 24 million figure).

26. Michelle Andrews, *The Impact of 'Sicko' on Popular Opinion About Healthcare Reform,* US NEWS, Aug. 31, 2007, *available at* http://health.usnews.com/health-news/articles/2007/08/31/the-impact-of-sicko-on-popular-opinion-about-healthcare-reform. For the underlying data, *see* The Henry J. Kaiser Family Foundation, *The Reach and Impact of "Sicko,"* http://www.kff.org/kaiserpolls/upload/7689.pdf.

27. *See generally* DANIEL T. RODGERS, ATLANTIC CROSSINGS: SOCIAL POLITICS IN A PROGRESSIVE AGE (1998); JAMES KLOPPENBERG, UNCERTAIN VICTORY: SOCIAL DEMOCRACY AND PROGRESSIVISM IN EUROPEAN AND AMERICAN THOUGHT, 1870–1920 (1986).

28. AXEL SCHAFFER, AMERICAN PROGRESSIVES AND GERMAN SOCIAL REFORM, 1875–1920, 193–94 (2000).

29. *See* PAUL STARR, THE SOCIAL TRANSFORMATION OF AMERICAN MEDICINE: THE RISE OF A SOVEREIGN PROFESSION AND THE MAKING OF A VAST INDUSTRY 243–57 (1982).

30. *See* JAMES T. MORONE, THE POLITICS OF HEALTH CARE REFORM: LESSONS FROM THE PAST, PROSPECTS FOR THE FUTURE 105 (1994). *See also* JACOB S. HACKER, THE DIVIDED WELFARE STATE: THE BATTLE OVER PUBLIC AND PRIVATE SOCIAL BENEFITS IN THE UNITED STATES (2002); Jacob S. Hacker, *The Historical Logic of National Health Insurance: Structure and Sequence in the Development of British, Canadian and U.S. Medical Policy*, 12 STUD. AM. POL. DEV. 57 (1998).

31. For a brief history of U.S. family reform efforts, see Steven K. Wisensale, *The White House and Congress on Childcare and Family Leave Policy: From Carter to Clinton*, 25 POL'Y STUD. J. 75 (1997).

32. Bill Clinton, first general election presidential debate (Oct. 11, 1992) (transcript *available at* http://www.presidency.ucsb.edu/ws/index.php?pid=21605#axzz1jw8vSJML) (introducing the Family and Medical Leave Act) (emphasis added).

33. Bill Clinton, first general election presidential debate (Oct. 11, 1992) (transcript *available at* http://www.presidency.ucsb.edu/ws/index.php?pid=21605#axzz1jw8vSJML (introducing his health reform proposal) (emphasis added).

34. For example, in the second presidential debate, candidate Clinton argued: *"We spend 30 percent more of our income than any nation on earth on health care. And yet we insure fewer people.* We have 35 million people without any insurance at all. I see them all the time. A hundred thousand Americans a month have lost their health insurance just in the last four years. *So if you analyze where we're out of line with other countries, you come up with the following conclusions:* No. 1, we spend at least $60 billion a year on insurance, administrative costs, bureaucracy and government regulation that wouldn't be spent in any other nation. So we have to have, in my judgment, a drastic simplification of the basic health insurance policies of this country. Be very comprehensive for everybody." Bill Clinton, second general election presidential debate (Oct. 15, 1992) (transcript *available at* http://www.presidency.ucsb.edu/ws/index.php?pid=21617#axzz1ksuNhlew) (emphasis added). Independent candidate Ross Perot also adopted a similar strategy of pushing for health reform by reference to foreign models. In that same Richmond, Virginia, debate Perot argued: "We have the most expensive health-care system in the world; 12 percent of our gross national product goes to health care. *Our industrial competitors who are beating us in competition spend less and have better health care. Japan spends a little over 6 percent of its gross national product, Germany spends 8 percent.* It's fascinating. You bought a front-row box seat and you're not happy with your health care, and you're saying we've got bad health care but very expensive health care." Ross Perot, second general election presidential debate (Oct. 15, 1992) (transcript *available at* http://www.presidency.ucsb.edu/ws/index.php?pid=21617#axzz1ksuNhlew) (emphasis added).

35. In introducing his health care proposal, President Clinton argued: "We're blessed with the best health care professionals on earth, the finest health care institutions, the best medical research, the most sophisticated technology...And in spite of all this, our medical bills are growing at over twice the rate of inflation, and the United States spends over a third more of its income on health care than any other nation on earth. And the gap is growing, causing many of our companies in global competition severe disadvantage. There is no excuse for this kind of system. We know other people have done better." President Bill Clinton, speech introducing health care reform to Congress. (Sept. 22, 1993) transcript *available at* http://millercenter.org/president/speeches/detail/3926 (last visited Oct. 2, 2011).

36. *See* Wisensale, *supra* note 31, at 83 (contrasting Clinton's decision to sign the FMLA in a highly publicized Rose Garden ceremony with his decision to sign the Defense of Marriage Act at midnight, alone in the Oval Office).

37. 1993 U.S.C.C.A.N. 54 (daily ed. Feb. 5, 1993) (statement of President Clinton).

38. *See* Wisensale, *supra* note 31, at 84.

39. For a narrative of what went wrong, see JACOB HACKER, THE ROAD TO NOWHERE: THE GENESIS OF PRESIDENT CLINTON'S PLAN FOR HEALTH SECURITY (1999).

40. *See* Paul Starr, *What Happened to Health Care Reform?* THE AMERICAN PROSPECT, Dec. 1994, at 20 (presenting several strategic miscalculations in negotiations for health

reform, from the perspective of a leading Clinton health advisor). *See also* Theodore Marmor & Jonathan Oberlander, *The Patchwork: Health Reform, American Style*, 72 Sci. & Med. 125, 126 (2011) (explaining that "the conventional wisdom was that the Clinton plan failed because of a series of mistakes and political mistakes").

41. Barack Obama, The Time Has Come for Universal Health Care (Jan. 25, 2007) (transcript *available at* http://usliberals.about.com/od/extraordinaryspeeches/a/ ObamaHealthIns.htm) (introducing his health care plan at the Families USA Conference in Washington, DC).

42. *Id.*

43. Barack Obama, remarks at the Selma Voting Rights March Commemoration in Selma, Alabama (March 4, 2007).

44. *Id.*

45. For examples of campaign speeches where Barack Obama made these arguments see Remarks at a Labor Day Rally in Manchester, New Hampshire (Sept. 3, 2007); Remarks at a Town Hall in Springfield, Missouri (July 30, 2008); Remarks at a Town Hall in St. Petersburg, Florida (Aug. 1, 2008); Remarks at a Town Hall in Titusville, Florida (Aug. 2, 2008); Remarks at Kettering University in Flint, Michigan (June 16, 2008); Remarks at Macomb Community College in Warren, Michigan (May 14, 2008); Remarks at the Building Trades National Legislative Conference in Washington, DC (Apr. 15, 2008); Remarks in Dover, New Hampshire (Sept. 12, 2008); Remarks in Newport News, Virginia (Oct. 4, 2008); Remarks in Pittsburgh, Pennsylvania (June 26, 2008); Remarks in Washington, DC: "Changing the Odds for Urban America" (July 18, 2007); Remarks on Health Care at the University of Iowa (May 29, 2007); Remarks to the Alliance for American Manufacturing in Pittsburgh, Pennsylvania (Apr. 14, 2008); Remarks with Senator Hillary Clinton in Unity, New Hampshire (June 27, 2008) (transcripts *available at* http://www.presidency.ucsb.edu/2008_election_speeches.php?ca ndidate=44&campaign=2008OBAMA&doctype=5000). Observe that these speeches were delivered in key swing states for the 2008 presidential campaign. In these most crucial electoral regions, the notoriously data-driven Obama campaign employed references to international models to persuade voters critical to the election outcome.

46. President Barack Obama, *Obama's health care speech to Congress*, N.Y. Times, Sept. 9, 2009, *available at* http://www.nytimes.com/2009/09/10/us/politics/10obama.text. html?pagewanted=all. The media extensively covered Obama's speech introducing healthcare reform. See, for example, Sheryl Gay Stolberg & Jeff Zeleny, *Obama, Armed With Details, Says Health Plan Is Necessary*, N.Y. Times, Sept. 9, 2009, *available at* http:// www.nytimes.com/2009/09/10/us/politics/10obama.html?ref=politics, a version of which appeared on the front page of the *New York Times* on Sept. 10, 2009.

47. President Barack Obama, *supra* note 45.

48. For these totals, and for tables 3.7, 3.8, and 3.9, the reference to a particular country, state, or region is the unit of analysis.

49. For a review of this literature, see Katerina Linos, Note, *When Do Policy Innovations Spread?*, 119 Harv. L. Rev. 1467 (2006).

50. *See* Donna R. Lenoff, & Sylvia M. Becker, *Family and Medical Leave Legislation in the States: Toward a Comprehensive Approach*, 26 Harv. J. Legis. 403 (1989); Jane Waldfogel, *Family Leave Coverage in the 1990s*, Monthly Lab. Rev., Oct. 1999, at 13–21.

51. *See, e.g.*, Michael S. Dukakis, *Hawaii and Massachusetts: Lessons from the States*, 10 Yale L. & Pol'y Rev. 397 (1992) (former Democratic presidential candidate explaining that while "practices in other countries like Germany and Canada have received considerable media attention lately and may influence the course of national health care reform here," we should also study the United States).

52. The unit of analysis for this figure is the statement, not the country. That is, if a Republican said we should not adopt family leave because labor regulation increases unemployment, and mentioned both France and Spain as examples, this would count as a single statement.

53. For example, in January 2009, the Commonwealth Fund issued a much-publicized study concluding that "policies in Switzerland and the Netherlands that achieve

near-universal coverage and low administrative costs can help inform the U.S. health care reform debate." Commonwealth Fund, *New Study: Swiss and Dutch Health Systems Can Provide Lessons for U.S. on Achieving Universal Coverage, Low Administrative Costs* (Jan. 16, 2009), http://www.commonwealthfund.org/News/News-Releases/2009/Jan/New-Study—Swiss-and-Dutch-Health-Systems-Can-Provide-Lessons-for-U-S—on-Achieving-Universal-Covera.aspx. *See also* Kieke G.H. Okma, Theodore R. Marmor & Jonathan Oberlander, *Managed Competition for Medicare? Sobering Lessons from the Netherlands,* 365 New Eng. J. Med. 287 (2011).

54. 155 Cong. Rec. S11853 (daily ed. Nov. 20, 2009) (statement of Sen. Conrad).

55. 156 Cong. Rec. S1953 (daily ed. Mar. 24, 2010) (statement of Sen. Feinstein); 155 Cong. Rec. S12059 (daily ed. December 1, 2009) (statement of Sen. Feinstein); 155 Cong. Rec. S11854 (daily ed. Nov. 20, 2009) (statement of Sen. Conrad).

56. 155 Cong. Rec. S12503 (daily ed. Dec. 5, 2009) (statement of Sen Ensign).

57. 156 Cong. Rec. E510 (daily ed. Mar. 25, 2010) (statement of Sen. Rep. Larson); 156 Cong. Rec. H1884 (daily ed. Mar. 24, 2010) (statement of Rep. Ryan); 156 Cong. Rec. S1848 (daily ed. Mar. 23, 2010) (statement of Sen. Bond); 155 Cong. Rec. S11826 (daily ed. Nov. 20, 2009) (statement of Sen. McConnell); 155 Cong. Rec. H12855 (daily ed. Nov. 7, 2009) (statement of Rep. Ryan); 155 Cong. Rec. H12881 (daily ed. Nov. 7, 2009) (statement of Rep. Dent).

58. 156 Cong. Rec. H1899 (daily ed. Mar. 21, 2010) (statement of Rep. Sanchez); 156 Cong. Rec. S1710 (daily ed. Mar. 18, 2010) (statement of Sen. Carper); 156 Cong. Rec. H1163 (daily ed. Mar. 4, 2010) (statement of Rep. Ellison); 155 Cong. Rec. S11850 (daily ed. Nov. 20, 2009) (statement of Sen. Harkin); 155 Cong. Rec. S11854 (daily ed. Nov. 20, 2009) (statement of Sen. Conrad).

59. 155 Cong. Rec. S11876 (daily ed. Nov. 20, 2009) (statement of Sen. Dorgan).

60. 155 Cong. Rec. S13661 (daily ed. Dec. 21, 2009) (statement of Sen. Harkin).

61. 155 Cong. Rec. S13677 (daily ed. Dec. 21, 2009) (statement of Sen. Kerry).

62. 155 Cong. Rec. S12501 (daily ed. Dec. 5, 2009) (statement of Sen. Chambliss).

63. 155 Cong. Rec. S11875 (daily ed. Nov. 20, 2009) (statement of Sen. Dorgan); 155 Cong. Rec. S11872 (daily ed. Nov. 20, 2009) (statement of Sen. Boxer).

64. 155 Cong. Rec. S11853 (daily ed. Nov. 20, 2009) (statement of Sen. Conrad).

65. 156 Cong. Rec. S6370 (daily ed. July 28, 2010) (statement of Sen. Barrasso); 155 Cong. Rec. S11838 (daily ed. Nov. 20, 2009) (statement of Sen. Barrasso).

66. 155 Cong. Rec. S12501 (daily ed. Dec. 5, 2009) (statement of Sen. Ensign).

67. 155 Cong. Rec. S12503 (daily ed. Dec. 5, 2009) (statement of Sen. Ensign); 155 Cong. Rec. S12144 (daily ed. Dec. 2, 2009) (statement of Sen. Ensign); 155 Cong. Rec. S11954 (daily ed. Nov. 21, 2009) (statement of Sen Bennett).

68. 156 Cong. Rec. S1944 (daily ed. Mar. 24, 2010) (statement of Sen. Kyl); 156 Cong. Rec. H1826 (daily ed. Mar. 21, 2010) (statement of Rep. Ryan); 155 Cong. Rec. S12587 (daily ed. Dec. 7, 2009) (statement of Sen. Coburn); 155 Cong. Rec. H12850 (daily ed. Nov. 7, 2009) (statement of Rep. Hensarling).

69. 156 Cong. Rec. S1967 (daily ed. Mar, 24, 2010) (statement of Sen. Grassley).

70. 139 Cong. Rec. S987 (daily ed. Feb. 2, 1993) (statement of Sen. Dodd).

71. 136 Cong. Rec. H2176 (daily ed. May 9, 1990) (statement of Rep. Snowe). Similar references are plentiful. For example, Rep. Payne (D-NJ) stated: "What do the Sudan, Burkina, Guinea-Bissau, and South Africa have in common with the United States? The one thing that those five countries have in common is that not a one of them has a family medical leave act. Every other country on the planet enacted some sort of a family medical leave act years and years and years ago." 136 Cong. Rec. H2083 (daily ed. May 8, 1990) (statement of Rep. Payne). Other references in this manner include 136 Cong. Rec. S8003 (daily ed. June 14, 1990) (statement of Sen. Mitchell) and 136 Cong. Rec. H2177 (daily ed. May 9, 1990) (statement of Rep. Unsoeld).

72. 137 Cong. Rec. E3862 (daily ed. Nov. 13, 1991) (statement of Rep Sanders).

73. 139 Cong. Rec. S873 (daily ed. Jan. 28, 1993) (statement of Sen. Boxer).

74. 138 Cong. Rec. H8226 (daily ed. Sept. 10, 1992) (statement of Rep. Sanders).

75. 137 Cong. Rec. S14134 (daily ed., Oct. 2, 1991) (statement of Sen. Hatch).

76. 136 CONG. REC. H2157 (daily ed. May 9, 1990) (statement of Rep. Slaughter); 136 CONG. REC. H2166 (daily ed. May 9, 1990) (statement of Rep. Clay).

77. 139 CONG. REC. H370 (daily ed. Feb. 3, 1993) (statement of Rep. Woolsey). 139 CONG. REC. H421 (daily ed. Feb. 3, 1993) (statement of Rep. Swett).

78. Compare JACOB S. HACKER, THE ROAD TO NOWHERE: THE GENESIS OF PRESIDENT CLINTON'S PLAN FOR HEALTH SECURITY (1996), with Jacob S. Hacker, *The Road to Somewhere: Why Health Reform Happened*, 8 PERSP. POL. 861 (2010).

Chapter 4

1. See generally ELLEN M. IMMERGUT, HEALTH POLITICS: INTERESTS AND INSTITUTIONS IN WESTERN EUROPE (1992); Jacob S. Hacker, *The Historical Logic of National Health Insurance: Structure and Sequence in the Development of British, Canadian and U.S. Medical Policy*, 12 STUDIES IN AM. POL. DEV. 57 (1998).

2. The terminology of goals, instruments, and instrument settings comes from Peter A. Hall, *Policy Paradigms, Social Learning and the State: The Case of Policymaking in Britain*, 25 COMP. POL. 275, 278–79 (1993).

3. OECD, HEALTH AT A GLANCE 2009: OECD INDICATORS, at 171 (2009).

4. Many alternative classifications of health care systems exist, but the distinctions proposed here appear and re-appear often. See David Mechanic & David A. Rochefort, *Comparative Medical Systems*, 22 ANN. REV. SOC. 239 (1996) for a review. While most health systems classifications are undertaken by experts in health policy or economics rather than in political science, political science also emphasizes this distinction. See, e.g., Jacob S. Hacker, *Review Article: Dismantling the Health Care State? Political Institutions, Public Policies and the Comparative Politics of Health Reform*, 34 BRITISH J. POL. SCI. 693 (2004).

5. P. Hussey & G.F. Anderson, *A Comparison of Single- and Multi-Payer Health Insurance Systems and Options for Reform*, 66 HEALTH POL'Y 215 (2003).

6. Preconditions for an NHS include a government with the ability to raise sufficient tax revenue and the commitment to spend the revenue on health care. These preconditions existed for OECD countries in the post–World War II period, but are not trivial considerations for other times and places. Hussey & Anderson, *supra* note 5.

7. Advanced industrialized countries listed here include all the OECD members except for Mexico, South Korea, Hungary, Poland, Turkey, the Czech Republic, and the Slovak Republic, whose different historical paths lead welfare state scholars to exclude them from their analyses.

8. Acute care beds were counted for this estimate and the estimates in Table 4.2.

9. Iceland, too, has an NHS. It was introduced through a series of gradual reforms between 1971 and 1974, but is not included as it is not an OECD country.

10. OECD, THE REFORM OF HEALTH CARE SYSTEMS: A REVIEW OF SEVENTEEN OECD COUNTRIES (1994).

11. NICHOLAS TIMMINS, THE FIVE GIANTS: A BIOGRAPHY OF THE WELFARE STATE 24–25 (2d ed. 2001)

12. Itziar Larizgoitia & Barbara Starfield, *Reform of Primary Health Care: The Case of Spain*, 41 HEALTH POL'Y 121, 123 (1997).

13. Mario Cueto, *The Origins of Primary Health Care and Selective Primary Health Care*, 94 AM. J. PUB. HEALTH 1864 (2004).

14. R. Passmore, *The Declaration of Alma-Ata and the Future of Primary Care*, 2 LANCET 1005 (1979).

15. WILLY BRANDT, NORTH-SOUTH: A PROGRAM FOR SURVIVAL (1980).

16. See Allyn Taylor & Douglas Betcher, *WHO Framework Convention on Tobacco Control: A Global Good for Public Health*, 78 BULLETIN OF WORLD HEALTH ORG. 920 (2000).

17. Donald D. Light, *Managed Competition, Governmentality and Institutional Response in the United Kingdom*, 52 SOC. SCI. & MED. 1167 (2001). Managed competition theories call for introducing incentives for and competition among providers of health care services, within an overall system of government financing and regulation of care.

18. Sarah M. Brooks, *Interdependent and Domestic Foundations of Policy Change: The Diffusion of Pension Privatization Around the World*, 40 INT'L STUD. Q. 273 (2005); Beth Simmons & Zachary Elkins, *The Globalization of Liberalization: Policy Diffusion in the International Political Economy*, 98 AM. POL. SCI. REV. 171 (2004).

19. Sales of newspapers, journals, and periodicals in U.S. dollars for the year 1975 were used to construct these weights, based on data from Source OECD, OECD International Trade by Commodity Statistics, *available at* http://www.oecd.org/document/25/0,37 46,en_2649_34241_1906706_1_1_1_1,00.html.

20. Source OECD, *supra* note 19.

21. Deutsche Presse-Agentur does not have the global influence of the other listed firms but operates as a major regional agency in Europe. Robert Stevenson, *Mapping the News of the World, in* A DIFFERENT KIND OF HORSE RACE: ESSAYS HONORING RICHARD F. CARTER 17 (Brenda Dervin & Steven Chaffee eds., 2003).

22. ROBERT STEVENSON & RICHARD COLE, FOREIGN NEWS AND THE NEW WORLD INFORMATION ORDER 53 (1994).

23. David Weaver et al., *The News of the World in Four Major Wire Services: A Study of Selected Services of the Associated Press, United Press International, Reuters and Agence France-Press, in* FOREIGN NEWS IN THE MEDIA: INTERNATIONAL REPORTING IN 29 COUNTRIES, at 85 (Annabelle Mohammadi et al. eds., 1987).

24. Weaver, *supra* note 23, at 86.

25. Weaver, *supra* note 23, at 78.

26. Stevenson & Cole, *supra* note 22.

27. Stevenson & Cole, *supra* note 22; LISBETH CLAUSEN, GLOBAL NEWS PRODUCTION (2003).

28. Hiromi Cho & Stephen Lacy, *International Conflict Coverage in Japanese Local Daily Newspapers*, 77 JOURNALISM & MASS COMM. Q. 830 (2000); Folker Hanusch, *Valuing Those Close to Us: A Comparison of German and Australian Quality Newspapers' Reporting of Death in Foreign News*, 9 JOURNALISM STUD. 341 (2008).

29. Susanne Janssen, *Foreign Literatures in National Media: Comparing the International Focus of Literary Coverage in Europe and the United States, 1955–2005*, 44 ARCADIA 352 (2009); Susanne Janssen, Giselinde Kuipers & Marc Verboord, *Cultural Globalization and Arts Journalism: The International Orientation of Arts and Culture Coverage in Dutch, French, Germany and U.S. Newspapers, 1955 to 2005*, 73 AM. SOC. REV. 719 (2008).

30. FOREIGN NEWS IN THE MEDIA: INTERNATIONAL REPORTING IN 29 COUNTRIES, at 41 (Annabelle Mohammadi et al. eds., 1987).

31. 1986 Eurobarometer (No. 14), at 51.

32. The only alternative public opinion questions available for Greece in the 1980s look to foreign languages spoken and foreign countries visited. These language and travel numbers likely reflect both Greek social elites' familiarity with foreign countries and Greek migrant workers' experiences with host destinations. Indicatively, 16% of Greeks had travelled to Germany as of 1980, and fewer than 10% of Greeks had visited any of the other European countries listed. As of 1987, the first year the question was asked, 25% of Greeks reported speaking English fluently, 7% reported speaking French fluently, 5% reported speaking Italian fluently, and 4% reported speaking German fluently.

33. The Spanish data are for 1986 because Spain was not a member of the EU and thus was not included in the 1980 version of this survey.

34. Chang Kil Lee & David Strang, *The International Diffusion of Public Sector Downsizing*, 60 INT'L ORG. 883 (2006).

35. Fabrizio Gilardi et al., *Learning from Others: The Diffusion of Hospital Financing Reforms in OECD Countries*, 42 COMP. POL. STUD. 549 (2009).

36. Lee & Strang, *supra* note 34, is perhaps the most thorough and interesting study of the importance of policy success in policy diffusion and indicates that only successes consistent with dominant theoretical models are imitated.

37. World Health Organization (WHO), The World Health Report 2000—Health Systems: Improving Performance 35 (2000). As described above, the WHO has been promoting universal coverage and fairness in health financing for many decades, in addition to its

work promoting reductions in infant mortality and improvements in life-expectancy. These goals were reiterated as ways to measure health system performance in this key 2000 report. I focus on health care outcomes here, rather than on access or financing, because decision-makers considering a National Health Service likely understand that this policy improves coverage and makes financing more equitable; they would not need evidence from abroad to understand this point.

38. Zachary Elkins et al., *Competing for Capital: The Diffusion of Bilateral Investment Treaties, 1960–2000*, 60 INT'L ORG. 811 (2006).

39. Simmons & Elkins, *supra* note 18.

40. Witold J. Henisz et al., *The Worldwide Diffusion of Market-Oriented Infrastructure Reform*, 70 AM. SOC.REV. 871 (2005).

41. Some work emphasizes ideational influences. *See, e.g.*, Mark Blyth, *Powering, Puzzling, or Persuading? The Mechanisms of Building Institutional Orders*, 51 INT'L STUD. Q. 761 (2007).

42. The shift from a social insurance system funded through taxes on labor to an NHS funded through general income taxes could also benefit businesses. However, I have found no evidence that conservative parties and business associations rallied in favor of NHSs.

43. *See* Charles H. Blake & Jessica R. Adolino, *The Enactment of National Health Insurance: A Boolean Analysis of Twenty Advanced Industrial Countries*, 26 J. HEALTH POL., POL'Y, & LAW 679 (2001); Hacker, *supra* note 4, at 695–96; Walter Korpi, *Power, Politics, & State Autonomy in the Development of Social Citizenship*, 54 AM. SOC. REV. 309 (1989).

44. John D. Huber, *How Does Cabinet Instability Affect Political Performance? Portfolio Volatility and Health Care Cost Containment in Parliamentary Democracies*, 92 AM. POL. SCI. REV. 577 (1998).

45. Theodore R. Marmor, & David Thomas, *Doctors, Politics and Pay Disputes: Pressure Group Politics' Revisited*, 2 BRITISH J. POL. SCI. 421 (1972).

46. ELIOT FREIDSON, PROFESSION OF MEDICINE: A STUDY OF THE SOCIOLOGY OF APPLIED KNOWLEDGE (1988).

47. ODIN ANDERSON, UNEASY EQUILIBRIUM (1968).

48. RUDOLPH KLEIN, THE NEW POLITICS OF THE NHS (5th ed. 2006); Hacker, *supra* note 4.

49. Immergut, *supra* note 1, at 39.

50. Peter Hall & Rosemary Taylor, *Political Science and the Three New Institutionalisms*, 44 POL. STUD. 936 (1996).

51. GEORGE TSEBELIS, VETO PLAYERS: HOW POLITICAL INSTITUTIONS WORK (2002).

52. Immergut, *supra* note 1.

53. Huber, *supra* note 44.

54. AREND LIJPHART, PATTERNS OF DEMOCRACY: GOVERNMENT FORMS AND PERFORMANCE IN THIRTY-SIX COUNTRIES (1999); Vicki Birchfield & Markus M. L. Crepaz, *The Impact of Constitutional Structures and Collective and Competitive Veto Points on Income Inequality in Industrialized Democracies*, 34 EUR. J. POL. RESEARCH 175 (1998).

55. Antonia Maioni, *Parting at the Crossroads—The Development of Health Insurance in Canada and the United States, 1940–1965*, 29 COMP. POL. 411 (1997).

56. ANA RICO, DECENTRALIZACIÓN Y REFORMA SANITARIA EN ESPAÑA (1976–1996): INTENSIDAD DE PREFERENCIAS Y AUTONOMIA POLITICA COMO CONDICIONES PARA EL BUEN GOBIERNO (1998).

57. PAUL PIERSON, DISMANTLING THE WELFARE STATE? REAGAN, THATCHER, AND THE POLITICS OF RETRENCHMENT (1994). For related work on employment discrimination, see Katerina Linos, *Path Dependence in Discrimination Law*, 35 YALE J. INT'L LAW 116 (2010).

58. Hacker, *supra* note 4.

59. Manfred Schmidt's 1999 study finds that spending on health care is correlated with a large senior population. Manfred G. Schmidt, *Warum die Gesundheitsausgaben Wachsen: Befunde des Vergleich Demokratisch Verfasster Lander*, 2 POLITISCHE

VIERTELJAHRESSCHRIFT 229, 238 (1999). In contrast, John Huber's 1998 study, which is sensitive to time processes and other methodological issues, does not find health care cutbacks to be shaped by population structure. Instead, he finds that cabinet volatility impedes health cost-cutting efforts. Huber, *supra* note 44.

60. A national solidarity coalition introduced this reform in Italy. Maurizio Ferrera, *The Rise and Fall of Democratic Universalism: Health Care Reform in Italy, 1978–1994*, 20 J. HEALTH POL., POL'Y, & LAW 275 (1995).

61. Hans Jürgen Puhle, *Mobilizers and Late Modernizers: Socialist Parties in the New Southern Europe, in* PARTIES, POLITICS, AND DEMOCRACY IN THE NEW SOUTHERN EUROPE (P. Nikiforos Diamandouros & Richard Gunther eds., 2001); Philippe C. Schmitter, *Organized Interests and Democratic Consolidation in Southern Europe, in* THE POLITICS OF DEMOCRATIC CONSOLIDATION: SOUTHERN EUROPE IN COMPARATIVE PERSPECTIVE (Richard Gunther et al. eds., 2001).

62. The year 1960 is used as a starting point, even though the UK National Health Service preceded this, because of substantial missing data on key covariates prior to 1960. The last observed adoption of a National Health Service in the OECD occurred in 1986. Luxembourg is not included in the models due to extensive missing data.

63. Nathaniel Beck et al., *Taking Time Seriously: Time-Series-Cross-Section Analysis with a Binary Dependent Variable*, 42 AM. J. POL. SCI. 1260 (1998).

64. Dependent variable observations consist in a series of zeros (marking country-years for countries that do not adopt an NHS), or a series of zeros ending in a 1 (indicating the country-year in which the country adopted an NHS).

65. JEFFREY M. WOOLDRIDGE, ECONOMETRIC ANALYSIS OF CROSS-SECTION AND PANEL DATA 706–07 (2001).

66. While row standardization is conventional in spatial econometrics it has both advantages and disadvantages and must be justified on theoretical grounds. *See* Thomas Plümper and Eric Neumayer, *Model Specification in the Analysis of Spatial Dependence*, 49 EUR. J. POL. RESEARCH 418, 428–31. In general, row standardization makes coefficients easy to interpret and compare. An important additional theoretical reason justifies row standardization in this case. Row standardization reflects the theoretical assumption that because citizens' attention spans are limited, the relevance of any particular foreign country's choices depends on how many other foreign countries' choices are presented to citizens. For example, the assumption made here is that citizens who are familiar with a single foreign country will respond more to information about that country's policies than will citizens who are also familiar with many other foreign countries. This specification of the weight matrix is consistent with this book's theoretical claim that where a single foreign model is presented to voters, it has more influence than when it is one among several foreign models. That being said, row-standardization obscures the fact that citizens of different countries receive different volumes of foreign news coverage.

67. For a more detailed treatment on estimating cross-sectional time-series models with spatial interdependence, see Robert J. Franzese Jr. & Jude C. Hays, *Spatial Econometric Models of Cross-Sectional Interdependence in Political Science Panel and Time-Series-Cross-Section Data*, 15 POL. ANAL. 140 (2007).

68. WHO, *supra* note 37, at 35.

69. Elkins et al., *supra* note 38.

70. World Bank, *World Development Indicators, available at* http://data.worldbank.org/data-catalog/world-development-indicators. Data for 1975 is used. Correlations among countries were based on nine major export categories. Correlations are ranked and each country's top three competitors are used in creating the trade competition matrix.

71. ROBERT J. FRANZESE, JR., MACROECONOMIC POLICIES OF DEVELOPED DEMOCRACIES (2002).

72. Immergut, *supra* note 1, at 7.

73. Franzese, *supra* note 71.

74. Hacker, *supra* note 4.

75. Huber, *supra* note 44.

76. This table was calculated using Gary King's Clarify software. All variables were held constant at their 75th percentile, except for right-wing government and number of parties, which were held constant at the 25th percentile. That is, the coefficients in Table 4.4 report how a change in each independent variable would alter the probability of adoption of an NHS in an environment that was already relatively favorable (had a relatively left-wing government, a relatively small number of parties in government, a relatively high prior health care coverage of the population, relatively many trade partners who already have NHSs, and at a time when NHSs are perceived as relatively successful in terms of low infant mortality). These variables are held at the 75th percentile rather than at their mean because the adoption of an NHS happens rarely and only happens when multiple conditions are relatively favorable.

77. Indicatively, a cabinet composed entirely of UK Labor Party ministers would score a 2.8 while one composed entirely of UK Conservative Party ministers would score a 7.7 on this index.

78. Results using a one-period lag are reported.

79. Results using a broad NHS definition are reported, but this distinction is made somewhat moot since the controversial New Zealand case is not included in the data set due to missing covariates.

80. Lee & Strang, *supra* note 34.

Chapter 5

1. *See, e.g.*, Paul Pierson, DISMANTLING THE WELFARE STATE? REAGAN, THATCHER, AND THE POLITICS OF RETRENCHMENT (1994) (emphasizing that welfare policy retrenchment in particular is typically a gradual process). For related work on path dependence in employment discrimination law, see Katerina Linos, *Path Dependence in Discrimination Law*, 35 YALE J. INT'L LAW 116 (2010).

2. KURT WEYLAND, BOUNDED RATIONALITY AND POLICY DIFFUSION: SOCIAL SECTOR REFORM IN LATIN AMERICA 13 (2007) (emphasizing the role of experts in spreading pension reforms).

3. Using the quantitative measures detailed in chapter 3, Greece's export profile looked most similar to those of Spain, Portugal, and Denmark. Spain's export profile looked most similar to those of Portugal, Greece, and Austria. While manufactured goods were a major export category for these and all other OECD countries, these countries differed from other OECD countries in that they also exported significant amounts of food. Additionally, they also exported unusually large amounts of travel and transport services.

4. Fabrizio Gilardi et al., *Learning and the Conditional Diffusion of Health-Care Cost-Sharing Policies in Europe* (working paper, 2010), *available at* http://www.fabriziogilardi.org/resources/papers/refprice_july2010.pdf.

5. *See, e.g.*, Federico Sturzenegger and Mariano Tommasi, *Introduction, in* THE POLITICAL ECONOMY OF REFORM 13 (Federico Sturzenegger & Mariano Tommasi, eds., 1998).

6. RUDOLPH KLEIN, THE NEW POLITICS OF THE NHS 1 (2001).

7. Just before World War II, there were 1334 voluntary hospitals and 1771 municipal hospitals. NICHOLAS TIMMINS, THE FIVE GIANTS: A BIOGRAPHY OF THE WELFARE STATE 103 (2nd ed. 2001). By World War II, the former were in financial and medical crisis. Their income from gifts and investments had fallen to 33% of revenue by 1938 (from 88% in 1891). *Id.* at 104. The balance was made up by patient payments, undermining these hospitals' mission. Klein, *supra* note 6, at 4. Doctors made their income from private patients while treating the poor for free. This restricted specialist care to prosperous parts of Britain. Timmins, *supra* note 7, at 105. Even the House Governor of Charing Cross Hospital had announced, as early as 1930, that hospitals relying on sweepstakes and competitions were unsustainable and that state-supported and state-controlled hospitals would be introduced within a decade. *Id.* at 104.

8. Jacob S. Hacker, *The Historical Logic of National Health Insurance: Structure and Sequence in the Development of British, Canadian and U.S. Medical Policy*, 12 STUD. IN AM. POL. DEV. 57 (1998).

9. DEREK FRASER, THE EVOLUTION OF THE BRITISH WELFARE STATE: A HISTORY OF SOCIAL POLICY SINCE THE INDUSTRIAL REVOLUTION (3d ed. 2003); Timmins, *supra* note 7.

10. The development of the British NHS is discussed thoroughly in an extensive secondary literature and thus is not further detailed here.

11. Fraser, *supra* note 9.

12. HARTLEY DEAN, WELFARE RIGHTS AND SOCIAL POLICY (2002).

13. Fraser, *supra* note 9.

14. *See* Fraser, *supra* note 9.

15. Pierson, *supra* note 1.

16. Klein, *supra* note 6, at 151.

17. Klein, *supra* note 6.

18. While Britain was a pioneer in introducing the purchaser/provider split into an NHS, U.S. economists developed ideas about managed care, which American health maintenance organizations (HMOs) practiced. For a more extensive treatment of the purchaser/provider split as a potential policy transfer, see Fiona O'Neill, *Health: The "Internal Market" and Reform of the National Health Service, in* POLICY TRANSFER AND BRITISH SOCIAL POLICY (David P. Dolowitz ed., 2000).

19. This is particularly true for Spain, Portugal, and Greece. Italy was a founding member of the European Community.

20. In contrast, Socialist-led administrations governed Portugal from the transition to democracy until the mid-1980s.

21. *See* Hans Jürgen Puhle, *Mobilizers and Late Modernizers: Socialist Parties in the New Southern Europe, in* PARTIES, POLITICS, AND DEMOCRACY IN THE NEW SOUTHERN EUROPE 268 (P. Nikiforos Diamandouros & Richard Gunther eds., 2001); Juan Luis Rodríguez Vigil, *Prólogo, in* LA DÉCADA DE LA REFORMA SANITARIA 9 (Francisco Ortega & Fernando Lamata eds., 1998).

22. EUROPEAN OBSERVATORY ON HEALTH CARE SYSTEMS, HEALTH CARE SYSTEMS IN TRANSITION: SPAIN 10 (2000); JOSEP A. RODRIGUEZ & JESUS M. DE MIGUEL, SALUD Y PODER 180–85 (1990).

23. Joseph B. Kelley, *Health Care in the Spanish Social Security System: Public-Private Relationships*, 14 INT'L J. HEALTH SERVS. 309 (1984); Servicio de Estudios Sociológicos del IESS 1979.

24. ANA GUILLÉN, POLÍTICAS DE REFORMA SANITARIA EN ESPAÑA: DE LA RESTAURACIÓN A LA DEMOCRACIA 358 (1996).

25. SIMA LIEBERMAN, GROWTH AND CRISIS IN THE SPANISH ECONOMY: 1940–93, at 150, 218 (1995).

26. *See* Ana M. Guillén & Laura Cabiedes, *Towards a National Health Service in Spain: The Search for Equity and Efficiency*, 7 J. EUR. SOC. POL'Y 319 (1997). Supplemented by European Observatory, *supra* note 22; Marisol Rodríguez et al., *An Update on Spain's Health Care System: Is It Time for Managed Competition?*, 51 HEALTH POL'Y 109 (2000).

27. Ana Rico, et al., *The Spanish State and the Medical Profession in Primary Health Care: Doctors, Veto Points and Reform Attempts, in* SUCCESS AND FAILURE IN PUBLIC GOVERNANCE : A COMPARATIVE ANALYSIS 238 (Paul Hart Bovens & B. Guy Peters eds., 2001).

28. Diario de Sesiones del Congreso de los Diputados no. 86, 5708, May 6, 1980.

29. Diario de Sesiones del Congreso de los Diputados no. 86, 5711, May 6, 1980.

30. ANA GUILLÉN, POLÍTICAS DE REFORMA SANITARIA EN ESPAÑA: DE LA RESTAURACIÓN A LA DEMOCRACIA 358 (1996).

31. PSOE, PSOE MANIFESTO (1977).

32. *Id.*

33. *Id.*

34. *Id.*
35. PSOE, PSOE MANIFESTO (1982).
36. *Id.*
37. J. Velarde Fuertes, EL TERCER VIRAJE DE LA SEGURIDAD SOCIAL EN ESPANA (1990).
38. RODRÍGUEZ & DE MIGUEL, *supra* note 22, at 100–06.
39. Itziar Larizgoitia & Barbara Starfield, *Reform of Primary Health Care: The Case of Spain,* 41 HEALTH POL'Y 121, 122 (1997).
40. *Id.*
41. Whereas PSOE had explicitly advocated for a National Health Service in its 1979 and 1982 Manifestos, in 1986, it called the reform a National Health System, to emphasize its plans for strong regional involvement. I use the term National Health Service throughout for clarity.
42. Diario de Sesiones del Congreso de los Diputados, at 9854.
43. General Health Law (B.O.E. 1986, 102) (Spain) [Ley 14/1986].
44. 338 Diario de Sesiones del Congreso de los Diputados 35, p. 10,325, daily ed., Oct. 8, 1985.
45. PNV Representative Gorroño Arrizabalaga, 245 Diario de Sesiones del Congreso de los Diputados, p. 10,946, daily ed., Oct. 31, 1985.
46. PSOE Representative Martin Toval, 215 Diario de Sesiones del Congreso de los Diputados, page 9870, daily ed., June 11, 1985.
47. AP/PP Representative Núñez Pérez, 339 Diario de Sesiones del Congreso de los Diputados, page 10,360, daily ed., Oct. 9, 1985.
48. *Id.*
49. PSOE, PSOE MANIFESTO (1989).
50. *Id.*
51. PETER MCDONOUGH, SAMUEL H. BARNES & ANTONIO LÓPEZ PINA, THE CULTURAL DYNAMICS OF DEMOCRATIZATION IN SPAIN 98 (1998).
52. José M. Maravall, *Economic Reforms in New Democracies: The Southern European Experience,* (working paper no. 22, Instituto Juan March de Estudios e Investigaciones, Madrid, 1991), at 13.
53. JUAN DÍEZ MEDRANO, FRAMING EUROPE: ATTITUDES TO EUROPEAN INTEGRATION IN GERMANY, SPAIN AND THE UNITED KINGDOM (2003).
54. *Id.*
55. PETER MCDONOUGH, SAMUEL H. BARNES & ANTONIO LÓPEZ PINA, THE CULTURAL DYNAMICS OF DEMOCRATIZATION IN SPAIN 103 (1998).
56. *Id.* at 88.
57. *Id.* at 115.
58. Rico, et al., *supra* note 27, at 246.
59. RODRÍGUEZ & DE MIGUEL, *supra* note 22, at 195.
60. ANA GUILLÉN, *supra* note 24, at 358 (1996).
61. E. Martín López, *Los Médicos Españoles y Su Ideología Professional,* 2 REVISTA DE SEGURIDAD SOCIAL 167 (1979).
62. Servicio de Estudios Sociológicos del IESS 1979; RODRÍGUEZ & DE MIGUEL, *supra* note 22.
63. ANA RICO, DECENTRALIZACION Y REFORMA SANITARIA EN ESPANA (1976–1996): INTENSIDAD DE PREFERENCIAS Y AUTONOMIA POLITICA OMO CONDICIONES PARA EL BUEN GOBIERNO 137 (1998).
64. Marciano Sánchez Bayle, *Evolución del Sistema Sanitario en España, in* EL SISTEMA SANITARIO EN ESPAÑA: EVOLUCION, SITUACION, ACTUAL, PROBLEMAS Y PERSPECTIVAS 54 (Marciano Sánchez Bayle ed., 1996).
65. Rodríguez et al., *supra* note 26.
66. Laura Cabiedes & Ana Guillén, *Adopting and Adapting Managed Competition: Health Care Reform in Southern Europe,* 52 SOC. SCI. MED. 1205, 1210 (2001).
67. Indeed, Catalonia introduced purchaser/provider split legislation in May 1990, immediately after the UK internal market reforms. Rico, *supra* note 63, at 449.

68. This article only examines postwar developments in social policy. The 1920s and 1930s are likely much richer in diffusion experiences. In these decades, Greece's liberal administrations, advised by the ILO, copied a wide variety of French and German labor legislation, while Spain's short-lived 2nd Republic (1931–1936) rapidly introduced social reforms other European countries had been fighting over for a century. *See* Georgios Tsalikis, *Η Θεμελίωση της (Αντι)Κοινωνικής Ασφάλισης στην Ελλάδα (1840–1940)*, in Η ασφάλιση υγείας στην Ελλάδα, επιμέλεια Κυριόπουλος, Γιάννης, Λιαρόπουλος Λυκούργος, Χρήστος Μπουρσανίδης, Χαράλαμπος Οικονόμου (2001); Antonis Liakos, *Welfare Policy in Greece (1909–1940)*, in Comparing Social Welfare Systems in Southern Europe (1997); David Strang & Patricia M.Y. Chang, *The International Labour Organization and the Welfare State: Institutional Effects on National Welfare Spending, 1960–1980*, 47 Int'l Org. 235 (1993); Rico, *supra* note 63.

69. Demetrios Venieris, *The History of Health Insurance in Greece: The Nettle Governments Failed to Grasp* 23–24 (LSE Discussion Paper No. 9., 1997).

70. *Id.* at 27.

71. Ν. Giannis, Τα Οικονομικά της Υγείας: Θεωρία και Πολιτική (2003); Ellie Tragakes & Nicholas Polyzos, *The Evolution of Health Care Reforms in Greece: Charting a Course of Change*, 13 Int'l J. Health Planning & Mgmt. 107 (1998); Konstantina Davaki & Elias Mossialos, *Plus ça Change: Health Sector Reforms in Greece*, 30 J. Health Pol., Pol'y, & Law 143 (2005).

72. Organization for Economic Cooperation and Development (OECD), OECD Health Systems: Facts and Trends 1960–1991, 247 (1993).

73. Interviews with ministers' advisors in Athens, Greece. (Mar. –Apr. 2004).

74. Interviews with Minister Avgerinos and ministers' advisors in Athens, Greece (Mar. –Apr. 2004).

75. *See* George Alogoskoufis, Francesco Giavazzi & Guy Laroque, *The Two Faces of Janus: Institutions, Policy Regimes and Macroeconomic Performance in Greece*, 10 Econ. Pol'y 147, 147 (1995).

76. I have italicized certain phrases for emphasis.

77. Introductory report to the bill for the National Health System, at 5.

78. *Id.* at 2.

79. *Id.* at 5.

80. *See, e.g.*, Demos Papademetriou, PASOK MP, PVE (Praktika tis Voulis twn Ellinwn) Aug. 23, 1983, at 1381; Athanasios Filippopoulos, PASOK MP, PVE Aug. 23, 1983, at 1359.

81. *See* Paraskevas Avgerinos, PASOK Health Minister, PVE, Aug. 24, at 1404; Athanassios Filippopoulos, PASOK MP, PVE Aug. 26, at 1529.

82. For example, Andreas Andrianopoulos, ND MP, criticized the introductory report to the National Health Service bill as "outdated Anglo-Saxon economics from the 1960s." PVE, Aug. 23, 1983, at 1427. Constantinos Printzos, ND MP, mentioned that the success of the UK and Swedish NHS was doubtful, and that he believed that no foreign system had been uniformly successful and thus worthy of direct imitation. PVE, Aug. 23, 1983, at 1373.

83. E.g., Diakos Manoussakis, ND MP, PVE, Aug. 24, 1983, at 1386.

84. *See* Vassilios Bemires, ND MP, PVE, Aug. 24, 1983, at 1389–90.

85. For example, both Vassilios Bemires, ND MP, and Paraskevas Avgerinos, the PASOK health minister, referred to Canada to support their arguments. PVE, Aug. 24, at 1390, 1392.

86. *See* Ioannis Varvitsiotis, ND spokesperson, PVE Aug. 24, at 1406. Vassilios Kontogiannopoulos, ND MP, also referred to long queues for hospital treatment in Sweden. PVE Aug. 24, at 1426. Aggelos Valtadoros, ND MP, referred to long queues outside pharmacies in Socialist countries. PVE Aug. 26, at 1469.

87. *See* Constantinos Kappos, spokesperson for the Communist KKE party, PVE, Aug. 24, 1983, at 1408.

88. For example, Paraskevas Avgerinos, the PASOK health minister, referred to Alma-Ata's "health for all by 2000" goal as a justification for his bill's goal to provide equal access to health services for all. PVE, Aug. 24, 1983, at 1399.

89. For example, according to an October 1984 MRB poll, 62 percent of Greeks thought the PASOK government had handled health care and social insurance issues well. In contrast, for every other issue studied in this poll, only a minority of Greeks thought well of the PASOK government. *See* Γιάννης Λούλης, Η Κρίση της Πολιτικής στην Ελλάδα: Εκλογές—Κοινή Γνώμη, Πολιτικές Εξελίξεις 1980–1995 (1995), at 92. See also *id.* at 48 (presenting similar poll findings for May and October of 1983).

90. Tsalikis, *supra* note 68, at 43.

91. Venieris, *supra* note 69, at 10.

92. Mick Carpenter, *On the Edge: The Fate of Progressive Modernization in Greek Health Policy*, 24 INT'L POL. SCI. REV. 257, 263 (2003); Venieris, *supra* note 69; Interviews with medical association leaders, in Athens, Greece (Apr. 6, 2004).

93. Franglinos Papadelis, president of the Athens Medical Association was also a close aide to Paraskevas Avgerinos, the PASOK minister drafting the National Health Service law. Interviews with several advisors to health ministers, in Athens, Greece (Mar. –Apr. 2004).

94. Interview with health minister advisor, in Athens, Greece (Mar. 10, 2004); interview with medical association vice-president, in Athens, Greece (Apr. 6, 2004).

95. Konstantina Davaki & Elias Mossialos, *Plus ça Change: Health Sector Reforms in Greece*, 30 J. HEALTH POL., POL'Y & LAW 143, 159 (2005).

96. Interview with medical association vice-president, in Athens, Greece (Apr. 6, 2004); interview with health policy expert, in Athens, Greece (Apr. 5, 2004).

97. Ellie Tragakes & Nicholas Polyzos, *The Evolution of Health Care Reforms in Greece: Charting a Course of Change*, 13 INT'L J. HEALTH PLANNING & MGMT. 107, 124–25 (1998).

98. Yannis Tountas, et al., *Reforming the Reform: the Greek National Health System in Transition*, 62 HEALTH POL'Y 15, 22 (2002).

99. Interviews with advisors to the health minister, in Athens, Greece (Mar. 19, 2004).

100. *See* Introductory Report, Bill for the Improvement and Modernization of the National Health System, Dec. 8, 2000, at 1.

101. *See* PVE, Jan. 22, 2001, at 3969.

102. *See* Athanassios Giannopoulos, ND Speaker, PVE Jan. 22, 2001, at 3970.

103. *See* Paraskevas Avgerinos, PASOK MP, PVE Jan. 22, 2001, at 3981. Christina Spyraki, PASOK deputy health minister, echoed this point. PVE Jan. 22, 2001, at 3982.

104. Puhle, *supra* note 21.

105. Rodríguez Vigil, *supra* note 21, at 11.

Chapter 6

1. ORGANIZATION FOR ECONOMIC COOPERATION AND DEVELOPMENT (OECD), EXTENDING OPPORTUNITIES: HOW ACTIVE SOCIAL POLICY CAN BENEFIT US ALL 60 (2005).

2. Desired family size is typically greater than actual family size. *See* OECD, *supra* note 1, at 65–67.

3. *See* Christopher J. Ruhm, *The Economic Consequences of Parental Leave Mandates: Lessons from Europe*, 113 Q. J. ECON. 285, 310–11 (1998). *See also* Christine Jolls, *Accommodation Mandates*, 53 STAN. L. REV. 290–300 (2000) (discussing the effects of the FMLA); Gillian Lester, *A Defense of Paid Family Leave*, 28 HARV. J.L. & GENDER 1 (2005) (reviewing empirical work concluding that paid leaves increase women's labor force participation, and arguing that this is normatively desirable); CATHERINE R. ALBISTON, RIGHTS ON LEAVE: INSTITUTIONAL INEQUALITY AND THE MOBILIZATION OF THE FAMILY AND MEDICAL LEAVE ACT (2010) (explaining how lack of information and uneven enforcement of leave laws influences uptake).

4. The 2% of GDP figure only captures direct payments to parents. Families in many countries get additional benefits through the tax code and through policies that are targeted

mostly, but not exclusively, to families, such as housing allowances. *See* OECD, OECD SOCIAL EXPENDITURE DATABASE (2004).

5. The terms family allowances and family benefits are used interchangeably.

6. Leaves for the care of infants and young children are called childcare leaves in this chapter, following Gauthier (1996). *See* ANNE GAUTHIER, THE STATE AND THE FAMILY: A COMPARATIVE ANALYSIS OF FAMILY POLICIES IN INDUSTRIALIZED COUNTRIES (1996). This distinction avoids the terminology "parental leave" which some governments use to refer to maternity leave and others to childcare leave. Many countries have introduced very short "paternity leaves" that give the father a few days off work surrounding the birth of a child. Similarly, some countries reserve parts of childcare leave for the father. While leaves generally give parents the choice to work or take care of family, many European laws include short mandatory periods of maternity leave.

7. The terminology of goals, instruments, and instrument settings comes from Peter Hall, *Policy Paradigms, Social Learning and the State: The Case of Policymaking in Britain*, 25 COMP. POL. 275, 278–79 (1993).

8. For a historical account of how key doctrines creating the modern European legal order were developed and accepted, see KAREN J. ALTER, ESTABLISHING THE SUPREMACY OF EUROPEAN LAW (2001). For a more general introduction to the EU legal system, see EU LAW: TEXT, CASES AND MATERIALS (Paul Craig & Grainne de Burca eds., 3d ed. 2002).

9. I study how well member states comply with these directives in a separate study. *See* Katerina Linos, *How Can International Organizations Shape National Welfare States? Evidence from Compliance with European Union Directives*, 40 COMP. POL. STUD. 547 (2007).

10. Laurence R. Helfer, *Understanding Change in International Organizations: Globalization and Innovation in the ILO*, 59 VAND. L. REV. 651 (2006).

11. Conversely, in the case of pension privatization models or health care cost-cutting, we should expect conservative actors to be especially receptive to international models. *See* Sarah Brooks, *Interdependent and Domestic Foundations of Policy Change: The Diffusion of Pension Privatization Around the World*, 40 INT'L STUD. Q. 273 (2005); Fabrizio Gilardi et al., *Learning from Others: The Diffusion of Hospital Financing Reforms in OECD Countries* 42 COMP. POL. STUD. 549 (2009).

12. *See* Kenneth Abbott et al., *The Concept of Legalization*, 54 INT'L ORG. 401 (2000).

13. The Pregnant Workers Directive (92/85/EEC) outlines health and safety protections, and provides for paid maternity leave of 14 weeks, time off for antenatal care, and protection against dismissal. The transposition deadline was October 1994; no member state had correctly transposed the directive before this deadline. *See* GERDA FALKNER ET AL., COMPLYING WITH EUROPE: EU HARMONISATION AND SOFT LAW IN THE MEMBER STATES 89 (2005).

14. The main changes brought about through the directive were an important expansion in coverage in the UK, an extension of leave by one week in Portugal, and an extension of (mandatory) leave by two weeks in Sweden. *See* FALKNER ET AL., *supra* note 13, at 91.

15. For a more extensive discussion of EU social directives and their impact on EU member state countries, see Linos, *supra* note 9. *See also*, Katerina Linos, *Path Dependence in Discrimination Law*, 35 YALE J. INT'L L. 116 (2010) (discussing European Court of Justice [ECJ] interpretations of EU directives and treaty provisions in the social policy field).

16. Constitution of the International Labour Organization, art. 389.3 and art. 389.19, June 28, 1919, 49 Stat. 2712, 225 C.T.I.A. 373 [hereinafter 1919 ILO Constitution].

17. Maternity and sickness insurance were often introduced together, and the available data do not distinguish between the two. Social Security Administration, *Social Security Programs Throughout the World* (1999), *available at* http://www.ssa.gov/policy/docs/progdesc/ssptw/.

18. Family benefit data are also based on Social Security Administration data. Social Security Administration, *supra* note 17. An important limitation of these data is that they do not fully capture provisions in the tax code designed to benefit families. Year

cutoffs in the graphs aim to put comparable numbers of countries in each bin; as Figure 6.3 shows, many countries adopted family benefits between 1940 and 1960, but the rate of adoption tapered off thereafter.

19. One might wonder whether countries adopted maternity leaves at the same time because they experienced common shocks, such as World War II. However, the slope of the line in Figure 6.4 suggests that countries were adopting maternity leave laws at the same pace between the 1930s and the early 1950s, and that the spike in the adoption of this policy began in 1952, the year of the ILO Convention.

20. *See generally*, ECONOMICS OF THE INDUSTRIAL REVOLUTION (Joel Mokyr ed., 1985).

21. WALLY SECCOMBE, WORKING-CLASS FAMILIES FROM THE INDUSTRIAL REVOLUTION TO THE FERTILITY DECLINE 40–49 (1993).

22. James Cronin, *Strikes and Power in Britain, 1870–1920, in* STRIKES, WARS, AND REVOLUTIONS IN AN INTERNATIONAL PERSPECTIVE 79–100 (Leopold H. Haimson & Charles Tilly eds., 1989)

23. AMERICA'S WORKING WOMEN: A DOCUMENTARY HISTORY 1600 TO THE PRESENT 158–78 (Rosalyn Baxandall & Linda Gordan eds., 1995).

24. For data on policy adoption, see Social Security Administration, *supra* note 17; for data on industrialization, see BRIAN MITCHELL, INTERNATIONAL HISTORICAL STATISTICS EUROPE 1750–2005 (2007).

25. ANNE GAUTHIER & ANITA BORTNIK, COMPARATIVE MATERNITY, PARENTAL AND CHILDCARE DATABASE, VERSION 2 (2001); ANNE GAUTHIER, COMPARATIVE FAMILY BENEFITS DATABASE, VERSION 2 (2003). It was also possible to use maternity leave weighted by the generosity of this leave. These measures correlate at .92, because maternity leave is well-compensated across OECD countries. Therefore little hinges on this choice. Maternity leave length is used because of the theoretical expectation that qualitative features of policies diffuse.

26. INTERNATIONAL LABOUR OFFICE. YEARBOOK OF LABOUR STATISTICS (various years); GAUTHIER, *supra* note 25.

27. New Zealand and Australia have subsequently introduced laws mandating paid maternity leave.

28. In particular, the value of sales of newspapers, journals and periodicals in United States for the year 1975 was used to construct these weights. ORGANIZATION FOR ECONOMIC COOPERATION AND DEVELOPMENT: OECD FACTBOOK (various years).

29. CONSTRUCTING WORLD CULTURE: INTERNATIONAL NONGOVERNMENTAL ORGANIZATIONS SINCE 1875 (John Boli & George M. Thomas, eds., 1999).

30. *Id.* at 41.

31. UNION OF INTERNATIONAL ASSOCIATIONS (UIA), YEARBOOK OF INTERNATIONAL ORGANIZATIONS (various years).

32. The available data indicates whether an international organization has any members in a country (1) or not (0), rather than indicating the number of members the organization has in a particular country. This measure was chosen because, at the 20% cutoff, a clear break in the data appears, whether it is adjusted for population size or not. Alternative ways of coding this variable yield substantially similar results.

33. *See, e.g.,* Jack Goldsmith & Eric A. Posner, *The New International Law Scholarship,* 34 GA. J. INT'L & COMP. L. 474 ("NGOs have no particular interest in forcing states to comply with international law as opposed to whatever goals or agendas those NGOs have."); *see also* JACK GOLDSMITH & ERIC POSNER, THE LIMITS OF INTERNATIONAL LAW 124–26.

34. Zachary Elkins, Andrew Guzman & Beth Simmons, *Competing for Capital: The Diffusion of Bilateral Investment Treaties, 1960–2000,* 60 INT'L ORG. 811 (2006); Beth Simmons & Zachary Elkins, *The Globalization of Liberalization: Policy Diffusion in the International Political Economy,* 70 AM. POL. SCI. REV. 171 (2004); Witold Henisz, Bennet Zelner & Mauro Guillen, *The Worldwide Diffusion of Market Oriented Infrastructure Reform,* 59 AM. SOC. REV. 861 (2005).

35. VARIETIES OF CAPITALISM: THE INSTITUTIONAL FOUNDATIONS OF COMPARATIVE ADVANTAGE (Peter Hall & David Soskice, eds., 2001).

36. World Development Indicators 2007, *available at* http://data.worldbank.org/products/data-books/WDI-2007. Data for 1975 is used in the analysis below. Correlations among countries' exports in nine major export categories were used to identify each country's top three competitors. *See* Elkins, Guzman, & Simmons, *supra* note 34.

37. More specifically, the regressions examine whether countries that are in the top 10 percent of this measure in particular years were imitated disproportionately. In an alternative coding, countries that were top performers throughout the period under study were marked as the template countries. Results did not differ.

38. The measure used records years elapsed since particular countries ratified the relevant ILO conventions.

39. George Downs, David Rocke & Peter Barsoom, *Is the Good News About Compliance Good News About Cooperation?*, 50 INT'L ORG. 379 (1996).

40. Olli Kangas and Joakim Palme, *Does Social Policy Matter? Poverty Cycles in OECD Countries*, 30 INT'L J. HEALTH SERV. 335 (2000); Karl Ove Moene & Michael Wallerstein, *Earnings Inequality and Welfare Spending*, 55 WORLD POL. 485 (2003).

41. Walter Korpi, *Power, Politics, and State Autonomy in the Development of Social Citizenship*, 54 AM. SOC. REV. 309 (1989); GOSTA ESPING-ANDERSEN, THE THREE WORLDS OF WELFARE CAPITALISM (1990); EVELYNE HUBER & JOHN STEPHENS, DEVELOPMENT AND CRISIS OF THE WELFARE STATE: PARTIES AND POLICIES IN GLOBAL MARKETS (2001); David Bradley, Evelyne Huber, Stephanie Moller, Francois Nielsen, & John D. Stephens, *Distribution and Redistribution in Post-Industrial Democracies*, 55 WORLD POL. 193 (2003).

42. Kimberly Morgan, *The Politics of Mother's Employment*, 55 WORLD POL. 259 (2003).

43. Kimberly Morgan & Kathrin Zippel, *Paid to Care: The Origins and Effects of Care Leave Policies in Western Europe*, 10 SOC. POL. 49, 65 (2003); ANNE GAUTHIER, THE STATE AND THE FAMILY: A COMPARATIVE ANALYSIS OF FAMILY POLICIES IN INDUSTRIALIZED COUNTRIES (1996).

44. EVELYNE HUBER & JOHN STEPHENS, DEVELOPMENT AND CRISIS OF THE WELFARE STATE: PARTIES AND POLICIES IN GLOBAL MARKETS (2001); *see also* Bradley et al., *supra* note 41.

45. EVELYNE HUBER, CHARLES RAGIN & JOHN STEPHENS, COMPARATIVE WELFARE STATES DATA SET (1997).

46. SUE THOMAS, HOW WOMEN LEGISLATE (1994); Lynda Erickson, *Might More Women Make a Difference?* 30 CAN. J. POL. SCI. 663 (1997); VALERIA O'REGAN, GENDER MATTERS: FEMALE POLICYMAKERS' INFLUENCE IN INDUSTRIALIZED NATIONS (2000).

47. Inter-Parliamentary Union (IPU) Report 1995, *available at* http://www.ipu.org/english/surv95.htm.

48. ORGANIZATION FOR ECONOMIC COOPERATION AND DEVELOPMENT: EMPLOYMENT OUTLOOK (various years).

49. GAUTHIER, *supra* note 25.

50. Robert Franzese & Jude Hays, *Spatial Econometric Models of Cross-Sectional Interdependence in Political Science Panel and Time-Series-Cross-Section Data*, 15 POL. ANALYSIS 140 (2007) [hereinafter Franzese & Hays, *Spatial Econometric Models*]; Robert Franzese & Jude Hays, *Empirical Models of Spatial Interdependence*, IN OXFORD HANDBOOK OF POLITICAL METHODOLOGY (Janet Box-Steffensmeier, Henry Brady & David Collier, eds., 2008) (describing estimation strategies for pooled cross sectional time series data) [hereinafter Franzese & Hays, *Spatial Interdependence*].

51. Nathaniel Beck, Kristian Skrede Gleditsch & Kyle Beardsley, *Space is More than Geography: Using Spatial Econometrics in the Study of Political Economy*, 50 INT'L STUD. Q. 27, 40 (2006); *see also* Franzese & Hays, "Empirical Models of Spatial Interdependence," *supra* note 50.

52. Olivier Blanchard & Justin Wolfers, *The Role of Shocks and Institutions in the Rise of European Unemployment: The Aggregate Evidence*, 110 ECON. J. C1 (2000).

53. Blanchard & Wolfers, *supra* note 52. This index comes from Huber, Ragin and Stephens, *supra* note 45, and summarizes national levels of federalism, presidentialism, strength

of bicameralism, single member districts or proportional representation, referenda, judicial review, and authoritarian legacies.

54. *See,* Franzese & Hays, *Spatial Econometric Models, supra* note 50, at 15; Franzese & Hays, *Empirical Models of Spatial Interdependence, supra* note 50; Nathaniel Beck, Kristian Skrede Gleditsch & Kyle Beardsley, *Space is More than Geography: Using Spatial Econometrics in the Study of Political Economy,* 50 INT'L STUD. Q. 27, 40 (2006).

55. *See,* Franzese & Hays, *Empirical Models of Spatial Interdependence, supra* note 50, at 23–24.

56. Franzese & Hays, *Spatial Econometric Models, supra* note 50, run Monte Carlo simulations for data sets exhibiting spatial correlation, where the number of cross-sectional units ranges from 5 to 40, the number of time periods from 20 to 40, and imperfections in the weight matrix are allowed for. When the diffusion coefficient is on the order of .1, the combined effect of a slight bias in the estimate of the coefficient and a somewhat bigger bias in the estimate of the standard error leads to a misestimation of the overall strength of diffusion between 10% and 30%. Samples where the number of observations over time is high relative to the number of observations over space, such as the one used here, permit the clearest separation of diffusion from common shock effects.

57. For additional specifications and robustness tests, see Katerina Linos, *Diffusion through Democracy,* 55 AM. J. POL. SCI. 678 (2011). Some specifications in *Diffusion through Democracy* are even more conservative than those presented here, in that they control for a baseline diffusion effect in the imitation of geographic neighbors.

58. *See, e.g.,* Fabrizio Gilardi et al., *Learning from Others: The Diffusion of Hospital Financing Reforms in OECD Countries,* 42 COMP. POL. STUD. 549 (2009); Kurt Weyland, *Theories of Policy Diffusion,* 57 WORLD POL. 262, 283–85 (2005).

59. See Franzese & Hays, *Spatial Interdependence, supra* note 50, for a discussion and methods to estimate long-run effects. As a robustness check, because the spatial weight matrix based on newspaper sales is new, the models were also run with a second set of spatial weights. This second specification tested whether countries that share a border emulate each other's policies disproportionately. Both measures assume that proximate countries are covered disproportionately in each others' news; however, the shared border specification assumes media relationships are symmetric, whereas the newspaper sales matrix assumes that larger countries are covered disproportionately. A measure of emulation based on a shared border also yields results that are positive, consistent, and statistically significant, but the coefficients based on newspaper sales weights are approximately double in size (results not shown).

60. The results distinguishing between pioneers and latecomers are very similar when model VI is used instead.

61. Theoretically it would be preferable to experiment with interaction terms between dates of adoption and each of the independent variables; however, the degrees of freedom this would require were not available here. Alternative cutoff points for distinguishing between early and late adopters, as expected, produced very similar results.

62. However, the global connectedness variables cannot be sensibly compared across the two groups, as the late adopters in this sample were not very internationally oriented. Specifically, for the late adopter sample, the bottom 80th percentile of country-years had no high INGO memberships and no ratifications of the relevant ILO conventions.

Chapter 7

1. *See* MANUELA NALDINI, THE FAMILY IN THE MEDITERRANEAN WELFARE STATES 46 (2003).

2. In contrast, as chapters 4 and 5 explain, the WHO issued its Alma-Ata Declaration in 1978.

3. *See generally* Antonis Liakos, *Εργασία και Πολιτική στην Ελλάδα του Μεσοπολέμου: Το Διεθνές Γραφείο Εργασίας και η Ανάδυση των Κοινωνικών Θεσμών* (1993).

4. *See, e.g.,* Federico Sturzenegger & Mariano Tommasi, *Introduction, in* THE POLITICAL ECONOMY OF REFORM 13 (Federico Sturzenegger & Mariano Tommasi, eds., 1998).
5. SUSAN PEDERSEN, FAMILY, DEPENDENCE AND THE ORIGINS OF THE WELFARE STATE: BRITAIN AND FRANCE 1914–1945, 37 (1993).
6. Jane Lewis & Sonya O. Rose, *"Let England Blush!": Protective Labour Legislation: 1820–1914, in* PROTECTING WOMEN: LABOR LEGISLATION IN EUROPE, THE UNITED STATES, AND AUSTRALIA 1880–1920, 91, 110 (Ulla Wikander et al. eds., 1995); NICHOLAS TIMMINS, THE FIVE GIANTS: A BIOGRAPHY OF THE WELFARE STATE 14 (1995).
7. PEDERSEN, *supra* note 5, at 37, 71, 73.
8. Efi Avdela, *To the Most Weak and Needy: Women's Protective Labor Legislation in Greece, in* PROTECTING WOMEN: LABOR LEGISLATION IN EUROPE, THE UNITED STATES AND AUSTRALIA 1880–1920, 290, 293 (Ulla Wikander et al. eds., 1995).
9. Liakos, *supra* note 3, at 31–32.
10. *Id.* at 96–105.
11. Avdela, *supra* note 8, at 295.
12. *Id.* at 297–98.
13. Law ΔΚΘ'/1912 «Περί Εργασίας Γυναικών και Ανηλίκων»; Royal Decree 14, "Περί Εκτελέσεως του Περί Εργασίας Γυναικών και Ανηλίκων ΔΚΘ' (υπ' αριθ. 4029) Νόμου, ως προς τα Εργοστάσια, Εργαστήρια, Εμπορικά Καταστήματα και Πρατήρια Παντός Είδους (Aug. 26, 1913).
14. Liakos, *supra* note 3, at 250; ILO Convention 3, Maternity Protection Convention (1919), *available at* http://www.ilo.org/dyn/normlex/en/f?p=1000:12100:0::NO::P12100_INSTRUMENT_ID:312148.
15. Law 2274/20, Article 3(c), Περί κυρώσεως της διεθνούς συμβάσεως της Διεθνούς Συνδιασκέψεως της εργασίας της Ουασιγκτώνος, περί εργασίας των γυναικών προ και μετά τον τοκετόν (ΦΕΚ 145/Α/1-07-1920).
16. Liakos, *supra* note 3, at 239–45 (providing detailed evidence for these conclusions, including documentation from the public legislative record, correspondence between Greek leaders, and correspondence between Greek leaders and the ILO); *see also* Antonis Liakos, *Welfare Policy in Greece (1909–1940), in* COMPARING SOCIAL WELFARE SYSTEMS IN SOUTHERN EUROPE, VOL. 3, 93 (1997) (offering a brief, English language account of Greek labor politics in the interwar period).
17. Liakos, *supra* note 3, at 293–300; *see generally* Avdela, Protecting Women: Labor Legislation in Europe, the United States and Australia, *supra* note 8.
18. Avdela, *supra* note 8, at 315.
19. *See* Liakos, *supra* note 3, at 224 (quoting Greek government documents circulated to ILO delegates in 1919 celebrating Greek legislative achievements protecting children and women).
20. RAFAEL ARACIL & ANTONI SEGURA, HISTORIA ECONÓMICA MUNDIAL Y DE ESPAÑA 196 (1995).
21. Alvaro Soto Carmona, *La Participacion de la Mujer en la Conflictividad Laboral (1905–1921), in* Ordenamiento juridico y realidad social de las mujeres, siglos XVI a XX, 287–88 (Maria Carmen Garcia-Nieto ed., 1986).
22. Maria Gloria Nuñez Perez, *La Implantacion y los Resultados del Seguro de Maternidad en la Segunda Republica, in* ORDENAMIENTO JURIDICO Y REALIDAD SOCIAL DE LAS MUJERES, SIGLOS XVI A XX, 363–64 (Maria Carmen Garcia-Nieto ed., 1986).
23. Ley de 13 de julio de 1922 (published in *La Gaceta de Madrid,* Jul. 15 1922).
24. Real Decreto de 21 de agosto de 1923.
25. Josefina Cuesta, *Hacia el Seguro de Maternidad: La Situacion de la Mujer Obrera en los Años Veinte* [*Towards Security Regulations of Maternity*], *in* ORDENAMIENTO JURIDICO Y REALIDAD SOCIAL DE LAS MUJERES, SIGLOS XVI A XX, 330, 335–36 (Maria Carmen Garcia-Nieto ed., 1986); NALDINI, *supra* note 1, at 81; Nuñez Perez, *supra* note 22, at 365.
26. Jerònia Pons Pons, LOS INICIOS DEL SEGURO SOCIAL DE SALUD EN ESPAÑA, 1923–1949. DEL SEGURO DE MATERNIDAD AL SEGURO OBLIGATORIO DE ENFERMEDAD 10 (2009), *available at* http://www.google.com/url?sa=t&rct=j&q=&esrc=s&s

ource=web&cd=1&ved=0CFcQFjAA&url=http%3A%2F%2Fdialnet.unirioja. es%2Fservlet%2Ffichero_articulo%3Fcodigo%3D2942283%26orden%3D0&ei=WT QpUL2OHePqiwLYr4GQCw&usg=AFQjCNF4Hzb13eWrkESTsKJpbxIdoqVTmQ &sig2=Tdpgvq6Fpe_W9_AqwyVs8Q.

27. *Id.*

28. Key accomplishments making permanent the social insurance fund's payment of leaves were Law 22 de marzo de 1929 and Real Decreto de 26 de mayo de 1931.

29. Lynn Karlsson, *The Beginning of a "Masculine Renaissance": The Debate on the 1909 Prohibition Against Women's Night Work in Sweden, in* PROTECTING WOMEN: LABOR LEGISLATION IN EUROPE, THE UNITED STATES AND AUSTRALIA, 1880–1920, 235, 238 (Ulla Wikander et al. eds., 1995).

30. *Id.* at 238–39.

31. *See* International Labour Organization, *available at* http://www.ilo.org/dyn/ normlex/en/f?p=1000:11200:1948536543888391::::P11200_INSTRUMENT_ SORT:4; International Labour Organization, Ratifications for Greece (providing dates of Greek ratification of ILO conventions), *available at* http://www. ilo.org/dyn/normlex/en/f?p=1000:11200:1948536543888391::NO:11200: P11200_COUNTRY_ID:102658.

32. *Id.*; International Labour Organization, Ratifications for Spain (last accessed Aug. 12, 2012) (providing dates of Spanish ratification of ILO conventions), *available at* http://www.ilo.org/dyn/normlex/en/f?p=1000:11200:0::NO:11200: P11200_COUNTRY_ID:102847.

33. International Labour Organization, Const. art. 389.3, 389.19 (June 28, 1919), 49 Stat. 2712, 225 C.T.I.A. 373.

34. For an analogous criticism, *see* George W. Downs et al., *Is the Good News About Compliance Good News About Cooperation?,* 50 INT'L ORG. 379 (1996).

35. There is also significant variation between, and even within, autocracies. Figure 7.1 shows the Primo de Rivera dictatorship in Spain in the 1920s to be more receptive to international standards than the Franco dictatorship. Consistent with much of the historical scholarship, more detailed analysis of the data shows that while the Franco regime was internationally isolated in its first two decades and did not ratify any ILO conventions until 1958, it was more open and ratified more conventions during its last two decades in power. This variation among dictatorships' engagement with international conventions is consistent with recent literature explaining that under some circumstances, even dictatorships must please domestic constituencies. *See generally,* Jessica Weeks, *Autocratic Audience Costs: Regime Type and Signaling Resolve,* 62 INT'L ORG. 35 (2008).

36. *See* ILO Convention 102, Social Security Minimum Standards Convention (1952), *available at* http://www.ilo.org/public/english/protection/secsoc/areas/legal/ conv102.htm.

37. *See* International Labour Organization, *Ratification of C102, Social Security Minimum Standards Convention (1952)* (last accessed Aug. 12, 2012), *available at* http://www.ilo. org/dyn/normlex/en/f?p=NORMLEXPUB:11300:6861602275439136::NO:11300: P11300_INSTRUMENT_ID:312247:NO.

38. *See* ILO Convention 102, *supra* note 37, art. 2.

39. The most important of these was a 1926 law giving various small benefits to families with eight or more children. Pilar Folguera Crespo, *Politica Natalista y Control de Natalidad en Espana Durante la Decada de los Veinte: El Caso de Madrid, in* ORDENAMIENTO JURIDICO Y REALIDAD SOCIAL DE LAS MUJERES 337, 350 (Maria Carmen & Garcia-Nieto Paris eds., 1986). However, Folguera Crespo finds the Rivera pro-family policies very different from those of Rivera's contemporary, Mussolini; they were milder in substance and public rhetoric and not accompanied by the establishment of profamily organizations. *Id.* at 348.

40. Gerardo Meil Landwerlin, *L'évolution de la Politique Familiale en Espagne: Du Salaire Familial à la Lutte Contre la Pauvreté,* 49 POPULATION 959 (1994).

41. *Id.* at 963.

42. "Families with many children" is a loose translation of "familias numerosas." Both the Spanish and Greek languages (πολύτεκνες οικογένειες) have special technical terms that mean "families with many children." These are redefined legislatively to conform to changing understandings of what constitutes a large family. Over time, the number of children necessary to qualify for these benefits declined.

43. Celia Valiente Fernández, *Olvidando el Pasado: La Política Familiar en España (1975–1996)*, 5–6 Gestión y Análisis de Políticas Públicas 151, 153–54 (1996).

44. Landwerlin, *supra* note 40.

45. *Id.* at 972.

46. N. 1910/44 (ΦΕΚ 229/Α/3–10–1944) «Περί κωδικοποιήσεως και συμπληρώσεως της Νομοθεσίας «περι προστασίας πολυτέκνων»».

47. *100,000 Ιδιωτικοί Υπάλληλοι Συνέρχονται Σημερον Εις το Επαγγελματικον Των Συνεδρίων*, Το Βήμα, Nov. 1, 1959, at 9.

48. Law 3868/1958 Νομοθετικό Διάταγμα 3868 Περί Συστάσεως Διανεμητικού Λογαριασμού Οικογενειακών Επιδομάτων Μισθωτών (1958).

49. Katerina Linos, *How Can International Organizations Shape National Welfare States? Evidence from Compliance with European Union Directives*, 40 Comp. Pol. Studies 547 (2007).

50. Although substantially involved in many areas of policy-making, labor unions were slow to embrace family-related demands. Until 1990, the General Federation of Greek Workers had not expressed any position on the family or on demographic issues. H. Symeonidou, *Greece, in* Family Policy in EEC Countries 159–60 (W. Dumont ed., 1990). However, in the 1990s, notably in 1993 and 2000, women delegates successfully negotiated for improvements in maternity leaves. Panagiota Petroglou, Καλές Πρακτικές για το Συνδιασμό Οικογενειακής Ζωής και Σταδιοδρομίας, Ελληνική Έκθεση (2000), *available at* http://www.kethi.gr/greek/meletes/GREEK_REPORT_FAMILY_LIFE (last accessed Apr. 10, 2007). Spanish labor unions were generally supportive of gender equality, but took little interest in family policy. Resolutions of UCG and CCOO confederation congresses from 1984 to 1994 contain very few references to leaves, benefits, or other family related policies. Celia Valiente, *Las Políticas de Cuidado de los Niños a Nivel Nacional en España (1975–1996) [Central-State Child Care Policies in Spain (1975–1996)]*, 50 Papers: Revista de Sociología 101, 118 (1997) [hereinafter Valiente, *Las Políticas de Cuidado de los Niños*]. Trade union feminists occasionally raised family policies in their preliminary negotiation demands, but these were often among the first items to be dropped. *Id.* at 117–18. Institutionally or numerically weak actors can become much more effective instruments for change when armed with foreign models.

51. Since the transition to democracy, Greek feminists have adhered to party lines. Kyriazis terms women's organizations as "appendages to the parties of the left." Nota Kyriazis, *Women's Employment and Gender Relations in Greece.* 55 Eur. Urb. & Regional Stud. 65 (1998). The Socialist women's group EGE (Union of Greek Women) was founded in 1976. EGE (Enosi Gunaikon Elladas) (2004), *available at* http://www.ege.gr. Estimated to have had more than 30,000 members at its peak, the EGE now has almost none. Interview with EGE leader, Athens, Greece (Mar. 2004). While partisanship deprived women's organizations of independence and unity, it provided women affiliated with the Socialist Party access to power. Within the state, PASOK created the Equality Council, later transformed into the General Secretariat for Equality, with feminists well represented in its staff. This body pressed for changes in legislation concerning women. An interview with the Council's leader during the 1980s suggests that foreign experiences were carefully studied, especially those of Sweden, but also those of France and Italy. International conventions were especially useful as the Equality Secretariat could ask the relevant minister to approve of the translated text and move on with ratification without much debate. *Id.* Spanish feminists were even more hesitant to take up family issues given the strong association between pro-natalism and the Franco dictatorship. An extensive literature outlines how Spanish feminists gained influence over policy by creating and infiltrating the national and regional "Women's Institutes." *See* Katerina

Linos, *Are Socialists a Woman's Best Friend? Equality Policies in the Spanish Regions*, 10 J. OF EUR. PUB. POL'Y 438 (2003) (providing a review of the literature). However, these bodies never prioritized family questions. Celia Valiente, *The Rejection of Authoritarian Policy Legacies: Family Policy in Spain*, 1 S. EUR. SOC'Y & POL. 95 (1996); Valiente, *Las Políticas de Cuidado de los Niños, supra* note 50.

52. Valiente, *Las Políticas de Cuidado de los Niños, supra* note 50, at 105, (citing Iglesias de Ussel).

53. In surveying parliamentary debates on family policy from the mid-1970s onward, I only found references to family organization importance in 1997. At that time, the opposition accused them of caving to Socialist government pressures by accepting the introduction of a means test for family allowances.

54. *See* JULIO IGLESIAS DE USSEL & GERARDO MEIL LANDWERLIN, LA POLÍTICA FAMILIAR EN ESPAÑA (2001) (discussing limited opposition to proposals that would permit untrained housewives to care for groups of children in Spain). *See also,* Julio Iglesias de Ussel, *La Familia, in* INFORME SOCIOLOGICO SOBRE LA REALIDAD DE ESPANA 415–547 (2000).

55. Marianne Sundström, *Sweden: Supporting Work, Family, and Gender Equality, in* CHILD CARE, PARENTAL LEAVE, AND THE UNDER 3s 171, 176 (Sheila B. Kamerman & Alfred J. Kahn eds., 1991).

56. Interview with Director, Research Center for Gender Equality, Athens, October 9, 2003.

57. Inheritance, marriage, divorce, and abortion rights were central feminist concerns, while labor unions were focused on rights to organize, wages, and terms of work.

58. *See* Remarks of Praktika Voulis ton Ellinon, Gr. Parl. Deb., at 1675–77 (Sep. 19, 1984). Efrosini Spentzari, the conservative New Democracy Party spokesperson, specifically criticized the government's bill for not fully implementing Convention 156, despite earlier commitments to do so. Diamantis Mavrodoglou, the Communist KKE Party spokesperson, also criticized the government for not fully incorporating Convention 156. *See id.* at 1678–79.

59. *See supra* Figure 5.3, Chapter 5.

60. *See generally* Gr. Parl. Deb. (Sep. 19 & 20, 1984).

61. Both Efrosini Spentzari, the spokesperson for the conservative opposition New Democracy Party, and Diamantis Mavrodoglou, the spokesperson for the Communist Party, KKE, agreed with the government bill in principle. *See* Gr. Parl. Deb., at 1676, 1678 (Sep. 19, 1984).

62. *See id.* at 1685 (remarks of Konstantinos Tsigaridas, member of the governing Socialist Party, PASOK; *see also* remarks of Evaggelos Yiannopoulos, minister of labor in the PASOK government, at 1683).

63. The government's bill did not cover public sector employees. Both the Communists and the conservatives criticized this "segregation of the workforce." *See id.* at 1675, 1679. Efrosini Spentzari, the spokesperson for the conservative opposition New Democracy Party, argued that an unpaid parental leave would be ineffective, as parents who took advantage of the leave would not only forego their salaries but would have to pay back to their employers any social security contributions corresponding to the period of their leave. *See id.* at 1676.

64. Both Efrosini Spentzari and Diamantis Mavrodoglou called for quick ratification of the ILO convention and expressed their support for the extension of the right to parental leave to all employees. *See id.* at 1675, 1679.

65. Evaggelos Yiannopoulos, minister of labor in the PASOK government, reassured the parliament that ILO Convention 156 was extensively discussed in the ministry. *See id.* at 1681.

66. Essentially, the PASOK government was hesitant to ratify the ILO convention as it did not want to impose the cost of parental leave on the public sector. In 1984, it proposed a bill that would only give unpaid leave to private sector workers. The government argued that technicalities relating to the state budget reform process prevented it from extending unpaid leave benefits to public sector workers. *See id.* at 1682 (remarks of Evaggelos

Yiannopoulos, minister of labor in the PASOK government). The Socialist government ratified the ILO Convention in 1988, thus extending the leave to public sector workers.

67. *See id.* at 1678, 1687.
68. *See id.* at 1676, 1686.
69. *See id.* at 1676.
70. Ley 8/1980, de 10 de marzo, del Estatuto de los Trabajadores. Boletín Oficial del Estado, núm. 64 de 14 de marzo de 1980, páginas 5799 a 5815.
71. Ley 3/1989, de 3 de marzo, por la que se amplía a dieciséis semanas el permiso por maternidad y se establecen medidas para favorecer la igualdad de trato de la mujer en el trabajo. Boletín Oficial del Estado, núm. 57 de 8 de marzo de 1989, páginas 6504 a 6505.
72. PSOE, PSOE MANIFESTO (1977).
73. *Id.*
74. PSOE, PSOE MANIFESTO (1986).
75. PSOE, PSOE MANIFESTO (1989).
76. *Id.*
77. Ley 3/1989, de 3 de marzo, por la que se amplía a dieciséis semanas el permiso por maternidad y se establecen medidas para favorecer la igualdad de trato de la mujer en el trabajo. Boletín Oficial del Estado, núm. 57 de 8 de marzo de 1989, páginas 6504 a 6505.
78. *Id.* at 6504.
79. *Id.*
80. *See generally* KATHRIN S. ZIPPEL, THE POLITICS OF SEXUAL HARASSMENT: A COMPARATIVE STUDY OF THE UNITED STATES, THE EUROPEAN UNION, AND GERMANY 17–20 (2009).
81. CELIA VALIENTE, SEXUAL HARASSMENT IN THE WORKPLACE : EQUALITY POLICIES IN POST-AUTHORITARIAN SPAIN, IN THE POLITICS OF SEXUALITY: IDENTITY, GENDER CITIZENSHIP 168, 172 (Terrel Carver & Véronique Mottier, eds., 1988).
82. PSOE Representative and Minister of Labor and Social Security Manuel Chaves González, 110 Diario de Sesiones del Senado, pages 5101–5102, daily ed., February 22, 1989.
83. *Id.*
84. *Id.* at 5102.
85. *Id.*
86. *Id.* at 5102–05.
87. *Id.* at 5103.
88. *Id.* at 5102.
89. Minoría Catalana Representative Rafael Hinojosa i Lusena, 110 Diario de Sesiones del Congreso de los Diputados, page 10144, daily ed., Mar. 2, 1989.
90. Representative Celia Villalobos Talero, 369 Diario de Sesiones del Congreso de los Diputados, page 12806, daily ed., Nov. 16, 1988.
91. 173 Diario de Sesiones del Congreso de los Diputados, page 10142, daily ed., Mar. 2, 1989 (presenting lower house vote of 3 votes against, 192 votes in favor, and 64 abstentions).
92. NALDINI, *supra* note 1; IGLESIAS DE USSEL & MEIL, *supra* note 54.
93. *See generally* Hans Jürgen Puhle, *Mobilizers and Late Modernizers: Socialist Parties in the New Southern Europe, in* PARTIES, POLITICS, AND DEMOCRACY IN THE NEW SOUTHERN EUROPE (P. Nikiforos Diamandouros & Richard Gunther eds., 2001).
94. IGLESIAS DE USSEL & MEIL, *supra* note 55, at 106.
95. Alianza Popular [AP], AP manifesto (1977).
96. *Id.*
97. AP, AP manifesto (1982).
98. AP, AP manifesto (1986).
99. *Id.*
100. IGLESIAS DE USSEL & MEIL, *supra* note 54, at 92–93.
101. *Id.* at 92–94.
102. *Id.* at 110.

Chapter 8

1. *See generally,* ANDREW GUZMAN, HOW INTERNATIONAL LAW WORKS: A RATIONAL CHOICE THEORY (2008) [hereinafter Guzman 2008].

2. *See e.g., Xinyuan Dai, Why Comply? The Domestic Constituency Mechanism,* 59 INT'L ORG. 363 (2005); Songying Fang, *The Informational Role of International Institutions and Domestic Politics,* 52 AM. J. POL. SCI. 304 (2008).

3. *See, e.g.,* Anu Bradford & Omri Ben-Shahar, *Efficient Enforcement in International Law,* 12 CHI. J. INT'L L. 375 (2012) (exploring the size of enforcement costs).

4. For general discussions on the questions of the democratic deficits international bodies may face, *see* Ruth W. Grant & Robert O. Keohane, *Accountability and Abuses of Power in World Politics,* 99 AM. POL. SCI. REV. 29 (2005); Anne-Marie Slaughter, *The Accountability of Government Networks,* 8 IND. J. GLOBAL LEGAL STUD. 367 (2001) [hereinafter Slaughter 2001]; Robert Dahl, *Can International Organizations be Democratic: A Skeptic's View?, in* DEMOCRACY'S EDGES (Ian Shapiro & Casiano Hacker-Cordon eds., 1999) (arguing that multilateral bodies may produce positive outcomes but threaten domestic democracy).

5. *See, e.g.,* Jed Rubenfeld, *Unilateralism and Constitutionalism,* 79 N.Y.U. L. Rev. 1971 (2004).

6. *See also* Jack Goldsmith & Darryl Levinson, *Law for States: International Law, Constitutional Law, Public Law,* 22 HARV. L. REV. 1793 (2009).

7. *See, e.g.,* John R. Bolton, *Should We Take Global Governance Seriously?* 1 CHI. J. INT'L L. 206 (2005) (criticizing international decision making in fields such as human rights, labor, health, and the environment as an attack on American popular sovereignty and constitutionalism).

8. *See, e.g.,* Michael N. Bartnett & Martha Finemore, *The Politics, Power and Pathologies of International Organizations,* 53 INT'L ORG. 699, 713 (1999) (stating that officials in international organizations "are the 'missionaries' of our time. Armed with a notion of progress, an idea of how to create the better life, and some understanding of the conversion process, many IO [international organization] elites have as their stated purpose a desire to shape state practices by establishing, articulating, and transmitting norms that define what constitutes acceptable and legitimate state behavior"). *See also* Robert Howse, *The Boundaries of the WTO: From Politics to Technocracy-and Back Again: The Fate of the Multilateral Trading Regime,* 96 AM. J. INT'L L. 98–106 (2002).

9. *See* John O. McGinnis & Ilya Somin, *Should International Law Be Part of Our Law?* 59 STAN. L. REV. 1176–77 (2007) (distinguishing between international law that has been incorporated into domestic law through statutes and treaties and "raw international law" which "has not been endorsed by the domestic political process" and therefore, they argue, generates much greater democratic deficits). *See also* Oona A. Hathaway, *International Delegation and State Sovereignty,* 71 LAW & CONTEMP. PROBS. 115, 120–24 (2008) (arguing that the tension between international law and domestic democracy is reduced when state consent to delegation is taken into account). *But see* Oona A. Hathaway, *Treaties' End: The Past, Present, and Future of International Lawmaking in the United States,* 117 YALE L.J. 1308–12 (2008) (proposing that the Treaty Clause be almost abandoned in order to better balance international law and democratic legitimacy concerns); OONA HATHAWAY, OUR FOREIGN AFFAIRS CONSTITUTION: THE PRESIDENT, CONGRESS AND THE MAKING OF INTERNATIONAL LAW (forthcoming) (highlighting that in the US, Congress has has increasingly delegated to the executive branch authority to make binding international agreements over important policy areas through executive agreements, without Senate participation).

10. *See* Anne-Marie Slaughter, *Global Government Networks, Global Information Agencies, and Disaggregated Democracy,* 24 MICH J. INT'L L. 1056 (2003) [hereinafter Slaughter 2003]. *See also* Slaughter 2001, *supra* note 4.

11. ANNE MARIE SLAUGHTER, A NEW WORLD ORDER (2004) [hereinafter Slaughter 2004].

12. *See* Slaughter 2003, *supra* note 10.

13. *See* Robert O. Keohane, Stephen Macedo & Andrew Moravcsik, *Democracy-Enhancing Multilateralism,* 63 INT'L ORG. 1, 2 (2009).

14. *See* Eyal Benvenisti, *Reclaiming Democracy: The Strategic Uses of Foreign and International Law by National Courts*, 102 Am. J. Int'l L. 241 (2008). On a related point, Daniela Caruso explains how private law can lend legitimacy to transnational institutions by creating an appearance of neutrality and distance from politics. Daniela Caruso, *Private Law and State-Making in an Era of Globalization*, 39 N.Y.U. J. Int'l L. & Pol. 71–74 (2006).

15. *See* Rosalind Dixon, *A Democratic Theory of Constitution Comparison*, 56 Am. J. Comp. L. 947–48 (2008).

16. *See generally* Fabrizio Gilardi, Katharina Füglister & Stéphane Luyet, *InterdependentWelfare States: The Diffusion of Hospital Financing Reforms in OECD Countries* (presented at The Diffusion of Policies and Institutions workshop, Cyprus, 2006).

17. *See, e.g.,* Eric Posner & Cass Sunstein, *The Law of Other States*, 59 Stan. L. Rev. 131 (2006).

18. *Id.*

19. *But see,* Máximo Langer, *Revolution in Latin American Criminal Procedure: Diffusion of Legal Ideas from the Periphery*, 55 Am. J. Comp. L. 617 (2007) (arguing, contrary to most of the diffusion literature, that reforms can spread from the periphery to the center and documenting this process in the case of criminal procedure reforms across Latin America).

20. *See generally* Peter Evans, *From Situations of Dependency to Globalized Social Democracy*, 44 Stud. in Comp. Int'l Dev. 318 (2009).

21. *See* Roderick M. Hills, Jr., *Compared to What? Tiebout and the Comparative Merits of Congress and the States in Constitutional Federalism*, in The Tiebout Model at Fifty: Essays in Public Economics in Honor of Wallace Oates 239 (William A. Fischel ed., 2006).

22. *See* Michael C. Dorf & Charles F. Sabel, *A Constitution of Democratic Experimentalism*, 98 Colum. L. Rev. 314 (1998); Gráinne de Búrca, *New Governance and Experimentalism: An Introduction*, Wis. L. Rev. 2 (2010): 228. For an analogous debate on whether the study of comparative law broadens or narrows the range of possible alternatives for policy-makers, *compare* Jeremy Waldron, *Dirty Little Secrets*, 98 Colum. L. Rev. 510, 510–20 (1998) *with* Roberto Mangabeira Unger, What Should Legal Analysis Become? (1996).

23. *See* Kenneth Abbott et al., *The Concept of Legalization*, 54 Int'l Org. 401, 401 (2000) (presenting obligation, precision, and delegation as the three most important dimensions of international agreements). For a broader discussion of how treaties are negotiated, *see, for example,* Oona Hathaway, *Why Do Nations Join Human Rights Treaties?*, 51 J. Conflict Resol. 588 (2007) (discussing the negotiation of human rights treaties); Anu Bradford, *International Antitrust Negotiations and the False Hope of the WTO*, 48 Harv. Int'l L.J. 383 (2007) (discussing the negotiation of trade and anti-trust treaties); Oona Hathaway, *Treaties' End: The Past, Present and Future of International Lawmaking in the United States*, 117 Yale L.J. 1236 (2008) (discussing the interplay between Congress and the executive as the United States negotiates treaties).

24. Prominent legal scholars typically define soft law by using the absence of legal formalities to distinguish soft law from hard law, on the one hand, and by emphasizing soft law's effects to distinguish it from non-law, on the other. *See, e.g.,* Jacob E. Gersen & Eric Posner, *Soft Law: Lessons from Congressional Practice*, 61 Stan. L. Rev. 573, 573 (2008) ("Soft law consists of rules issued by lawmaking bodies that do not comply with procedural formalities necessary to give the rules legal status yet nonetheless influence the behavior of other lawmaking bodies and of the public."); Andrew T. Guzman & Timothy L. Meyer, *International Soft Law*, 2 J. Legal Analysis 171, 174 (2010) ("We define soft law as those nonbinding rules or instruments that interpret or inform our understanding of binding legal rules or represent promises that in turn create expectations about future conduct."); Dinah Shelton, *Introduction: Law, Non-Law and the Problem of "Soft Law,"* in Commitment and Compliance 1, 2 (Dinah Shelton ed., 2000) (arguing that soft law is non-binding law that contains "a normative element that leads to expectations of compliance"). This book examines empirically what these definitions assume,

namely whether soft law in fact influences state choices, and whether the nature of this influence sufficiently distinguishes soft law from non-law. For additional discussions of the tradeoffs between hard and soft law, *see also* JACK GOLDSMITH & ERIC POSNER, THE LIMITS OF INTERNATIONAL LAW 91–100 (2005) (outlining why states sometimes prefer treaties and at other times use non-legal agreements); Kenneth W. Abbott & Duncan Snidal, *The International Standards Process: Setting and Applying Global Business Norms, in* INTERNATIONAL STANDARDS AND THE LAW (Peter Nobel ed., 2005).

25. *See, e.g.,* Katerina Linos, *When Do Policy Innovations Spread?,* 119 HARV. L. REV. 1467 (2006) (discussing the European open method of coordination).

26. *See, e.g.,* Slaughter 2004, *supra* note 11.

27. *See generally,* Kevin E. Davis, Benedict Kingsbury & Sally Engle Merry, *Indicators as a Technology of Global Governance,* 46 L. & SOC. REV. 71 (2012).

28. *See, e.g.,* Andrew T. Guzman & Timothy L. Meyer, *International Soft Law,* 2 J. LEGAL ANALYSIS 171 (2010). Some scholars are even more critical of soft international law, suggesting that it is not merely less effective but could undermine the effectiveness of hard international law and the international legal system as a whole. *See, e.g.,* Prosper Weil, *Towards Relative Normativity in International Law?,* 77 AM. J. INT'L L. 413, 423 (1983). *But see* Douglass Cassell, *Inter-American Human Rights Law, Soft and Hard, in* COMMITMENT AND COMPLIANCE 393 (Dinah Shelton ed., 2000) (suggesting that hard and soft international law instruments were equally effective at improving human rights compliance in the Organization of American States); Steven R. Ratner, *Does International Law Matter in Preventing Ethnic Conflict?,* 32 N.Y.U. J. INT'L L. & POL. 591 (2000) (arguing that distinctions between hard and soft law are not particularly salient in the work of the Organization for Security and Cooperation in Europe [OSCE] High Commissioner on National Minorities).

29. *See, e.g.,* Abbott & Snidal, *supra* note 24; GOLDSMITH & POSNER, *supra* note 24. *See also* Rachel Brewster, *Unpacking the State's Reputation,* 50 HARV. INT'L L.J. 231 (outlining the mechanisms through which reputation can influence government behavior).

30. *See, e.g.,* THOMAS FRANCK, THE POWER OF LEGITIMACY AMONG NATIONS 24 (1990); *see also* Abram Chayes & Dinah Shelton, *Commentary, in* COMMITMENT AND COMPLIANCE 521, 526 (Dinah Shelton ed., 2000).

31. *See, e.g.,* Dinah Shelton, *Editor's Concluding Note: The Role of Non-binding Norms in the International Legal System, in* COMMITMENT AND COMPLIANCE 554, 554–55 (Dinah Shelton ed., 2000).

32. *Id.* (arguing that an important advantage of soft law is that agreements can be reached quickly). For arguments that governments may prefer informal agreements because they can reach these quickly and avoid ratification hurdles, *see* Andrew T. Guzman, *The Design of International Agreements,* 16 EUR. J. INT'L L., 579 (2005); Guzman 2008, *supra* note 2, at 126–42; Charles Lipson, *Why Are Some International Agreements Informal?,* 45 INT'L ORG. 495 (1991).

33. *See, e.g.,* Christopher Joyner, *Legal Status and Effect of Antarctic Recommended Measures, in* COMMITMENT AND COMPLIANCE (Dinah Shelton ed., 2000) (suggesting that Antarctic Treaty consultative meeting recommendations prompted countries to assume more extensive environmental obligations than they would have assumed through binding law instruments); Erika Schlager, *A Hard Look at Compliance with "Soft" Law: The Case of OSCE, in* COMMITMENT AND COMPLIANCE (suggesting that the fact that the Helsinki Final Act was non-binding allowed Soviet block countries to agree to more extensive human rights norms than would have otherwise been possible in 1975); Jon Birger Skjaerseth, Olav Schram Stokke & Jorgen Wettestad, *Soft Law, Hard Law, and Effective Implementation of International Environmental Norms,* 6 GLOBAL ENVTL. POL'Y 104 (2006) (presenting cases studies that showed it was easier to reach agreement on substantively ambitious soft law than on hard law on the questions of protecting the northeast Atlantic, constraining fisheries subsidies, and containing long-range transboundary air pollution).

34. Allyn Taylor & Douglas Bettcher, *WHO Framework Convention on Tobacco Control: A Global "Good" for Public Health*, 78 BULLETIN OF THE WORLD HEALTH ORGANIZATION 920 (2000).

35. *See* Ryan Goodman & Derek Jinks, *How to Influence States: Socialization and International Human Rights Law*, 54 DUKE L. J. 621, 656–74 (2004) [hereinafter Goodman & Jinks, *Socialization*].

36. *See, e.g.,* Oona A. Hathaway, *Do Human Rights Treaties Make a Difference?*, 111 YALE L.J. 1935, 2024 (2002).

37. *See* Goodman & Jinks, *Socialization, supra* note 35, at 667.

38. We know that democracies comply substantially more with soft law in at least one area—banking. *See* Daniel E. Ho, *Compliance and International Soft Law: Why Do Countries Implement the Basle Accord?*, 5 J. INT'L ECON. L. 647 (2002).

39. Jeffrey T. Checkel, *Why Comply? Social Learning and European Identity Change*, 55 INT'L ORG. 553, 563 (2001).

40. *See, e.g.,* Thomas Risse, *Let's Argue: Communicative Action in World Politics*, 54 INT'L ORG. 1 (2000); Christian Joerges & Juergen Neyer, *From Intergovernmental Bargaining to Deliberative Political Processes: The Constitutionalisation of Comitology*, 3 EUR. L.J. 273 (1997); Christian Joerges & Juergen Neyer, *Transforming Strategic Interaction into Deliberative Problem-Solving: European Comitology in the Foodstuffs Sector*, 4 J. EUR. PUB. POL'Y 609 (2005). For broader discussions of socialization and its impact on the diffusion of norms, *see* Ryan Goodman & Derek Jinks, *International Law and State Socialization: Conceptual, Empirical, and Normative Challenges*, 54 DUKE L.J. 983 (2005); Derek Jinks, *The Translation of Global Human Rights Norms: The Empirical Dimension*, 41 TEX. INT'L L.J. 415 (2006); Ryan Goodman & Derek Jinks, *Incomplete Internalization and Compliance with Human Rights Law*, 19 EUR. J. OF INT'L L. 725 (2008).

41. *See* International Labour Organization, constitution (1919). *See also* Laurence R. Helfer, *Understanding Change in International Organizations: Globalization and Innovation in the ILO*, 59 VAND. L. REV. 651 (2006).

42. For a more extensive discussion of these procedures, see Helfer, *supra* note 41 at 684–85.

43. *See, e.g.,* Francis Maupin, *International Labour Organization Recommendations and Similar Instruments, in* Commitment and Compliance (Dinah Shelton ed., 2000) (noting that while ILO conventions are ratified by few countries, many countries adopt principles developed in these conventions). *See also*, Helfer, *supra* note 41.

44. MARGARET E. KECK & KATHRYN SIKKINK, ACTIVISTS BEYOND BORDERS 26–29 (1998). *See also* Margaret E. Keck & Kathryn Sikkink, *Transnational Advocacy Networks in International and Regional Politics*, 51 INT'L SOC. SCI. J. 89 (1999). Kenneth Roth, executive director of Human Rights Watch, has made this claim most forcefully, arguing that human rights advocates should prioritize gross violations of civil and political rights, rather than entering debates about social and economic rights, because "the core of our methodology is our ability to investigate, expose, and shame." Kenneth Roth, *Defending Economic, Social and Cultural Rights: Practical Issues faced by an International Human Rights Organization*, 26 HUM. RTS. Q. 63 (2004). *See also* James H. Lebovich & Erik Voeten, *The Politics of Shame: The Condemnation of Country Human Rights Practices in the UNCHR*, 50 INT'L STUD. Q. 861 (2006).

45. Goodman & Jinks, *Socialization, supra* note 35, also emphasize this point, and argue that theories of state acculturation also lead to the conclusion that human rights activists could broaden the range of their advocacy efforts.

INDEX

Figures and tables are indicated by an italic *f* or *t* following the page number.

A

Adolino, Jessica, 39, 205n43
African countries, adoption of social
    insurance programs, 6, 7*f*
agency, 16–17, 27–29
Alma-Ata Declaration (1978), 8, 11, 68,
    76, 97, 102, 107, 109, 116, 121,
    183, 195n61
Alonso, Palacios, on National Health System,
    109, 195n61
American exceptionalism, 176, 196n70,
    198n13
Anderson, Kenneth, on foreign law adoption,
    27, 190n5
Australia, media coverage in, 20
Austria, export profile of, 98, 207n3
Avgerinos, Paraskevas, 116–117,
    123–124

B

Benvenisti, Eyal, on international
    organizations, 180
Berlin Conference (1890), 153, 155, 156
Bevan, Aneurin, 99
Beveridge Plan, 75, 101*t*, 114
Binding vs. non-binding international
    agreements, 182–183
Blake, Charles, 39, 205n43
Britain
    health care policy reform in, 99–100, 100*t*
    maternity leaves in, 130, 212n14
    National Health Service in, 68
    purchaser/provider split, 100, 101*t*, 113, 124,
      208n18
    support of UN in, 197n1
    voluntary vs. state-controlled hospitals, 99,
      207n7

C

Calabresi, Steven, on foreign law
    adoption, 27
case study evidence, use of, 9–10, 176, 96, 98,
    126, 150, 173, 176, 177
Catalonia
    maternity leaves in, 156
    purchaser/provider split legislation,
      209n67
child care leave, vs. parental leaves, 212n6
Children's Health Insurance Program, Volden's
    study of, 195n59
Clarify software, 207n76
Clinton, Bill, on healthcare reform, 22, 55–56,
    57, 58, 64, 200n34, 200n35
cognitive shortcut models, 15, 16
competition model, 14–16, 86, 139–140
conditionality, 15
Congressional policy debates
    arguments presented, 61–65, 62*t*
    countries referenced, 59–61, 60*t*, 61*t*
    frequency of foreign models, 57–58
    partisanship and, 58–59
contestation, effectiveness of, 9, 25,
    199n24
Conyers, John, 195n58
county-to-country diffusion vs. yardstick
    competition, 32, 197n83
cross-national regressions, use of, 9, 176
Current Population Survey vs. Knowledge
    Networks sampling, 197n6

D

decision-making
    international networks for, 1
    Scharfstein and Stein model, 197n84
decoupling, 30